WINES OF THE
RHÔNE VALLEY

WINES
OF THE
RHÔNE VALLEY

A Guide to Origins

ROBERT W. MAYBERRY

ROWMAN & LITTLEFIELD
Publishers

ROWMAN & LITTLEFIELD

Published in the United States of America in 1987
by Rowman & Littlefield, Publishers
(a division of Littlefield, Adams & Company)
81 Adams Drive, Totowa, New Jersey 07512

Library of Congress Cataloging-in-Publication Data

Mayberry, Robert W., 1938–
  Wines of the Rhône Valley.

  Bibliography: p. 202
  Includes indexes.
  1. Wine and wine making—Rhône River Valley
(Switzerland and France) 2. Wine and wine making—
France. I. Title.
TP553.M38 1987   663′.2′0094458   87-16516
        ISBN 0-8476-7430-4

88 90 91 89 87
 2 4 6 7 5 3 1

Printed in the United States of America

Contents

──────── PART IV   THE NORTHERN RHÔNE VALLEY ────────

Acknowledgments

ONLY WITH THE COOPERATION of the winegrowers and professionals of the Rhône valley could this book have been written. As an amateur of wine, I have depended on repeated personal visits with hundreds of them for basic information and the opportunity to taste. From the very beginning, this cooperation has been freely, universally, and unpretentiously given. Thus I owe a debt of fundamental gratitude to persons genuinely too numerous to name. I ask for their understanding if I mention only a very few for special thanks.

For friendship, good counsel, and tasting companionship over the years I want to thank Romain Bouchard, René Maisonneuve, and Bruno Sabatier. Jean-Pierre Saltarelli has been a valued colleague. Red Hauenstein and Father Henri Michel have been family, as is Joe Slack, who has driven to docks and airports more times than he probably cares to remember. I have always enjoyed the understanding and support of my mother and father, and of my parents-in-law.

I owe much for opening doors before I had written even a single article to Mary Lyons of Food and Wines from France, and to Pierre Ligier, then director of the Interprofessional Committee of the Côtes-du-Rhône. It was through him, as I recall, that I first met M. Mézières of the Institut Technique du Vin, who has always been willing to answer a non-technician's technical questions. Friend and fellow teacher Robert Burns has generously shared his knowledge and love of circum-alpine France. Others to whom I am grateful for taking my work seriously during crucial times include Chip Delsenser, Patrick Fegan, Stephen Grant, Field Reichardt, Leo Renaghan, Dick Scheer and the Ann Arbor Friends of Wine, Pete Stern, and Rebecca Wasserman.

Grand Valley State College has twice provided sabbatical leaves, and I owe particular thanks to Adrian Tinsley and to Forrest Armstrong for that most precious thing to an academic, the support of one's Dean. Photography students David Ferris and Robert Braendle graciously and skillfully printed the black-and-white photographs from color slides.

I owe hearty thanks to Senior Editor Paul Lee of Rowman & Littlefield for his interest in this book, and to my reader, Harm de Blij. The manuscript benefited from the textual editing of Associate Editor Janet Johnston. Don Blackburn did me the favor of critiquing the chapters on *cépages* and vinification. As much as I have tried to do my homework and report well what those more knowledgeable have told me, I feel the burden of responsibility for any errors that remain in those and other sections. All judgments of taste are my own.

Finally, there are no words with which I can sufficiently express appreciation to my wife, Rosalind Srb Mayberry. She has aided, she has participated—witness her photographs—but the whole truth is that the project itself would have been impossible without her. We have been sustained by our daughter, Katherine, who gives us joy.

Robert W. Mayberry
Grand Haven, Michigan
July 1987

Abbreviations

ABBREVIATIONS used throughout the book are explained here. Other abbreviations used only in particular chapters are explained within those chapters.

Frequently mentioned AOCs

AOC = *Appellation d'Origine Contrôlée*
   The words mean "controlled name of origin." Besides specifying exactly where and from what kinds of grapes the wine must be grown, the controls referred to derive from those "loyal, local and constant" vinegrowing and winemaking usages that are held responsible for producing a wine of that origin's recognizable identity or type.

CDL = Côtes du Lubéron
   Soon to be a regional AOC of the southern Rhône valley, just south of the Côtes du Ventoux, extending over 33 communes on the north and south slopes of the Montagne de Lubéron between the Calavon and Durance Rivers. Because for most of the duration of this study these wines were VDQS and not AOC, the area as a whole is not included.

CDR = Côtes du Rhône
   The principal regional AOC of the French Rhône valley, extending over 163 communes (towns) on both sides of the river, roughly between Vienne in the north and Beaucaire in the south, an area of approximately 52000 hectares. While in principle it could come from anywhere within this zone, wine bearing only the regional AOC is overwhelmingly a product of the southern *(méridional)* group of the two into which the CDR is traditionally divided.

CDT = Coteaux du Tricastin
   A regional AOC of the southern Rhône valley, extending over 22 communes on the left bank of the Rhône just north of the southern CDR, roughly in the area between Suze-la-Rousse and Montélimar.

CDV = Côtes du Ventoux
   A regional AOC of the southern Rhône valley, extending over 51 communes largely south of the Mont-Ventoux and east of the left bank CDR, an area of approximately 5000 hectares.

Other Categories of Wine

VDN = Vin Doux Naturel
   The words mean "natural sweet wine." They are applied to a category of wines so called because their sweetness is obliged to come from stopping the fermentation by the addition of alcohol while some of the natural sugar of the must (grape juice) remains

unfermented. Certain AOCs have been granted specifically to VDN produced in delimited areas, e.g., Muscat de Beaumes-de-Venise.

VDP = Vin de Pays

The words mean "wine of the country," meaning a definable local neighborhood or vicinity. They apply to a superior category of table wine allowed to carry an indication of its geographical "provenance," either that of a department or of a particular, legally defined zone of production.

VDQS = Vin Délimité de Qualité Supérieur

The words mean "delimited wine of superior quality." In intent this is a rank or grade of regionally reputed, controlled-origin wines conducted according to similar principles but just below the quality level and more general reputation of AOC wines. In effect it has become a training ground for passage into AOC on the part of "country wines" with a record of improved quality and expanding reputations.

VDT = Vin de Table

The words mean table wine, but in France this is the legal category for *vin ordinaire* without indication of geographical origin or provenance. In some regions of France only VDT may be produced, but in an AOC area like the CDR, the sources of VDT include vineyards outside the delimited AOC area, grape varieties that are not permitted in AOC wines, including hybrids, and production in excess of AOC regulations.

Grape Varieties (Cépages)

Below, S = southern Rhône, N = northern Rhône, R = red *cépage,* and W = white *cépage.*

BR = Bourboulenc
SW used for its distinctive aroma and freshness.

CN = Counoise
Rare SR, among the permitted 13 of Châteauneuf-du-Pape.

CR = Carignan
Regularly productive SR entering chiefly into certain regional CDR reds for color and tannin, and for the same reasons even into *cru* rosés.

CS = Cinsault
SR used on all AOC levels for refinement and aroma of reds, finesse in rosés.

CT = Clairette
Dominant SW. Has a pink *(rose)* variant.

GR = Grenache
Dominant SR.

GR blanc = Grenache blanc
SW used for body and richness, limited in CDR-Villages.

MR = Marsanne
NW dominant in the middle valley. Also SW for aroma in certain CDRs.

MV = Mourvèdre
SR used for aroma, structure, and longevity.

MD = Muscardin
Rare SR, apparently native to Châteauneuf-du-Pape.

PC = Picardan
Rare SW, among the permitted 13 of Châteauneuf-du-Pape.

PL = Picpoul
Rare SW. Has red and pink variants.

RS = Roussanne
NW of middle valley. Also SW in certain Châteauneuf-du-Papes and CDR-Villages
for aroma and structure.

SY = Syrah
Sole NR. Also SR used for color, aroma, and tannin.

UN = Ugni blanc
SW used chiefly in certain regional CDRs for acid support and floral aroma.

VA = Vaccarèse
Rare SR, among the permitted 13 of Châteauneuf-du-Pape.

VN = Viognier
NW of the northern valley. Condrieu is 100% VN. A limited percentage is used to
refine Côte-Rôtie. Also experimental SW.

Vinification Methods

CL = Classic Method
Sometimes called Bordeaux method, in it all the grapes are usually crushed and,
more important, destemmed before *encuvage* (being placed in the vat).

CM = Integral Carbonic Maceration
In this method the grapes are placed in the vat still on their stems. None are crushed
except on the bottom of the vat by weight of the bunches above, and the vats have been
filled beforehand with CO_2.

days = days of *cuvaison*
In red winemaking, *cuvaison* is the leaving of the liquid in the vat with the solid
matter while the must ferments into wine, and color and tannins are extracted,
principally from the skins.

OT = Old-time or "Ancient Method"
In it the grapes are left on the stems and some are lightly crushed and some not
before *encuvage* (30% to 70% whole grape berries to start). The grapes may be carried
directly to the vats (OT1) or passed through pieces of mechanical apparatus designed to
approximate the same result (OT2).

ST = Standard Method
The orthodox modern method in the Rhône valley. The grapes are left on the stems
or only a part destemmed, and crushed before *encuvage*.

Miscellaneous

* = the wine is recommended

Entry followed by commentary in bold-face = the producer is recommended

H = the producer or the wine is highly recommended

ha = hectare of land
   100 ares, the equivalent in round numbers of 2.47 acres.

hl = hectoliter of wine
   100 liters, the equivalent in round numbers of 26.42 U.S. gallons.

INAO = *Institut National des Appellations d'Origine des Vins et Eaux de Vie*
   National Institute of Controlled Names of Origin of Wines and Spirits.

% = percentage in the plantation
   When used with the abbreviations for *cépages* in the entries on individual producers, unless otherwise indicated.

Qrt = *quartier*
   A traditionally identified, small geographical zone or district within a town *(commune)* on the official survey map of France *(cadastre)*. In the Rhône valley, qrt names are used for indicating the location of vineyard sites (Larmat 1944).

Introduction: Origins

"There is a harmony among all things and the places where they are found."
—Waverly Root

T HE WORD "ORIGINS" is used in this book to describe where and what a wine comes from. Included in the idea is first and foremost the place where the wine, or rather the grapes, grew. Once the place is definitely located (or delimited, as the French say), "origins" is widened to include the environment of the place as a habitat for grapes to grow in. This is what the French mean by *terroir*, which as everyone knows includes soil, but which actually includes climate, terrain, and microclimate as well. Obviously "origins" includes the grapes themselves, especially their kind or variety, for which the French word is *cépage*. Some people even include the *cépage* as a factor in *terroir*, since grapes have to grow in a place to whose natural conditions they are adapted and which, when they have been made into wine, they are said to express. The recognizable expression of its origins in the sensory characteristics of a wine is referred to by the French as the wine's *originalité* (originality). So "origins" finally includes by whom and by what artistry the grapes have been transformed into a wine that may constitute such an expression. This brings us back to the beginning, because if the maker of the wine also grew the grapes, then we can know exactly where the wine came from.

This book is a guide to sources of bottled Rhône wines whose origins can be determined. Commentary is therefore limited for the most part to estate-bottled, grower-produced wines. In fact, extensive geographically organized commentary is provided in bold-face on the wines of some 300 personally recommended private and cooperative producers. Structural and taste characteristics of each wine are indicated to the best of the author's first-hand experience. These descriptions are a composite of tasting notes accumulated during his 38 months of residence in the Rhône valley on nine occasions since 1974. They are attempts to represent the originality of the wines in the sense explained above. Vintages are mentioned less for their own sake than for some typical or perhaps exceptional aspect they reveal of a wine's identity.

Following each comment, origins of the wine are traced as exactly as possible, at least by a person outside the wine industry and trade. In this context it should be remembered that quantitative information on the wine estates has been obtained in every case from the owners. Some owners quote exactly from their ledgers, others round off from memory. The point has not been to put statistics on the record, but to allow approximate comparisons among the estates.

Almost 200 briefer entries locate additional properties belonging to those who receive full commentary, locate other cooperatives and where their wine comes from, and indicate the most particular wines available from *négociants* of the type whose principal business is merchandising wine they have bought from its producers.

Now second only to Bordeaux in the production of AOC wine, the Côtes du Rhône is the only one of the "big three" French sources of non-sparkling wine in popular perception to lie predominantly, overwhelmingly in the Mediterranean climate zone. These proportions are respected in the attention paid by this book to the southern majority of Rhône wine producers. For many consumers estate-bottled southern Rhônes will be an unfamiliar category of wines, many of which until recently were sold in bulk by their producers to shippers for eventual presentation to the consumer in an anonymous form. It is to solve the problem of consumer unfamiliarity with their original characteristics that a geographical organization of the commentary has been adopted. The consequence is that neighboring southern wines are in many cases shown together as belonging to identifiable subregions for the first time.

Yet beyond their history of bulk sale, there is a problem about the very origin of these wines that must be faced. Serious barriers to the full appreciation of even estate-bottled southern Rhônes are raised against all such "vernacular" wines (to use Hugh Johnson's well-chosen term) by widely shared "international" assumptions about wine quality. To these assumptions, vernacular wines from Mediterranean countries, when they can be found in their original state, are a standing challenge on behalf of regional prerequisites for appreciating, again in Johnson's terms, "that most precious attribute of wine, variety." A person cannot simply take for granted that everything he or she associates with wine quality from the study of one region will apply without modification to another, where nature may impose somewhat different necessities for the achievement of quality upon the winemaker.

Thus the assumption that favors wines from cool climates over wines from hot climates will not help us much to enjoy southern Rhônes, because the southern Rhône valley is hot.

Likewise we will have to work around the assumption that grape varieties (*cépages*) that originated in cool northern Europe are inherently superior no matter where planted to those that originated in the Mediterranean south. That is because, with the principal exception of Syrah, the main southern Rhône *cépages* are natives of the Mediterranean basin, *cépages* that are well adapted to the quasi-desert conditions of the summer in a climate of the two-season, Mediterranean type. Grown at the crop levels associated with "noble" varieties elsewhere (2⅓ to 3⅓ tons per acre) and dry-farmed except by special permission to irrigate only in emergencies, the red *cépages* produce wines that have softer tannins than maritime climate Bordeaux, less acid than continental climate Burgundy, and more alcohol than either. The low acidity requires that the wine be produced in impeccably clean rather than romantic facilities, along with such other rigorous protections against oxidation as extracting as few as possible of the grosser sort of oxidizable tannins that can come from the Grenache variety. When so produced, the advantage of these *cépages* to quality is that their taste interest is on the whole enhanced rather than suppressed by a dominance of alcohol among the structural elements of the wine.

For the same reason southern Rhônes made from a single *cépage* are characteristically "extreme climate"; that is, boldly fruity and exaggerated in some dimension adverse to balance. It is to achieve balance that traditional wines from the southern Rhône valley are in principle and in intent *vins d'assemblage* (generics) and not *vins de cépage* (varietals), 13 different *cépages* being permitted by law in Châteauneuf-du-Pape, 23 in regional Côtes du Rhône. In addition to considerations of balance, some of the historic *cépages* are more resistant to oxidation than Grenache. All this is particularly challenging to the residual

American assumption that favors wines made from a single variety over wines made from several.

Bordeaux, which permits 6 *cépages* in its red wines, might have helped us learn a lesson on varietals. Where it may create a barrier to appreciating Rhônes is its influence over our assumptions about winemaking. We tend to think red winemaking, with the exception of Beaujolais and something called carbonic maceration, always begins by destemming and crushing the grapes. Yet in the southern *and* northern Rhône valley, as elsewhere in eastern France, the grapes are often left on the stems, and many producers try to leave a portion of the grapes uncrushed. Traditional in the south as an aid to temperature control, this practice is now also recognized as permitting the extraction of finer tannins from the local varieties.

Perhaps strongest in England, if not California, is the assumption that aging in an oak barrel, especially a Bordeaux-sized, new oak barrel, adds nuances and subtleties a wine would not otherwise have. The familiar taste of oak is omitted by choice in many southern Rhônes because the growers wish to avoid the oxidation a small barrel can give a wine made from Mediterranean *cépages* in a hot, dry climate. No wood at all or large reused casks *(foudres* or *demi-muids)* are preferred to new small barrels *(pièces)*. Often revealed when not masked by oxidation are wooded nuances, usually subtler than oak, the *cépages* themselves can contribute to the wine.

Like other wines which derive their character from the specific habitats in which they are grown, southern Rhônes remind us that the important factors for wine quality may differ and be arranged differently in different locations. These factors are important precisely because they meet the demands made upon the ideal of quality by the circumstances of origin. This is also the principle behind France's laws of *appellation d'origine contrôlée*. Under these laws, which were virtually invented by the growers of Châteauneuf-du-Pape, more is controlled about an appellation than where the wine comes from, although that is specified exactly. By itself this would only be an indication of provenance from a French point of view. Nor is an *appellation contrôlée* a guarantee of quality in an absolute or abstract sense. Rather it regulates precisely those quality factors traditionally reponsible for producing a wine of that origin's type. These factors stem on the one hand from the natural conditions of a definable place comprehended by the concept of *terroir,* and on the other from the "loyal, local and constant" viti- and vinicultural practices of the resident *vignerons* who have preserved the identity of their wines over time. This degree of control, transferred from tradition to law, is accepted by French growers because the recognizable originality of their product is understood to be the common property of its producers.

The result is that all making and judging of wine in France takes account of a wine's origin. Knowledge of original types requires familiarity with them among the judges so that everybody involved has an idea of what the wine from a particular place is supposed to be. The French do not favor indiscriminate mixing of different types of wine in a blind tasting. They would not assume, for instance, that wines made from even the same prestigious grape variety, say Cabernet Sauvignon, are necessarily of the same type, if the wines are from California, Australia, and Bordeaux. This is not just sour grapes.

From the French point of view, a taster should know in advance whether the wines in a tasting are truly comparable before he marks them on the same scale. Otherwise he might downgrade a Cabernet-franc from Chinon for failing to have the richness of a St.-

Emilion, or the Cabernet-franc-dominant St.-Emilion for lacking the pungent calcareous nose of a Chinon. Origin bears on the judgment of a wine's analytic components as well. Many a southern Rhône is best balanced in high relief, that is, with an alcohol level that would kill the fresh fruitiness of a Beaujolais. The value and significance of alcohol is different in the two types, as is the purpose for which one might use "whole berries" in the fermentation of both wines. That tasting is truly blind in which the origin of the wines is not understood, even if the labels are exposed.

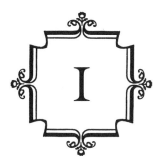

I

THE SOUTHERN RHÔNE VALLEY
IN GENERAL

Demi-muid oak cask. Reused casks of this and the even larger *foudre* size are employed much more often than burgundian-size small barrels *(pièces)* by those in the southern Rhône valley who age their wine in wood. Photo courtesy of Rosalind Srb.

Chateau La Nerte
CHATEAUNEUF-DU-PAPE

APPELLATION CHATEAUNEUF-DU-PAPE CONTROLÉE

RÉCOLTE 1971

Alor que lou moust de la Nerto
Sautourlejo e ris dins lou got...
*Quand le moût de la Nerte
Vibre et rit dans le verre....*
MISTRAL

E. & F. MOTTE
PROPRIÉTAIRES
RÉCOLTANTS

CHATEAUNEUF-DU-PAPE (Vse)

CUVÉE LES CADETTES

Mise en bouteille au Château

CHATEAU LA NERTHE
RÉCOLTE 1984

Alor que lou moust
de la Nerto
Sautourlejo e ris
dins lou got...

*Quand le moût de
la Nerte
Vibre et rit dans
le verre...*
MISTRAL

Chateauneuf du Pape
APPELLATION CHÂTEAUNEUF-DU-PAPE CONTRÔLÉE

Mis en bouteille au Château

Château la Nerthe - Propriétaire-Récoltant à Châteauneuf-du-Pape - Vaucluse - France

75 cl

PRODUCT OF FRANCE

1
Tradition Revisited

IN APRIL 1985 Château La Nerthe, an historic Châteauneuf-du-Pape property, changed hands. Two large French *négociant* firms, David et Foillard of nearby Sorgues and Société Richard, the latter a specialist in distribution, replaced the families Motte and Leclerc in the society that owns La Nerthe. Alain Dugas, who directs David et Foillard's Côtes-du-Rhône estate at Sérignan, Domaine de la Renjarde, will now also direct La Nerthe.

Included in the sale was the 1984 wine for estate-bottling, already assembled by consulting oenologist Noël Rabot. In it he had increased the percentage of some of the 13 permitted *cépages* besides Grenache. In addition, the 1984 was given a much shorter passage in cask before bottling than was the practice under the former owners. The result of only these two changes is, to my taste, a finer, more tightly structured, more aromatic wine likely to cause an outcry in quarters that have upheld the familiar inky, fiery, massive almost all-Grenache La Nerte as *the* traditional Châteauneuf-du-Pape. It is clear that restoration of the *h* to the château's name is not the only change the new owners have in mind.

This most famous Châteauneuf estate, with 58 hectares in vine, is found just east of Fines Roches across the same little north-south oriented valley that runs south through La Solitude. The soil is sand mixed with clay and fewer of the famous Châteauneuf cobblestones than at nearby Fortia.

The property once belonged to Le Commandant Ducos, leader in the reconstitution of the vineyards of Châteauneuf after phylloxera (the vine louse from North America that almost destroyed European vine varieties everywhere in the world). His formula for the ideal composition of La Nerthe is often quoted.

> For warmth, richness and fat: Grenache and Cinsault, 2/10 maximum. For solidity, conservation and color, with a straightforward and thirst-quenching flavor: Mourvèdre, Syrah, Muscardin, and Vaccarèse, 4/10. For vinosity, agreeability, freshness, and a distinctive bouquet: Counoise and Picpoul, 3/10. For finesse, fire, and brilliance— white grapes: Clairette and Bourboulenc, 1/10. [Le Roy 1932, paraphrase and translation by the author.]

This followed the Mediterranean tradition of winemaking that calls for multiple *cépages,* including white grapes in the red wine, to make a balanced wine from elements each one of which by itself would exhibit too pronounced an "extreme climate" character.

This tradition would have been hard to follow at La Nerte in recent years. *Encépagement* of the vineyard at the time of sale stood at 85% to 90% Grenache; 5% for the ensemble of Mourvèdre, Counoise, and Cinsault; 5% Syrah; and 3% Clairette. Thus for Rabot to increase the Syrah to 20% in an *assemblage* representing less than half the estate's 1984 production required using the total output of Syrah, even with the aid of that vintage's shortage of Grenache.

7

More important for the long term at La Nerthe is that change back to balance will extend to the vineyard, where the next few years will see the same restoration of a more diversified plantation as has already occurred at such other reputed Châteauneuf estates as Domaine de Mont-Redon, Clos des Papes, and Château de Beaucastel. (In composition of the wine the latter has moved from 90% Grenache in the 1949 to 30% each of Grenache and Mourvèdre in the 1984.) Director Dugas's aim for La Nerthe's plantation is to arrive at around 60% Grenache, 15% Syrah, 10% Mourvèdre, 5% Cinsault, plus smaller amounts of Clairette, Counoise and other minor *cépages* for the red. Grenache blanc, Bourboulenc, and Roussanne will be added to Clairette for the estate's white. It is only the recent excess, not the quality of the Grenache of which oenologist Rabot is critical. The product of the old vines at La Nerthe is notable for good acidity and low PH, Rabot says, and among the clones are almost certainly those selected by Ducos.

The contribution of the other *cépages* to making a Châteauneuf less dense and fiery is especially noticeable in this case because an orthodox vinification of crushed but not destemmed grapes had not been changed. In fact, at Rabot's instigation the *cuvaison* (vatting time) had actually been lengthened from 8 or 10 days to 12. Moreover, press wine is now incorporated in the wine for estate-bottling, which was not the case under the former owners.

During their era, however, the practice now abandoned was to store the wine 3 years or more in oak casks, a duration more often regulated by pace of sales than by taste qualities. At the same time, a single wine was not assembled from the different *cuves* (vats), so that the *négociants* who even in recent years bought 60% or more of the estate's production could have their choice of raw materials. The lack of *assemblage* produced considerable variation from one bottling to another in the wine that remained to La Nerte for bottle sale. In all this La Nerte had simply retained the early 20th-century system of dependence during hard times on bulk sale of blending wine that initially drove the Châteauneuf growers to overplant Grenache. Many remember and in effect still cite as "traditional" the characteristics of this blending wine. What it meant to the genuine tradition was explained long ago by the Baron LeRoy, founder of the Châteauneuf-du-Pape appellation.

> Before the [First World] War, the greater part of the harvest of Châteauneuf-du-Pape was bought by Burgundy, where it served to strengthen the wines of that beautiful viticultural province, and also to correct the excess of their acidity in certain years. Under the influence of the *négociants* of that region, who held to the course of at one and the same time getting rid of eventual competitors and of having a blending wine that corresponded exactly to their desires, the majority of proprietors little by little abandoned the greater part of the old *cépages* to conserve only the Grenache, which ended up by constituting 80 to 100% of the *encépagement*. Thus it is that one saw certain Châteauneufs wear out prematurely and become "rancid" after a few years, and that at the same time, *body, warmth, and color were exaggerated to the detriment of finesse and bouquet*. [LeRoy 1932, author's emphasis and translation.]

Because of the circumstances of new ownership, La Nerthe now becomes only the latest example of the continuing, post-World War II change in the character of Châteauneuf-du-Papes and other southern Rhônes from blending wine to estate wines. Private growers now account for 37% of the whole region's production, and for 90% of

More than half of Châteauneuf-du-Pape's wine is still sold in bulk *(en gros)* to shippers *(négociants),* some of the most important of whom merely condition and sell it over again in bulk. It leaves the producer's *cave* in tank trucks *(camions-citernes),* in this case for Switzerland, the biggest importer of Rhône wines. Photo courtesy of Rosalind Srb.

Châteauneuf's. In many other *domaines* the quest for bouquet, finesse, and longevity has already proceeded apace, because to the origin legally guaranteed by *appellation contrôlée,* estate-bottling adds the commercial requirement that wines made from the most localized materials must be balanced and complete enough individually to be enjoyed on their own. Each of the diverse personalities of the resulting wines represents a particular grower's interpretation of what it takes to create that kind of interest in a southern Rhône. A review of the reasons for differences of style among wines that share a common origin will provide a basis for the commentaries on individual wines in this guide.

2

Estates and Growths

THE ANGLO-AMERICAN IMAGE of a wine estate tends to derive from Bordeaux. Thus our commerce and our reference books have by and large made familiar the names of southern Rhône estates whose property, essentially in one piece, surrounds a substantial enough countryside dwelling to qualify for the magic word *château*. Just such a single, *château,* or Bordeaux-style estate is Château La Nerthe. These large single estates are instances of what the social scientist calls "dispersed habitat," referring to the dwelling places, not the properties. The single estates tend to be located on the plains and plateaus of the southern Rhône valley, and at some point in their history have usually been the property of powerful aristocratic families, in some cases a pattern extending back to the villa system of Roman times. In proportion to the total number of estates at Châteauneuf and elsewhere in the Rhône valley, the Bordeaux-style estates are not typical. Equally rare is that the original character of their wines derives from a contiguous *terroir* within the *cru* or appellation area in which they are produced.

More typical of hillside sites and peasant ancestry are the dispersed or village estates, similar to those in Burgundy. The owner lives and has his *caves,* not in a *château* out in the vineyards, but in the village. To this anyone can testify who has wandered up and down Châteauneuf-du-Pape and seen the dozens of placards over modest basement entrances announcing the names of winemakers. The dispersed estate is an instance of what the social scientist calls "grouped habitat," again referring to the dwelling places. The property is made up of separate pieces or parcels of land scattered about in several or even many *quartiers* on the map of the neighboring territory. Besides working his own properties, an owner may also sharecrop parcels belonging to friends, neighbors, or other members of his own family. A representative case a decade ago, except that the estate is on the large side, was that of the maker of a first-rate Châteauneuf-du-Pape who personally owned 14 hectares in 22 parcels and who sharecropped an additional 24 hectares in 10 parcels owned by his sons.

The original character of village wines, then, derives in effect from a sampling of the *terroirs* of the *cru* or appellation area within which they are produced. Much as they employ multiple *cépages* for the same purpose, the owners of village estates usually assemble the wines of the various parcels to achieve a balance and synthesis of their characteristics. This is in keeping with the ancient origin of the village estate system, which was a sharing among members of the community of the different characteristics of the land belonging to it.

As a result the *quartiers* of a village like Châteauneuf-du-Pape are divided, as are the *lieux-dits* and *climats* of Burgundy, among multiple owners. About Burgundy, as we shall see, many writers speak of this as a division of the "vineyards," since the same *lieu-dit* or *climat* name may appear on the labels of wines from the several different owners who each own a part. At Châteauneuf-du-Pape the village estates themselves are spoken of as cut up ("morcellé"), doubtless because no *quartier* names can appear on the label as an origin of the wine. Nor have any of the *quartiers,* unlike certain *lieux-dits* of Burgundy, been classified as *crus* or growths. The owners of village estates have consistently maintained that classifying them would be to the detriment of Châteauneuf-du-Pape as *the* cru, as would any classification of properties, which in addition would favor the châteaus to the disadvantage of the village estates. Inadvertently they may have contributed thereby to the damaging perception that, by comparison to other regions, there are no growths in the Rhône valley. It is therefore important to recognize that this honorific notion of a "growth" is somewhat different in each of the principal winegrowing regions of France.

A *cru* or "growth" in Bordeaux is somebody's property, usually more or less surrounding the principal dwelling or *château* for which it is named. Some but not all of these growths, i.e., properties, have been classified as "great" according to the reputation of their product by one of the several local systems, the oldest being that of 1855 for the Gironde (Haut-Médoc and Sauternes). Château Montrose from the town of St.-Estèphe, for example, is classified as a "second great growth" in the 1855 classification.

Geographically named vineyard sites comprised in whole or in part by the properties do not usually appear on Bordeaux labels. This helps to make the usually favorable statement in English and American books that "vineyards in Bordeaux have one owner" true by definition, since "vineyard" in this case refers to property. Because *appellations d'origine contrôlées* are regarded in French law as the common property of those who employ them, they have not been extended to private properties, even the classified ones, in Bordeaux. This is why the AOC of Château Montrose is St.-Estèphe.

In the Côte d'Or of Burgundy, geographically named vineyard sites, locally called *lieux-dits* and in some cases *climats,* do appear on the label. Some but not all of these named places have been classified as *crus* or growths according to the reputation of their product. There are two grades in ascending order, *premier cru* or *grand cru* (first growth

Evidence of dispersed *(morcellé)* properties and traditional mixed-crop agriculture shows on the hillside at St.-Maurice-sur-Eygues (Drôme). Photo courtesy of Rosalind Srb.

or great growth). Le Chambertin is a *lieu-dit* in the town of Gevrey-Chambertin that has been classified as a "great growth."

Somebody's property is usually called a *domaine,* and is most often dispersed among scattered parcels in several *lieux-dits.* Domaine Damoy and Domaine Armand Rousseau each own a part of Chambertin. (Johnson 1983.) This makes the somewhat detrimental statement in English and American books that "vineyards in Burgundy have multiple owners" true as a fact in this case, since "vineyard" now refers to a named place. There is no classification of private properties in Burgundy. Since their ownership is shared, the names of the places that have been classified as growths are given their own *appellations d'origine contrôlées.* The AOC of Chambertin is Chambertin. The names of the *grands crus* stand alone, those of the *premiers crus* are added to that of their commune in type of a regulated size, as in Gevrey-Chambertin Clos St.-Jacques, where Domaine Armand Rousseau also own a part.

In the Rhône valley, as in the similar Beaujolais system, the word *cru* (growth) is customarily applied to a locality historically recognized for the reputation of its product and subsequently granted its own local *appellation d'origine contrôlée* (for example, Châteauneuf-du-Pape and Côte-Rôtie). The unit of classification therefore is a geographically named place as in Burgundy (Côte d'Or), but larger in this case than the vineyard site and sometimes, as in the examples, covering parts of several political units.

Unless they are among the few of the château type, we have seen that properties in the Côtes du Rhône, as in Burgundy, are usually dispersed, and are called *domaines* on the label, except in the northern Rhône where the grower simply uses his name. As in Burgundy, but not in Bordeaux, there is no classification of private properties. As in Bordeaux, but not in Burgundy, geographically named vineyard sites do not appear on the label except occasionally when added to that of a growth in the northern Côtes du Rhône. *Quartier* names are not so employed in the southern Rhône, unless they happen to have been incorporated as a sort of brand, when the practice was legal, into the name of a *domaine,* for example the Domaine de Beaurenard at Châteauneuf-du-Pape.

3
Southern Climate and *Cépages*

────────── THE PRINCIPLE OF MULTIPLE *CÉPAGES* ──────────

MY FRIENDS from California, perhaps conditioned by the Santa Anna wind, sometimes forget that the mistral of the southern Rhône valley is a prevailing north wind. It blows cool enough even in summer to cause people to put on sweaters and the restaurant owners to close doors and windows just when (from an American point of view) the temperature is becoming comfortable.

Are the descriptions of grape varieties in many of our standard wine books similarly conditioned by the California growing experience? If so, it might explain why so little is found in these books to prepare one for the idea of producing intensely fruity—as compared to simply powerful—and distinctive wines from the varieties of the southern Rhône. Yet it is often the bold fruit character of clean, unoxidized southern Rhônes that most surprises a person who is tasting them for the first time. It is a little like seeing a favorite painting with the varnish removed. As a Michigan wine merchant exclaimed over a Visan, "When you put your nose in the glass, they are right there."

The fact is that growers and technicians in the southern Rhône valley describe their Mediterranean climate grapes very differently than do the books. Far from producing coarse and neutral wine, each variety *(cépage)* by itself, they say, tends to produce a wine that is exaggerated in both its virtues and defects. The locals believe that this peculiar intensity, like that of the ingredients of Provençal cuisine—garlic, virgin olive oil, fresh truffles, wild thyme, rosemary, and sage—, reflects the extremes of a dry, windy climate.

Channeled through the Rhône valley by the mountains on either side, the mistral blows most forcibly in the south, where it clears and dries the weather. This allows the sun to beat down ferociously during the long periods of summer drought. The mistral and the sun create the quasi-desert conditions normal to the growing season. It is the brilliant illumination in such a dry climate (the famous Provençal light of the painters) as much or more than the heat which makes these conditions so favorable to the ripening of grapes. In addition the evaporative power of the mistral is said to concentrate the solutions of sugar and extract inside the ripening grapes.

The mistral also protects against late spring frosts, which are especially dangerous because the vines are no longer dormant. It plays a major role all season long in the battle against fungus diseases, to which the vines, being adapted to drought, are particularly susceptible. Thus the best vintage years in the southern Rhône have the most mistral, I have been consistently told. Bad years see too much moisture, the worst form being mugginess after rain that is not succeeded quickly enough by mistral. So important is the mistral to the character of southern Côtes du Rhône wines that being sheltered from the mistral by the Mont-Ventoux is one reason the neighboring Côtes du Ventoux vineyards are not included within the Côtes du Rhône. On the other hand, slopes in the Côtes du

Rhône with a northward exposure produce some of the region's biggest wines—Gigondas and the Laudun from St.-Victor-la-Coste, for example.

Except for the thunderstorms, which often occur about August 15th, the torrential rains of the region tend to be concentrated around the vernal and autumnal equinoxes. If the autumn equinoctial rains coincide with the harvest period, the vintage is at risk. Best is if the harvest is gathered before the rains begin, or if it extends beyond them into what the locals call the "arrière saison," the back season, late autumn. Then when the mistral blows it is downright cold. In the southern Rhône valley the *caves de vinification*, or the fermentation vats themselves if the estate is so-equipped, must be heated as often as cooled, in either case to avoid "stopped" fermentation.

The stringent crop restrictions of the *appellation contrôlée* laws further intensify the extreme climate character of southern Rhône wines. No one would consider growing Grenache and the other varieties at anything but the same low levels of productivity that are insisted upon for the more prestigious varieties of other regions. Thirty-five hectoliters of wine per hectare of land is the maximum production normally permitted for most *crus* and Côtes-du-Rhône-Villages (2¹/₃ tons of grapes or 1889 bottles of wine per acre). Fifty hectoliters is permitted for regional Côtes du Rhône (3¹/₃ tons or 2699 bottles per acre) (Livingstone-Learmonth and Master 1983).

So the view in the southern Rhône is that while a single *cépage* might be capable of producing good wine by itself in some northern climates, wine produced in the south from a single Mediterranean *cépage* would almost certainly be out of balance. Each variety needs the compensating presence of an ensemble of companions to produce a balanced composition from its own bold strokes. In red wines, Grenache is for body and alcohol, and for the fruit and smell judged typical. Syrah is for color, fragrance and greater longevity. Cinsault lowers the alcoholic degree, and refines the body and fragrance. Also for finesse, the white grapes Grenache blanc, Clairette, and Bourboulenc are sometimes vinified with the red ones. Mourvèdre is for structure. These are currently the most important *cépages* among the "principal" 13 permitted in regional Côtes-du-Rhônes.

TASTING FOR THE *CÉPAGES*

The following pages are an attempt to characterize the wine produced from each of the important southern Rhône *cépages* when grown in that *terroir*. The reader should remember, however, that in the region itself, tasting unassembled wine from a single variety has a technical interest more than an aesthetic one. Other than the very moment of the *assemblage*, the opportunity to taste a single varietal wine rarely arises, even for a frequent visitor. Such a wine is almost never thought of as complete in itself. The characteristics to be described are usually regarded, rather, as components in the more important "original" or appellation character of a fully assembled wine. Even the practice of vinifying the *cépages* separately is by no means universal. In fact, the tradition is the contrary. As the president of a cooperative winery once asked me, by way of explanation, "Would Monsieur make a stew by cooking the meat, the carrots, and the onions in different pots?"

This attitude once extended to the plantation itself. In old vineyards parcels can still be found in which the various *cépages,* sometimes both red and white, are field-blended *(plants mêlés)* together. The practice was to replace each wornout plant of the dominant *cépage* with a different *cépage.* This was said to give a distinctive and superior aroma to the resulting wine because of the harvesting together of grapes at different stages of ripeness.

Today most *cépages* are planted separately, the better to apply needed sprays to each and to harvest each at the optimum moment. With some of the multiple *cépages* ripening in the second "epoch," as the French categorize varieties, and some in the third (and some are late third at that), the harvest at any one place in the southern Rhône takes about a month to complete. The usual order for harvest of reds is Syrah, Cinsault, Grenache, Carignan, and Mourvèdre.

Nevertheless, a few nearly pure *cépage* wines are recommended under the heading of each *cépage* to help the reader recognize the contributions of each to assembled wines.

RED *CÉPAGES*

Grenache

The Grenache originated in Spain and was widely planted in the Vaucluse by the middle of the 19th century. After the phylloxera epidemic it was planted almost to the exclusion of other *cépages* in places such as Châteauneuf-du-Pape whose wine at that time was bought primarily by *négociants* to "improve" Burgundies. Though susceptible to poor fruit set *(coulure),* Grenache is still everywhere the dominant variety, or *cépage de base.* It does well in dry, windy conditions and can produce, depending on the *terroir,* the year, and how late it is picked, a wine of 15% to 16% of alcohol without chaptalization (the addition of sugar to the must during fermentation in order to raise the eventual alcohol percentage of the wine). As one grower said, "Grenache is our chaptalization."

Being the universal base, Grenache enters into wines of very different types, and its taste characteristics are modified accordingly. The flavor of the red wine varies from raspberry in lighter, earlier picked wines, through red currant, blueberry, and elderberry, to black cherry in heavier, later picked ones. Around Valréas the reds taste like peaches, as do many reds and rosés of the Gard. Grenache fragrances are often resinous of pine, cedar, or juniper, with black pepper, and in some years roses or violets. Licorice, truffles, and a generally Burgundian nose can emerge with age.

Grenache acidity tends to be low, especially off the hotter soils, and the bigger wines can be blurred in outline by being both heady and astringent, thick with what the French call gross tannin—especially if the tannin has been extracted by the heat of fermentation rather than by alcohol. Such a wine is at risk of turning orange prematurely and developing a maderized smell (so called because it is thought to make a wine resemble madeira).

One way of handling this risk is to turn it to stylistic advantage by deliberately pre-oxidizing the red wine to a controlled degree during the course of barrel-aging. Technically, such a wine is said to be in the "forme oxidative," and its taste, having nothing to do with bottle age, is what will be meant when certain growers ask a visitor if he likes "old wines." The mingling of this slight maderization with the smells of late-harvested grapes and of storage in casks must be regarded as a typical element, primarily in certain Châteauneuf-du-Papes and Gigondases. It is only going further in the same direction to make deliberate maderization the basis of the pure Grenache VDN of Rasteau, especially the wood-aged Rasteau Rancio.

Another approach is to minimize the risk of oxidation to Grenache-based wines. This is the theme that unifies a range of recent developments in southern viticulture and winemaking. These include the resurgence of planting multiple *cépages,* light or only partial crushing of the grapes before vinification, and diminishing or eliminating wood-aging—especially at estates where a large capital investment, dubious from the point of view of quality, would have to be made by a winemaker new to estate-bottling. A specific "point" of oxidation suffices to make what most people would recognize as the typical "exuberant" Grenache nose of a southern Rhône. At the same time the need to balance Grenache in a wine with other grapes should not lead us to attribute the greatness of southern Rhônes solely to the other grapes. The high quality of southern Rhône wines is directly attributable to the quality of Grenache as a *cépage noble* when grown in southern Rhône *terroirs.*

Try:

CDR **Domaine des Treilles** of Montbrison-sur-Lez (see "CDR of the Pre-Alps"). Shows that a complete wine can be made from practically pure Grenache in the cooler fringe areas of the southern Rhône.

Gigondas **Domaine du Grand Montmirail** (see Gigondas). Also succeeds with a 100% Grenache by keeping it out of wood.

Châteauneuf-du-Pape **Château Rayas** (see Châteauneuf-du-Pape). 100% red Grenache except for field-blended Grenache blanc and Clairette.

Syrah

The *cépage* of Côte-Rôtie and Hermitage, Syrah has origins that some believe extend by way of the Phocaean Greeks back to ancient Persia and the city of Shiraz, while others say it is equally ancient, but indigenous to the northern Rhône area of Gaul where the Allobrogian tribe lived. Since the 18th century, the use of Syrah has been advised in Provence, and it was planted at Condorcet in Châteauneuf-du-Pape in 1860. In the southern Rhône valley, it produces deep purple, almost black wine, which is firm and with a pronounced, almost jam-like, fruitiness of cassis (black currant) or black raspberry. Fragrances of black or even bell pepper and green olive can be startling and seem especially powerful in wine from young vines.

Picking Syrah somewhat earlier than many southern growers are used to, from the point of view of the desired alcohol, allows the Syrah to contribute a subtler, more leafy, mint or menthol-sage herb fragrance. Agreement seems to be growing that Syrah, a northern *cépage,* retains its character best in cooler and more northerly parts of the southern Rhône, as it also does, many growers observe, on sandy soil, siliceous like the granite of the north. Others counsel a shorter fermentation of partially destemmed grapes for Syrah grown in calcareous soil.

"La petite Syrah" is the name used in the Rhône valley for what is taken to be the true Syrah by comparison to a less fine, more productive clone called "grosse Syrah."

(This must not be confused with the name Petite Sirah on California labels, which refers to a variety that some authorities believe is not Syrah at all.)

Syrah has more and finer tannin than Grenache, and the Syrah wine keeps well. Nevertheless, the immediately attractive fruit of southern-grown Syrah causes it to be used in Côtes du Rhône *nouveaux*. Paradoxically, it is also said to give an early impression of maturity to the aroma of a wine.

Try:

CDT **Domaine de la Grangeneuve** "Cépage Syrah" (see Coteaux du Tricastin). 100% Syrah.

CDR **La Serre du Prieur** of Suze-la-Rousse (see *Château de l'Estagnol* in "CDR of the Lower Aygues and Garrigues"). 80% Syrah, 20% Grenache.

CDR-Villages Vacqueyras **Domaine Le Clos des Cazaux,** "Cuvée des Templiers" (see Vacqueyras). Regularly distinguished by its 75% or so proportion of Syrah from the same producer's 80% or so Grenache "Cuvée St.-Roch."

Carignan

Also of Spanish origin, Carignan was grown for its color, tannin, and regular productivity before Syrah was widely planted in the south. Although susceptible to fungus diseases, it is resistant to drought. Giving a frankly purple and somewhat hard wine, it has a pronounced cherry-lozenge fruitiness when young, a hint of saltiness, and tendencies toward bitterness and the development of an exaggerated licorice smell if not handled well.

Carignan is not allowed in Châteauneuf-du-Pape at all and is limited, along with the other secondary *cépages,* to 10% in CDR-Villages. It continues to be a factor in some regional CDR, where up to 30% is allowed, and is highly regarded in rosés. It responds well to vinifications of red wine that leave some berries whole (CM and OT). Carignan achieves its greatest distinction at low levels of productivity, from old vines on hillside sites.

Try:

CDR **Domaine Martin de Grangeneuve** (see "CDR of the Lower Ouvèze and Plan de Dieu"). Uses high percentages of Carignan in its small-barrel-aged *vins de garde* (wines that keep well).

CDR **Le Château** (see Cairanne). Its distinction is caused in part by its old hillside Carignan component, a vine in too high a proportion in the vineyard for the wine to be Villages.

Cinsault

Not everyone believes Cinsault, an old *cépage* of Languedoc, belongs among the *cépages* called "noble" in the southern Rhône. M. Paul Avril does not plant it for his Châteauneuf-du-Pape of Clos des Papes because it has too high a proportion of juice to skins. Elsewhere, I have been told that Cinsault wine in vat and cask is particularly susceptible to "reduction." The opposite of oxidation, this reaction occurs in the absence of air and can produce, among other unpleasant smells in a wine, that of rubber tires.

At Domaine de Mont-Redon, however, I have tasted Cinsault wine of great elegance. Light red or "clear" in color, soft, refreshing, the Cinsault wine there smells like violets. So does the amazingly dark and concentrated Cinsault from CDR Château de la Fonsalette, which supports the opinion that hillside sites and low productivity are the conditions for Cinsault's best results.

Cinsault, like Carignan, produces very high quality rosé, and minimum requirements for Cinsault are written into the rules of the great rosés Tavel and Lirac. So delicious is the Cinsault as a table grape that one grower in the Tricastin plants it in the interior of his vineyard, lest passers-by driving along the highway stop to help themselves. Cinsault is said to be called Black Malvoisie in California (Galet 1979).

The reputation of Cinsault was not helped among southern growers by its confusion with an undistinguished *cépage* called the "Plant droit." Apparently some nurserymen sold stock of this "Cinsault droit," whose plant is erect, instead of the true Cinsault, called "couché" (reclining) because its branches flop over.

Try:

The Lirac rosé of **Domaine des Causses & Ste.-Eynes** at Roquemaure (see Lirac). 90% Cinsault.

Châteauneuf-du-Pape **Domaine de la Solitude** (see Châteauneuf-du-Pape). A Châteauneuf with more than the usual Cinsault until 1984.

CDV **Domaine St.-Sauveur** of Aubignan (see Côtes du Ventoux). Regularly distinguished from the same producer's CDR by a high proportion of Cinsault, where the CDR has none.

Mourvèdre

Mourvèdre (apparently planted in California under its Catalonian name Mataro) is the most reserved, aristocratic *cépage* of the south. Yet another *cépage* of Spanish origin, it has been so long planted in Provence that it is often regarded as a native. It was the Mourvèdre, in particular, according to the judicial committee of experts appointed to define the Châteauneuf-du-Pape appellation, that lost its former place there to the overplantation of Grenache (Dufays, n.d.). Documents show that it was also strongly planted at Rochegude (Drôme) before phylloxera (Charnay 1985).

Somewhat the opposite of Syrah, then, Mourvèdre is a distinctly southern *cépage*, the *cépage* of Bandol, for example. It is a late mid-season ripener, after Grenache, but its reputation as such comes partly from the early post-phylloxera era, when there was difficulty in finding the right rootstock on which to graft it. Since the French believe less in the inherent superiority of northern *cépages* than in the superior results of planting a *cépage* near the northern limit of its growing zone, some would say that Mourvèdre's aroma is finer and more intense in the Côtes du Rhône than farther south. Most agree, however, that it does best in more southerly parts of the southern Rhône, especially with the heat of a westward exposure and when planted in clay soil with cobblestones on top to conserve moisture below.

A vine of low productivity when planted in infertile soil, Mourvèdre produces a wine that, when young, is dark red, firm, clean, and concentrated rather than thick. To some tasters it has a metallic contact and is "square" rather than "round" in its youth. While the fragrance is at first unforthcoming, one can liberate from it a red-plum or red cherry fruit and the scent of lavender or broomflower by swirling the glass. Mourvèdre seems to contribute vanilla to wines that have never seen oak. Growers have told me that this is because its wood is thick and mature by the time the fruit is ripe. Others believe that it is important to keep Mourvèdre out of barrel altogether to preserve the subtlety of its aroma.

Each year M. Paul Avril assembles a sample *cuvée* of Grenache/Mourvèdre that consistently tastes more Bordeaux-like from cask than does a comparison *cuvée* of Grenache/Syrah. The latter seems almost flagrantly fruity by comparison. At Beaucastel in 1977, the late M. Jacques Perrin served me a bottled Syrah/Cinsault/Mourvèdre *cuvée* from 1952 that tasted for all the world like a St.-Estèphe. The director of the Cave des Coteaux of Cairanne says that the contribution of Mourvèdre to a wine is above all a structure that seems to bring out the best of all the *cépages*.

Try:

CDR-Villages St.-Gervais **Domaine Ste.-Anne** 1983 (see "CDR-Villages of the Northern Gard"). 70% Mourvèdre.

CDR-Villages Rasteau **Château de Trignon** (see Gigondas). Is regularly 50% Grenache and 50% Mourvèdre, by contrast to the same producer's CDR-Villages Sablet at 50% Grenache, 40% Syrah, and 10% Cinsault.

Châteauneuf-du-Pape **Château de Beaucastel** (see Châteauneuf-du-Pape). Following the sequence of vintages here will show the effect of increasing the proportion of Mourvèdre. The composition in 1949 was 90% GR; in 1972, 75% GR, 15% SY; in 1973–74, 55% GR, 10% MV, 15% SY, 10% CS; in 1978, 50% GR, 15% MV, 15% SY, 3–4% CS; in 1980, 50% GR, 20% MV, 10% SY, 10% CS; and in 1984, 30% GR, 30% MV, 20% SY, 5% CS.

Counoise, Muscardin and *Vaccarèse* are other red *cépages* to which reference will be made.

WHITE *CÉPAGES*

Clairette

Clairette is widely planted throughout southern France, of which it is probably a native. It does well in meager soil on hillside sites. Like Grenache among the reds, it is the *cépage de base* of the southern Rhône whites, giving the fruit and freshness which define the type, vinosity, and alcohol support. Also like Grenache it is susceptible to oxidation, and was once used for desert wines. Its presence among the red *cépages* in old-fashioned field-blended parcels shows that it played an historic role in refinement of red wines. Left on the stems and hung up to dry very slowly in an attic or barn, it is an excellent table grape, more in a familial than in a commercial context.

Lately I have noticed an interesting Chardonnay resemblance in certain Clairettes—lemon-vanilla, and a reduction one also finds in Riesling. There can also be pears with a tinge of banana (the banana is said to be present even in the unfermented juice), almonds, and something metallic. The metal is exaggerated and the bananas turn brown if the wine is not protected from oxidation.

There is a less aromatic rose-colored variant of this *cépage*.

Try:

CDR **Domaine de l'Olivet** at Bourg-St.-Andéol (see "CDR of the Northern Gard and Southern Ardèche"). A wood-fermented pure Clairette blanc from both colors.

CDR **Chartreuse de Bonpas** blanc from Caumont-sur-Durance (see "CDR South of Châteauneuf-du-Pape"). A pure Clairette of some delicacy.

Châteauneuf-du-Pape **Château La Nerthe** (see Châteauneuf-du-Pape). Until 1984 the white has been 100% Clairette, very Chardonnay-like in that year.

Bourboulenc

The Bourboulenc has been a factor for a long time in the vineyards of the Vaucluse, where it is regularly cited in documents of the 16th century. Its earlier origins are apparently unknown. Its greatest importance for many years was at Châteauneuf-du-Pape, where it is still part of the triumvirate for whites, along with Clairette and Grenache blanc. Now it is being more widely planted elsewhere in the south as an accessory *cépage* capable of augmenting aroma and local distinctiveness, especially under modern white winemaking conditions. Only a moderate producer, it must be planted on just the right rootstock to avoid excess of its normally vigorous vegetation.

Bourboulenc's effects are fairly pronounced. It smells of flowers and bitter almond, with a little vanilla and fresh-cut green apple from near the skin. Since apples are a common oxidized smell in white wines, it is important to remember that fresh apple is varietal in this case, and to protect the wine from any oxidation that would push it over to the heavier, browned-over apple flesh. With maturity the flowers and apples seem to diminish, and the nuttiness and vanilla to prevail.

Try:

White CDR **Château de l'Estagnol** at Suze-la-Rousse (see "Lower Aygues and Garrigues"). A particularly perfumed and delicate 100% Bourboulenc.

White CDR of **Domaine de la Réméjeanne** at Sabran (see "CDR of Northern Gard and Southern Ardèche"). 50% Bourboulenc until its Clairette comes into production.

Grenache blanc

With some of the characteristics of Grenache noir—high alcohol and susceptibility to oxidation—the white variant is apparently less subject to bad fruit set. It makes an important contribution to richness, roundness, and body in a southern white, and for this reason Domaine de Nalys at Châteauneuf-du-Pape—with the advantage that the percentages of the *cépages* are unregulated in their AOC—usually has a good one-third Grenache blanc in its *assemblage*.

It is another southern white *cépage* in which the advantages of modern winemaking reveal aromatic potentialities hitherto unattainable. Once when I was invited to taste with some technicians, we were all fooled into taking a cool-fermented, blocked malolactic pure Grenache blanc from Rasteau for a big, minerally, leafy-grassy Sauvignon blanc from the upper Loire, a side of its nature I have since seen in similarly treated examples.

Grenache blanc is limited to 10% of the plantation in a CDR-Villages white.

Try:

CDR blanc from **Domaine de la Guicharde** at Mondragon (see "CDR of the Massif d'Uchaux"). 100% Grenache blanc.

White 1981 Châteauneuf-du-Pape **Domaine de Nalys** (see Châteauneuf-du-Pape) of the *cuvée* bottled for Alexis Lichine. 70% Grenache blanc.

Ugni Blanc

Ugni blanc is none other than the variety called St.-Emilion in the Cognac and Armagnac regions of France, where its high acidity suits it to the production of wine for distillation into brandy, and Trebbiano Toscano in Italy. It is thought to have been brought to the Vaucluse from Italy during the Avignon papacy in the 14th century. Another theory is that it may have been brought from the middle east by ancient Greek sailors to the coasts of all the regions where it is now found.

Like Carignan, Ugni blanc is capable under fertile conditions of producing an enormous crop that risks being green because it is a very late midseason ripener. As a result, its image as having any kind of potentiality for nobility has suffered. It is one of the secondary *cépages* limited to a 10% maximum as a group in plantations for CDR-Villages and 30% maximum for CDR.

Nevertheless, the principle of *terroir* maintains that nobility in a *cépage* is always in relation to a particular environment for which it is suited, and there are areas of the southern Rhône where Ugni, to my taste, may be giving its best results—especially on the slopes of the northern Gard, and pre-alpine sectors of the Vaucluse. Well-handled examples can exhibit an enormous florality, probably of violets, and a somewhat metallic crispness with a good mineral feel such as are found in whites of the upper Loire. Handled less well, or when too old, the color is yellow, the metallic taste is heavy, and the violets turn into geraniums.

Try:

White CDR **Château de Boussargues** from Sabran (see "CDR of the Northern Gard and Southern Ardèche"). 100% Ugni blanc, made extra crisp as a shellfish wine.

White CDR **Domaine de Roquevignan** (see Rochegude). Handles Ugni blanc successfully in a richer style.

Picardan, Picpoul, Marsanne, Roussanne, and *Viognier* are other white *cépages* to which reference will be made.

4

Vinification Methods

D IFFERENCES OF STYLE among producer-bottled Rhône wines occur because growers differ from one another in the mix of *cépages* in their *assemblages,* because of the *terroirs* in which the grapes have been grown, and because the growers differ from one another in their methods of vinification. Nevertheless, vinification has dominated contemporary discussion of style differences in the Rhône valley, perhaps because people are apt to give more credit to technique than to nature, and also because they tend to be romantically skeptical of anything alleged to be "untraditional" where the making of Rhône wines is concerned. So the question often arises about someone's vinification, is it "traditional" or is it "carbonic maceration"?—on the assumption that the latter is responsible for a lighter style of wine.

Before we discuss this question, we need to review, at least in layman's terms, the principal methods of red wine vinification that are employed at present in the whole of the Rhône valley. For this purpose it is useful to distinguish two key terms for what goes on in the *cuvaison* (vatting) of a red wine. The wine turns into wine because of *fermentation,* the conversion of sugar in the juice by yeast enzymes into alcohol. The wine turns red and tannic because of *maceration,* the extraction of coloring matter from grape skins, and of tannins from skins and to some extent from stems, if they are present in the process.

CLASSIC VINIFICATION

The method most often referred to as "classic" in the southern Rhône is also called Bordeaux method. It is marked by the destemming of the grapes at the beginning of the vinification process. The grapes are usually crushed as well.

In the south the method has its chief home in cooperatives, where its use reduces the volume of solids to be handled, thereby facilitating the movement of must (the mass of unfermented juice and skins) through pumps and pipes, and the removal of *marc* (pomace) from the fermentation vats, in industrial-scale operations. Actual fermentation is quite rapid in this method, because all the sugar is released immediately. This cuts down the time available for maceration, unless, as in Bordeaux itself, it is allowed to continue a while after the fermentation is finished. But the rapidity helps the cooperatives to empty the vats quickly to make space for the next batches of grapes. Though not all cooperatives use the classic method, the fact that many do, and that cooperatives still produce 63% of all CDR wines, means there is a large volume on the market of red CDR in a lighter style that has nothing whatsoever to do with use of carbonic maceration.

Classic vinification is increasing among private producers who harvest their grapes mechanically. As a general rule, with exceptions depending on the sophistication of the machine and the nature of the *cépage,* a mechanically collected harvest is automatically destemmed. One knowledgeable estimate is that 10% of all CDR is now mechanically harvested. Some of these growers will not crush the grapes further than is implicated by removing the stems, so there is now a "whole berry" version of fermentation without the stems, sometimes loosely styled "semi-carbonic maceration." For reasons that have already been discussed in relation to the Grenache *cépage,* there are also private growers who, although they harvest traditionally, employ CL to eliminate gross stem tannins from their wines.

More common than the Bordeaux method among traditional small producers in eastern France is vinification of grape bunches that have not been destemmed. This is what is meant in the Rhône valley by "traditional" vinification. The term by itself is not always helpful, since each winemaker would like to say that his own method is the traditional one, and since vinification with the stems nowadays takes three different forms, which will be discussed in the next three sections.

STANDARD VINIFICATION

In the standard or orthodox modern method in the southern Rhône, bunches of grapes that have been left on their stems are initially crushed and, in the archetypal case, pumped to the fermentation vats, typically closed. (I follow the French in saying vats— *cuves*—for both open and closed fermenters. The latter are usually called "tanks" in the U.S.) Because of the solids, actual fermentation with this method takes somewhat longer than with CL, giving more opportunity for maceration to go on simultaneously with fermentation. But the sugar being released all at once creates the risk that a grosser tannin will be extracted by heat from stems, rather than a finer one by alcohol from skins.

Some grapes may be destemmed depending on the *cépage,* and on the size, density, and health of the grapes on the bunches. From here on, a host of improvements in the vinification process, made possible by modern equipment, and applicable to CL method as well, have relieved ST of the burden of its bad image: squashed berries and broken stems forced through the hoses to arrive at the vat as a frothing jam of oxygen and gross tannins. Crushers can be flexible and gentle, so that berries are just burst *(éclaté)* and not squashed *(écrasé).* Pumps with the least possible force can be employed, and wherever possible gravity can replace pumping when moving must or wine from one place to another. The further these improvements go in this direction, the more ST resembles the second version of the following method, whose influence they probably reflect.

OLD-TIME VINIFICATION

In the most traditional vinification currently practiced in the northern Rhône, whole bunches of grapes are brought in wooden comports called "beneaux" to the cellar. Perhaps a few grapes will have been crushed if the bunches were occasionally tamped down in the comports to make room for more. Otherwise the intact bunches will be emptied without further manipulation into the open wooden vats. Any other crushing will occur gradually during the *cuvaison,* when from time to time the *vigneron* climbs into the vat, supported by wooden rails across the top, to punch down the floating cap of skins and stems with his feet. Technically this operation is called *pigeage,* but colloquially it is often called *foulage à pieds* (foot treading or crushing). It is an operation that must be performed with great caution in a well-ventilated place, because fermentation is producing carbon dioxide, which being heavier than air, rests in a potentially smothering layer in the space over the cap, even in an open vat.

As the amount of juice increases and the cap diminishes in the thickness required to support his weight, the *vigneron* may switch over to a wooden tamper for the *pigeage.* In France, regionality governs even technique, as a local variant of the method at Côte-Rôtie will remind us. There, after a few rounds of *pigeage,* some winemakers place a grid of planks in the vat above the cap and below the surface of the liquid, to keep the cap submerged. Where this barrier is not employed, one can reach into the vat with a pitchfork at any point in the process and fish out bunches that have a certain number of intact grape berries, by then characteristically rust-colored, still clinging unbroken to their stems.

The outward color is a sign that inside these whole berries, smothered by CO_2 in the surroundings of the fermenting mass, pigment has actually been extracted from their skins into their juice by internal maceration. At the same time, a host of complex, aroma-producing autolytic (self-digestive) enzymatic processes have occurred, collectively called anaerobic metabolism. If by carbonic maceration one means this anaerobic metabolism inside a grape, then it is worth noting that before the name itself was given, carbonic maceration, principally "in the liquid phase," had always been an offshoot of the most archaic traditional vinifications for the making of *vins de garde* in the northern Rhône and Burgundy—and in the Rioja and Piedmont as well (Dunn-Meynell 1984; Amerine and Joslyn 1970). Perhaps because people have heard so often that the purpose of carbonic maceration is to make light wines for early drinking, the term is rarely used to refer to OT vinification in the northern Rhône.

In the similar current practice in the southern Rhône, instead of wooden *beneaux,* the grapes are carried in plastic cases, built so that they can be stacked on top of one another without compressing the grape bunches within. There is no tamping down in the cases, but instead the bunches are passed through the rollers of a cylindrical roller crusher placed directly above the vat. The rollers are set widely apart so that many grape berries pass through unbroken, and other bunches are not put through at all. Instead of open wooden vats, closed cement or stainless steel ones are used. Closed vats made of cement are a reasonable approximation of the south's most traditional vats, which were carved directly into the bedrock or built out of blocks or slabs of the local calcareous rock. Since vats of this kind do not permit climbing into them for *pigeage,* pumping liquid from the bottom over the floating cap of skins and stems *(remontage)* is used instead, to keep the cap moist and below the surface, and to crush the grapes gradually during the course of *cuvaison.* As in the northern version of this method, some grape berries remain intact a long time during this process, and in them and in the "grape" sense we can say that carbonic maceration has occurred. Yet for reasons that almost sound accusatory, and often include allusions to Beaujolais, outsiders often call this vinification itself carbonic or semi-carbonic maceration when it is practiced in the south.

Perhaps this is because among some producers it was replaced for a while, beginning in the 1920s, by the method I call ST, which of course earned itself the name "traditional." This method with its then complete crushing led, we are told by M. Henri

Traditional closed vat made of stone slabs is exposed by house restoration in hamlet of Fontbonne, Vacqueyras (Vaucluse). Another vat of the same sort, still under the house, is dated 1739. Photo courtesy of Katherine Mayberry.

LeRoy, present owner of Château Fortia, "to elevations of temperature that the *old-time practice of incomplete crushing, leaving numerous berries whole,* had a tendency to limit" (LeRoy 1970, author's emphasis and translation).

The old-time practice helps control temperature because it slows down actual fermentation. To the advantage of the solids (the sugar is a smaller proportion of the mass) it adds the advantage of partial initial crushing (the sugar is released slowly). Simultaneous maceration time is increased (which will be anaerobic inside any as-yet-unbroken berries) under conditions that lead to the extraction of finer, unoxidized tannins. To the consequently unmasked "primary" or varietal aromas will be added a seasoning of "secondary" whole-berry aromas from those that come through intact. These are the advantages, when working with the high sugars and oxidizable tannins of Grenache in the climate conditions of southern *terroirs,* that have led to the old method's revival in the southern Rhône. Sometimes equipment is used—stainless vats to which bunches are delivered in overhead gondolas on rails—that makes it look innovative. But following M. LeRoy's language, I shall call both the southern and northern variants, old-time vinification in the first sense (OT1). In the region one also hears the French for "ancient method" applied to this practice of direct lodgement in the vats of whole grape bunches only partially crushed to begin with.

In the south and to a lesser extent in the north (e.g., at Crozes-Hermitage), the wide-spread use of certain other items of new equipment allows an approximation to OT1. This combines a bin for hauling grapes or a reception quay for receiving them that empties itself of the bunches by means of an augur *(vis sans fin)* with a pump that pushes the bunches along through a hose or pipe toward the vat by the turning of an ovoid wheel *(pompe à l'olive)* rather than the back and forth force of a piston. Usually the only crushing given the grapes is what occurs by the passage of the bunches through these two pieces of apparatus. Where the intent and the result is to "leave numerous berries whole," I call this version old-time vinification in the second sense (OT2). This version and a reformed ST can sometimes so strongly resemble each other that they are only arbitrarily distinguishable.

——— INTEGRAL CARBONIC MACERATION ———

In the 1930s some French scientists tried to keep grapes from spoiling by holding them under an atmospere of carbon dioxide. For commercial purposes the fruit did not keep well, but when the grapes were crushed and the juice fermented, the wine was good and had a very intense and distinctive aroma. By accident what they had discovered was anaerobic metabolism, the principle behind what had all along been going on unnoticed—except by Pasteur—in the grapes that came through OT vinification intact. Once carbon dioxide was found to be responsible, it was easy to turn "fruit preservation" into a technique of vinification that systematically preceded all deliberate crushing and normal fermentation of the juice by internal maceration of the grapes in an atmosphere of carbonic gas (André 1976). This was the invention of integral carbonic maceration or carbonic maceration "in the gaseous phase."

In this method, bunches of grapes on their stems and uncrushed (except for those that are by weight at the bottom of the vat) are carefully placed from the top into vats previously filled with carbon dioxide. The vats are then kept closed, so that in strictest application there is neither *pigeage* nor *remontage.* Crushing occurs at the end of the process, so alcoholic fermentation is completed after the wine has been drawn off the marc.

A lot of the work to perfect this vinification went on in the south of France, because it offered obvious advantages to protect the *cépages* of that climate against oxidation, to control temperature—in fact it works best at a high temperature—and to enhance aromatics. Nevertheless, if what is meant by carbonic maceration is a vinification and not a "grape event," it is by far the rarest of the principal kinds of vinification employed in making Rhône wines at the present time, even as the "grape event" is widespread in the Rhône and other regions.

Authorities on the subject have told me that despite frequently written linkage between the two, CM as a vinification is rarely employed in Beaujolais, where much more common is a shortened OT1 (4 to 6 days). Perhaps (which would be the reverse English of the reference in the southern Rhône) the intended linkage with Beaujolais is to the grape event. Whether or not the purpose of using OT in the Rhône resembles its purpose in the Beaujolais is best judged by looking, first at the *cépages* and *terroirs* to which the method is applied, and then at the length of *cuvaison* practiced by the Rhône growers in this guide.

Only in the latter respect might a skeptic conclude that old-time vinification is not practiced at Châteauneuf-du-Pape today the way it was at the turn of the century. While the *cuvaisons* are still long, now no one seals the partially crushed bunches into the vat with plaster and sand over the lid and goes off to hunt while the wine macerates until Christmas. *Châteauneuvois* who have heard of those days say that when the vats were reopened, the wine was sometimes wonderful, sometimes spoiled. Understandably the *vignerons* of the present are not inclined to gamble in this way with their livelihood.

5

Côtes du Rhône Appellations
and the *Terroir*

S ERIOUS WINE DRINKERS know there is a difference between Médocs and Pomerols and why. They may even successfully distinguish Graves-St.-Emilions from Côte-St.-Emilions, even as in Burgundy they will not confuse Côte de Nuits with Côte de Beaune, nor either with a Beaujolais. It is probably more difficult for them to differentiate the *terroirs* of the Rhône valley. At best a sense of the large difference between the northern, continental climate *(septentrionales)* and the southern, Mediterranean climate *(méridionales)* Côtes du Rhônes may have become clear.

Lack of information about regional differences within the vast southern zone, now source of 97% of the production of all Côtes-du-Rhônes and principally responsible for more than tripling Rhône production since World War II, seriously impedes appreciating them in the way one appreciates the other great wines of France, namely as original expressions of their *terroirs*. To advance that kind of appreciation, this book will later identify subregions into which neighboring wines of the southern Rhône can be grouped. First a somewhat larger picture of how *appellations contrôlées* relate to *terroirs* is needed.

—— LOCATION OF *LES CÔTES DU RHÔNE MÉRIDIONALES* ——

At Donzère (Drôme), on its course south from Lyon, the Rhône suddenly emerges from a gorge between cliffs and flows out into a spacious valley, really a basin. Its floor spans plains and ascends plateaus and slopes along tributary rivers to either side of the Rhône all the way from the southern pre-Alps on the east to the foothills of the Cévennes mountains on the west. From here south to about Beaucaire (Gard), the vineyards of *les Côtes du Rhône méridionales* stretch about as far from east to west as they do from north to south.

If one has followed *route nationale* 86 down the river from St.-Péray, one has already left granite behind for limestone country. South of Donzère one enters a zone where the gray-green of olive trees, wild thyme, rosemary, and lavender and the windowless north sides of tile-roofed farmhouses speak clearly of a Mediterranean climate. On the plateau of Donzère, in the area of the adjacent appellation Coteaux du Tricastin, and again near Orange (Vaucluse), the mistral wind achieves record levels of velocity. Not only is the mistral the prime reason the air of the south is bright and the climate dry, it is a also a factor in making the differences of *terroir* among southern Rhône wines occur both horizontally and vertically. Horizontal differences reflect origin on the east or west bank of the Rhône river. These will be spoken of later. Vertical differences are those that reflect

28

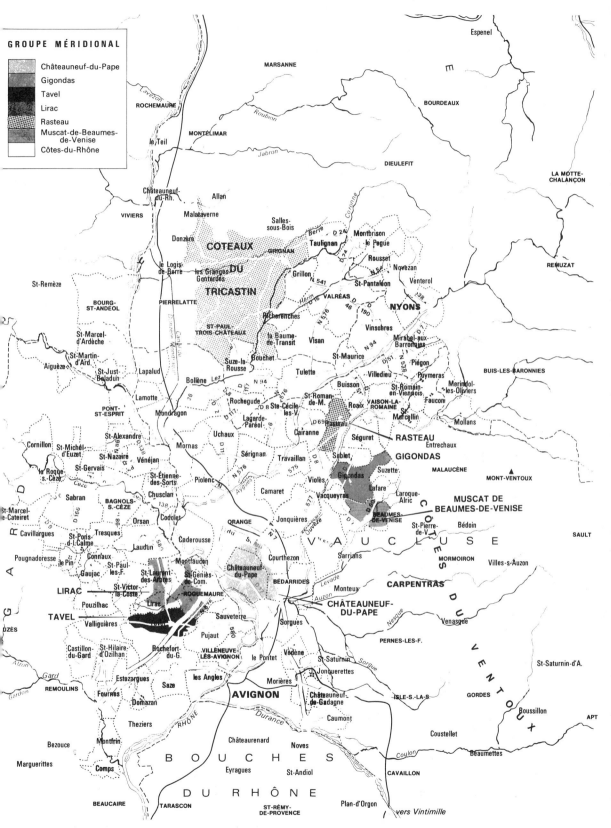

Les Côtes-du-Rhône, Groupe Méridional. Reprinted with permission from *Atlas de la France Vinicole L. Larmat*. Copyright 1976, *Revue du vin de France*.

the terrain. In broad outline, two fundamental associations with the terrain provide the underlying logic of *appellation d'origine contrôlée* in the southern Rhône. One is between topography and soil. The other connects topography with the hierarchy of specificity and quality in the AOC system.

TOPOGRAPHY AND SOIL

Southern Côtes-du-Rhônes are grown on essentially two kinds of land, plateaus and *coteaux* (slopes). Low-lying river bottom-land with recent alluvial soil has been excluded from the AOC. As always, "poor" soil for growing other crops is best for high-quality wine-grape production.

The plateaus, also called *terrasses* in the southern Rhône, are broad expanses of tableland at varying levels of elevation, covered by ancient alluvial soil, well drained and mineral rich. This is made up chiefly of rounded quartzite *cailloux* (pebbles)—the larger ones of cobblestone size—swept down from the Alps by the Rhône or one of its tributaries as the glaciers of the ice ages melted. The stones rest on a bed of mixed clay, gravel and sand, the proportions among which vary from place to place and with the exact geological origin of the subsoil.

Since the Rhône valley is so wide in the south, the slopes that concern us are not, as in the north, directly along the Rhône itself, but overlook its principal tributaries, the Lez, Aygues, and Ouvèze on the left (east) bank, the Cèze and the Tave on the right (west). On these slopes are found a scattering of cobblestones, but mostly chips, shards, and slabs of the local limestone or limey sandstone rock mixed with decomposed sandstone and calcareous clay.

TOPOGRAPHY AND SOUTHERN RHÔNE AOCs

Under the French system of *appellation contrôlée,* the more particular a wine's controlled name, the higher the minimum standards of quality the wine must meet to earn its name (these standards now include a compulsory taste test for all appellations). There are three levels of increasing particularity and quality in the hierarchy of appellations for the Côtes du Rhône as a whole. (a) The most general name is Côtes du Rhône by itself, which indicates a regional wine, in the wine trade sometimes misleadingly called a generic wine. In principle it could come from anywhere in the whole area of the Côtes du Rhône, 163 communes in all, but as we shall see, that is not the case in fact. (b) Restricted in origin to 74 communes and therefore higher on the scale of quality are the Côtes-du-Rhône-Villages. (c) At the top of the scale are 12 localities the names of which may appear by themselves on the label. With some simplification, a direct relationship can be drawn for the south between topography and these levels in the AOC system.

Regional CDR

A large area delimited for simply the regional AOC Côtes du Rhône are the low *terrasses,* given to monoculture of vine only since World War II. These are found east of the first line of higher plateaus along the Rhône, in the southern Drôme and Northern Vaucluse departments (left bank). CDR are also grown on plateaus along the Rhône south of Châteauneuf-du-Pape on the left bank, and south of Tavel (Gard) on the right. Some regional CDR is grown on north-facing slopes, and on foothills in the cooler eastern and western fringes of the AOC area.

Regional CDR represents about 80% of all wine produced in the Côtes du Rhône. It is overwhelmingly a southern product, especially since the postwar extension of the Crozes-Hermitage and St.-Joseph areas onto the northern zones that used to produce only regional wine. More than half the land producing regional CDR is in the department of the Vaucluse alone, another 25% or so is in the southern Drôme, and about 20% in the Gard (Lavigne 1977). Regional CDR is grown at a normal maximum of 50 hectoliters per hectare from 23 permitted *cépages,* with top limits since l957 of 30% of any plantation placed upon Carignan and upon the ensemble of secondary *cépages.*

CDR-Villages

Wine with the AOC Côtes-du-Rhône-Villages now comes in two categories. With one of 17 permitted commune names appearing on the label, and (as an option) hyphenated to CDR instead of the term "-Villages" within the phrase *"appellation . . . contrôlée,"* Villages is a wine essentially of the coteaux. (Adjacent plateau land above or below the slopes is sometimes included.) Twenty-seven communes, all in the south, are actually involved in the production of this category, because some of them have been grouped under the single name of a neighbor. Thus Vacqueyras (Vaucluse) covers two communes, Laudun (Gard) three, Beaumes-de-Venise (Vaucluse) four, and Chusclan (Gard) five.

The second category of CDR-Villages, starting with the 1983 *récolte* (harvest), comes from 47 more *méridionales* communes whose names are not permitted to appear on the label. By analogy to classical Villages terrain and soil, only certain delimited parcels in these communes have been added to the area for Villages. Until the present, CDR-Villages has represented about 7% of all Côtes du Rhône production. Besides indicating a more precise origin, this AOC also demands higher minimum standards of quality—in some respects equal to those of a *cru*—than does regional CDR. The proportion of permitted *cépages* in the plantation is regulated: Grenache 65% maximum; Carignan and all the other secondary *cépages* 10% maximum; and Syrah, Cinsault, and Mourvèdre, singly or together, 25% minimum. Productivity is reduced to a norm of 35 hectoliters per hectare (2¹/₃ tons per acre). The natural alcohol minimum is raised from 11% to 12.5%. In short, CDR-Villages is intended to be a more distinctive, more substantial, longer-keeping wine than regional CDR—a fact that, perhaps by false analogy with Beaujolais-Villages as a quaffing wine, has not penetrated consumer awareness.

The latter difficulty, coupled with another in the rules, poses a tough choice between quality and economics for a grower with parcels of land entitled to produce Villages wine. Since 1974 the rules have allowed for only one AOC to be declared per "surface" per year (no more "cascade" of overproduction downward through successively lower AOCs). So each year the grower must decide for each of his recorded parcels whether to harvest it at the Villages rate of productivity or at the higher regional rate. Since the price obtainable for Villages has never consistently established itself as more than marginally superior to that for regional CDR, less Villages is usually declared in years with abundant harvests (e.g., 1980).

The significance of the mistral for the coteaux is twofold, depending on which way the slopes incline the vineyard. Exposure to the north is into the teeth of the mistral (which makes for concentration), for example, Laudun from St.-Victor-la-Coste. Exposure to the south can provide some shelter, and sometimes a heat pocket, for example, Vinsobres. In addition, slopes give good air-drainage protection against such moisture-related problems as spring frosts, *coulure,* and rot. The clay of the slopes is a cool soil, good for body and acidity in a wine, as *calcaire* (lime) is said to be for aroma. Sand is a factor for finesse, for example, at Sablet and Vacqueyras.

Local AOCs

The *crus* of the southern Rhône are the wines named for specific localities. Apart from VDN, these are Châteauneuf-du-Pape and Gigondas (Vaucluse), Tavel and Lirac (Gard). All include high plateaus in their areas. (Adjacent slopes are also included and even some mountain land in the Dentelles de Montmirail at Gigondas.)

Wines with local AOCs account for approximately 12% of all the Côtes du Rhône production. Of this, only about 24% is grown in eight northern localities. Fully 40% of all locally named wine is from Châteauneuf-du-Pape alone (Le Plâtre et Sarfati 1983). Minimum quality standards for these AOCs vary somewhat but are uniformly elevated. A brief survey includes reduced productivity (35 to 42 hectoliters per hectare), regulation of the percentages of *cépages* (Lirac, Tavel, Gigondas), minimum alcohol of 12.5% (Châteauneuf-du-Pape and Gigondas), and the strictest rule in France against overproduction (Châteauneuf-du-Pape).

The high plateaus are fully exposed to the mistral. And in general, the higher the plateau, the bigger the cobblestones, which makes for a hot soil (though at the same time it protects against evaporation of valuable moisture from below). The result is concentrated, high-alcohol wine, usually smelling of *garrigues* (provençal scrub growth and wild herbs). It takes a special effort not to harvest overripe grapes from these sites, so some growers seek to produce a wine with late harvest character. Others pick earlier and stress the special importance in the circumstances of balancing low-acid Grenache with other *cépages.*

DIFFERENCES BETWEEN THE TWO BANKS OF THE RHÔNE

Vertical differences among the southern Rhône *terroirs* reflect features of the landscape that occur throughout the Côtes du Rhône *méridionales.* Horizontal differences reflect a variation in climate between the two banks of the Rhône. This variation is largely a story, again, of that river's tributaries.

The climate on the left bank (Vaucluse and southern Drôme) is drier, partly because, like the Rhône River itself, its left bank tributaries, the Lez, Aygues, and Ouvèze, originate in the Alps. This means that their rise and fall in water-level tends to parallel

Springtime high water on the Ouvèze River at Roaix (Vaucluse). Photo courtesy of Rosalind Srb.

that of the Rhône. They run high with alpine melt-water when the Rhône is running high, and are almost dry when the Rhône is running low.

An additional reason for less ambient humidity on the left bank is the orientation of the tributaries there. They flow from northeast to southwest, the lower Ouvèze even north-northeast to south-southwest. So the valleys of these rivers, especially that of the Ouvèze, become like the Rhône, corridors for the mistral. The concentrating effect is particularly felt on the north-facing slopes and on the open *terrasses* (the two coincide at Gigondas and on the north side of Châteauneuf-du-Pape). The broad expanse of wide-open spaces jutted into by higher plateaus, hills, and the jagged peaks of the Dentelles de Montmirail, give the area an atmosphere something like the American Southwest, most noticeable perhaps at sunset when the whole landscape shades from crimson to lavender.

The right bank tributaries, Ardèche, Cèze, and Tave, originate in the Cévennes. Their rise and fall in water-level is therefore less parallel to that of the Rhône than is the rise and fall of the left bank tributaries. The consequence is a little more and more constant ambient humidity in the Gard, a tendency that is reinforced by the geographical orientation of these tributaries *vis-à-vis* the mistral. The right bank tributaries flow nearly west to east, athwart the mistral, which enhances the sheltering effect for south- and east-facing slopes. This and a more general irregular hilliness in the Gard, compared to the definite contrast of broad *terrasses* with slopes in the Vaucluse, may be the prime reason why red wines of the Gard are often both firmer and more delicate, leaner and more Bordeaux-like, than the sometimes more robust, sometimes huge and less sharply defined reds from the Vaucluse. Other differences, both natural and cultural, seem to have accumulated to reinforce this primary distinction.

On the east bank, many exposures face the westward quadrant, and hence the heat of afternoon sun. This is to the advantage of alcohol and to the detriment of acidity. On the west bank, many exposures face the eastward quadrant, providing morning light at the same time the air is richest with carbon dioxide. This is to the advantage of aroma. (The eastern zone of Châteauneuf-du-Pape also sees eastward exposure.) Finesse is also contributed by a greater prevalence of sandy soil in the Gard, which makes erosion a cultivation problem in some areas.

The *encépagement*—number and proportion of the *cépages* in the vineyards—is more diverse on the right bank than on the left, which like the climate and soil differences helps to make the best wines of the right bank somewhat more elegant. Plantations in the Gard are often 50% Grenache or less, compared to the 70% Grenache that is frequent in the Vaucluse (Le Plâtre et Sarfati 1983). This diversity has two rather different causes. The vineyards of the Gard with older vines contained significant numbers of field-blended Carignan, secondary *cépages*, Aramon, and French-American hybrids. The latter two, in particular, were present because, immediately after phylloxera, many *vignerons* of the Gard followed the lead of the rest of Languedoc and grouped together into cooperatives specializing in the production of table wine, *vin ordinaire*. Since 1936 and the institution of AOC, to produce AOC wine has required replacing hybrids and Aramon, and the excess proportion, according to the new rules, of secondary *cépages* and Carignan. As this process has gradually gone on, the required substitutions have retained the underlying diversity, as well as being one of the causes, besides expansion of the vineyards and AOC areas elsewhere, of augmented CDR production (Charnay 1985). Nevertheless one still finds numerous private growers and cooperatives in the Gard who produce more table wine than AOC wine. (Cooperatives producing less than 20% AOC have not been included in this guide.)

In the vineyards with newer vines, like many at Tavel and Lirac, reconstitution after they were destroyed by phylloxera did not occur until after World War II, or even until after the arrival of the repatriated French ("pieds noirs") from North Africa. By this time diversity of initial plantation was insisted upon by the INAO who, by 1953, controlled "rights of plantation other than for replacement." They required a high proportion of the "ameliorative" *cépages,* as Syrah, Cinsault, and Mourvèdre are called.

In the Vaucluse, meanwhile, the growers' recourse after phylloxera was more apt to be production of blending wine for the Burgundian commerce, which, in the days before

AOC, bought Grenache wine from slopes and Carignan from plains to strengthen the northern product in body, alcohol and color. Both being *cépages* that were admissable in the transition to AOC, gross dominance of Grenache and a high proportion of Carignan in the vineyards, and the sale by their producers of 80% of all Côtes du Rhône wines in bulk, were the legacy delivered to the AOC.

APPELLATION TAVEL CONTROLÉE

CHÂTEAU D'AQUERIA

MIS EN BOUTEILLES AU CHÂTEAU

TAVEL
ROSÉ

JEAN OLIVIER, SOCIÉTÉ CIVILE AGRICOLE, PRODUCTEUR, TAVEL

CANTO PERDRIX

TAVEL

APPELLATION TAVEL CONTROLÉE

Mise en Bouteilles à la Propriété   "e" 75 cl

MEJAN-TAULIER PROPRIÉTAIRE TAVEL-GARD-FRANCE

Imp. LAFFONT - AVIGNON   CREATION MONA Yves

RÉCOLTÉ PAR LES PÈRES   DE LA SAINTE FAMILLE

Tavel

APPELLATION TAVEL CONTROLÉE

Château de Manissy

TAVEL (GARD)

0.75

DOMAINE DE LA GENESTIÈRE

TAVEL

APPELLATION TAVEL CONTRÔLÉE   70 cl

MIS EN BOUTEILLE AU DOMAINE

GEORGES BERNARD PROPRIÉTAIRE A TAVEL (GARD)

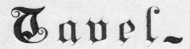

Tavel

LE PALAIS

APPELLATION TAVEL CONTROLÉE

ODOYER CHARLES
PROPRIÉTAIRE-RÉCOLTANT
30126 TAVEL
(GARD) - (FRANCE)

75 CL

Prieuré de Montézargues

Tavel

Appellation Tavel Controlée

Mis en bouteille au Prieuré

75 cl

-Allauzen- Propriétaires Récoltants-
Groupement Agricole Familial & Foncier - 30126 Tavel
France

CONTENTS 750 ml   ALCOHOL 12,5 % BY VOLUME

Domaine Le Vieux Moulin

MARQUE DÉPOSÉE N°160.

MIS EN BOUTEILLE A LA PROPRIÉTÉ

Tavel

APPELLATION TAVEL CONTROLÉE

G.a.e.c. les fils de Gabriel Roudil - Propriétaire-Récoltant 30126 Tavel France

CHATEAU DE TRINQUEVEDEL

TAVEL

APPELLATION TAVEL CONTROLÉE   75 cl

MIS EN BOUTEILLE AU CHATEAU

F. DEMOULIN, PROPRIÉTAIRE-RÉCOLTANT A TAVEL (GARD) FRANCE

SOUTHERN SUBREGIONS AND PRODUCERS

THE RIGHT BANK

Ardèche wine festival, held annually near Bourg-St.-Andéol (Ardèche).
Photo courtesy of Robert Burns.

Château d'Aqueria

LIRAC

FRANCE 75 cl

Appellation Lirac Contrôlée

Mis en Bouteille au Château

JEAN OLIVIER SOCIÉTÉ CIVILE AGRICOLE PRODUCTEUR A TAVEL 30126

Cuvée Ancienne Viguerie

DOMAINE

DU

Château Saint-Roch

Lirac

Appellation Lirac Contrôlée

ANTOINE VERDA & FILS

Propriétaire-Récoltant à Roquemaure (Gard)

FRANCE

Mise en bouteilles du Château

75 cl e

Domaine du Devoy

LIRAC

75 cl

APPELLATION LIRAC CONTRÔLÉE

MIS EN BOUTEILLE AU DOMAINE

LOMBARDO Frères, PROPRIÉTAIRES A St-LAURENT-DES-ARBRES (30126)

FRANCE

LES QUEYRADES

LIRAC

APPELLATION LIRAC CONTRÔLÉE

73 cl

Domaine André MÉJAN, Propriétaire, Récoltant à TAVEL (Gard).

1983 *Laudun* 75 cl

Côtes-du-Rhône

Appellation Côtes-du-Rhône Contrôlée

mis en bouteille à la propriété

Faraud et Fils Viticulteurs à Saint-Victor-la-Coste

30290 Laudun (France)

Imp. Legrand - Bagnols

PRODUCED AND BOTTLED IN FRANCE

Domaine des Moulins

Imported by PALMA CELLARS, INWOOD, NEW YORK

CÔTES·DU·RHÔNE

APPELLATION COTES DU RHONE CONTROLÉE

Red Table Wine Contents 750 ml

ALCOHOL MIS EN BOUTEILLE PAR

12,5% BY VOLUME GEORGES DUBŒUF

NÉGOCIANT A ROMANÈCHE-THORINS (SAONE-ET-LOIRE) FRANCE

DOMAINE PELAQUIÉ

1978

LAUDUN

Appellation COTES DU RHONE Contrôlée

Mis en bouteille au Domaine 75 cl

EMMANUEL et LUC PELAQUIÉ (GAEC) SAINT-VICTOR LA COSTE - 30790

Produce of France

IMP. PLUMELLE - ORANGE

CHATEAU d'ORSAN

1983

CÔTES DU RHONE

Appellation Côtes du Rhône Contrôlée

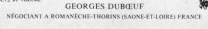

RÉCOLTÉ PAR

JOSEPH BRUNEL PROPRIÉTAIRE A ORSAN (GARD)

Distribué et mis en bouteille par 75 cl

LES GRANDES SERRES NÉGOCIANT A CHATEAUNEUF DU PAPE (Vse) FRANCE

6

Southern and Central Gard ("La Côte du Rhône")

FOR GEO-CLIMATIC and historical reasons, the right bank group of wines divides into two subregions: a southern and eastern group, the earliest in the southern Rhône to harvest, and a more northerly and westerly group.

To the south and east the climate is somewhat warmer and drier and the soils lighter, the *terroir* having a long recognized "vocation," as the French would say, for softer red wines and excellent rosés. These are close to the very kind of wines, then known as *clairet,* for which the area was renowned when it was called La Côte du Rhône.

La Côte du Rhône was a specific geographical, cultural, and administrative unit within Languedoc in the kingdom of France. Its spirit of autonomy and a connection with Provence were reinforced by being under the ecclesiastical sway of the bishop of Avignon, a city just across the Rhône, but then outside France. For vinous purposes the Côte stretched from the area of modern AOC Tavel to that of Chusclan. Its highly regarded wines were shipped from the river port of Roquemaure. Rules that were very specific by the early 18th century required that the letters CDR be branded on the barrels in which the wine was shipped and that wine from outside the CDR zone be barred from entry. Châteauneuf-du-Pape was once refused (Gouron n.d.).

Clairet, the ancestor of both red and rosé, was made from red *cépages,* with perhaps a few white for finesse, which were given only a short maceration to extract a "clear" (light) red color (hence the name). Then the juice was drawn off and fermented without the skins and stems. Areas that differed in the length of maceration and hence the darkness of color given their wines are roughly marked today by the boundary between AOCs Tavel and Lirac.

No doubt owing to the fame this proto-appellation CDR had already acquired, by the middle of the 19th century certain merchants and authors began to refer to "Côtes du Rhône" wines from the left bank and from the north. Unlike those of La Côte du Rhône, these were wines that until then had not been grouped under a single umbrella.

CRU: TAVEL

The sign on the roof of the cooperative Cave les Vignerons de Tavel says "Tavel 1ᵉʳ Rosé de France." It is easy to see as one reaches the outskirts of the village when coming the few miles west from the Rhône or from Avignon on the other side. The *vignerons* who bring their grapes to be vinified at the *cave* are responsible for about half the supply of all Tavel.

At one time, the Tavel Syndicate of Growers were more hesitant to identify Tavel as a rosé. Not long after its founding, the Syndicate wrote in a 1905 pamphlet that "the fine wines of Tavel . . . are of a pretty color, clear golden ruby, very lively, and not rosés" (Moison 1974). The same pamphlet refers to Tavel's "rich nuance of topaze mixed with ruby sparkling in the glass," to me a nuance that resembles the ripe blush on the skin of a peach. (Just as the wines now called "blushes" are too light, most American rosés are too dark to meet the color ideal of a Tavel.)

Present-day AOC regulations permit only what we now call rosé wines to bear the Tavel name. The moral of the pamphlet story, though, is this: whatever we may think of other rosés, Tavel needs to be appreciated as its own distinctive type, a direct successor to the tradition of making "clairet" wines that predate by centuries the vogue for the word rosé. Presence of both orange and blue reflections in the color is part of Tavel's typicity. So is complete dryness.

Uses of Rosé

Southern France, old Languedoc and Provence, is the native home of many bone-dry, medium to light colored rosés, including Tavel (Gard) and the other southern Rhône rosés. The uses of rosé at table in this region give some credence to both of the half-truths that often impede serious appreciation of rosé wines. One is that rosé is both red and white ("it goes with any food") and the other is that it is neither red nor white ("it can't make up its mind").

In the southern Rhône, for instance, rosé often accompanies dishes, like seafood, that in other regions might call for a white. One reason is that very little white wine, only about 2% of all Côtes du Rhônes, is made. Until recent technical advances even less was good, owing to the difficulty of working with low-acid Mediterranean *cépages* in a hot climate. Some winemakers overused sulfur, either to save acidity by blocking the malolactic fermentation, or simply to prevent oxidation. These wines led many locals to suspect that no white wine could be "natural." In the circumstances, the rosés were usually a better bet, and they remain better suited to the strong seasoning of some of the typical dishes—*soupe de poisson* with saffron and garlic-laden *rouille*, or salt cod with the garlic mayonnaise called *aioli*—which could overwhelm even a well-made white.

The summer heat of a Mediterranean climate is the reason why rosés are also substituted for southern Rhône reds. Rosés are served cold. More crucial is the weighty style of many reds. At the prevailing daytime temperatures of the region, 90° to 100° F, a Châteauneuf or Gigondas at 14% alcohol (plus wood age) is just not bearable.

Two Basic Methods for Making Rosé

The resemblances between rosé wines and both reds and whites make rosé a genuine third type. Like whites, rosés are produced by fermentation of the grape juice alone, after separation from the skins and stems. Like reds, they owe their color and tannins to some contact with the skins of red grapes. That is, although some white grapes can be used in making a rosé—as in making Rhône reds like Côte-Rôtie, Hermitage, and Châteauneuf-du-Pape—red grapes must be employed.

Of the two basic methods for vinifying rosé, the one called *pressurage direct* (direct pressing) or *vinification en blanc des raisins noirs* accentuates the resemblance of rosés to whites. In this method, the grapes are brought from the harvest directly to the wine press *(pressoir)*, perhaps having first been passed through a crusher. The grape skins are not allowed to macerate in the juice. Instead the juice is merely stained with skin color to the desired extent before fermentation by regulating the duration and force of the *pressurage*. Many Côtes de Provence rosés are produced by direct pressing (André 1976).

The method called *la saignée partielle de la cuve* (partial bleeding of the vat) accentuates the resemblance of rosés to reds. Here, the juice to be fermented into rosé is drawn off, or bled, from a vat in which the remaining juice and *marc* will be left to ferment into red wine. The extent of coloration is regulated by the length of time the juice for rosé remains in contact with the macerating skins (usually 12 to 36 hours) before "la saignée." This is the way most rosés are made in the Côtes du Rhône.

Tavel's Multiple Juices

The basic methods for making rosé produce only two of the three basic juices that may enter into composition of a Tavel. What this book will call "juice A" is obtained by the direct pressing of grapes of either color.

"Juice B" owes its color to having been left in contact with the skins of red, or red and white, grapes for a period of maceration. Although the drawing off of this juice from the maceration vats is sometimes called "la saignée" at Tavel, the term does not signify, as it does elsewhere, that most juice is left behind to be made into red wine. Two kinds of juice B need to be distinguished. In the case of B1, the grapes are placed in the vat for maceration after having been crushed (but not destemmed). In the case of B2, the grape bunches are partially crushed, sometimes only by their own weight in the vat, and therefore contain a proportion of whole berries.

"Juice C" is obtained from the macerated grape pomace that remains after "la saignée." Though a *pressoir* is employed in this operation, the press is not advanced to those pressures that produce "vin de presse" in the technical sense (locally called "3rd press"). Indeed, at the time of vinification, an amount of press juice together with lees and "bourbes" (precipitated impurities) equal to 10% of an estate's Tavel harvest must be declassified and eliminated from the production of any wine to be called Tavel.

While a few Tavels are made entirely from juice A, most, and the most classic, are multiple juice wines, composed either of juices B + C or even of B + C further adjusted for color and balance by addition of a little juice A. This use of B + C distinguishes Tavel from almost all other rosés. It further weights the rosé balance in a Tavel toward the red side, and is a benefit, I believe, of restricting the AOC Tavel to rosé wines.

As an example, consider Château de Trinquevedel, perhaps the most complexly made of all Tavels. Eight different *cépages* are planted on this 26–hectare estate. Each of the principal ones—Grenache, Cinsault, and Clairette—is handled a different way, so that all the possible juices actually enter into the composition of Trinquevedel. Clairette, a white *cépage* with a pink-colored variant, is pressed directly (juice A). Cinsault, a red grape with a high proportion of juice to its tender skins, is crushed over the vat to avoid pumping, and then held under an atmosphere of carbon dioxide for 24 hours of maceration before the juice (B1) is drawn off. The bunches of Grenache, a red grape, are placed uncrushed into the vat for a maceration of whole berries, also under CO_2, for up to 72 hours (juice B2). Juice is obtained from the *marc* of the red grapes by employing a pneumatic press, for the most even and gentle pressure (juice C).

Finally, it may be the use of B + C in classic Tavels that explains their reputed longevity. While some contemporary producers and consumers of Tavel stress drinking it in its first year, I remain of the old opinion that its hint of tannicity often asks that a Tavel be ripened to full peachiness in bottle. Optimum development seems to be achieved at about three years. A Tavel also benefits from a serving temperature that is not really ice-cold, as well as from a 30 to 45 minute breathing time before serving, to liberate the subtle floral, nutty, resinous, and even honeyed elements of the bouquet. In short, Tavel is the adult rosé.

Multiple Cépages

As the example of Triquevedel illustrates, Tavel is not a "varietal" wine, but one assembled for balance from multiple *cépages,* as are other wines of the southern Rhône. Following a period of overplantation of Grenache and Clairette, and an underplantation of Cinsault, Tavel is seeing a contemporary resurgence of the tradition of multiple *cépages*. While Grenache is absolutely necessary for truth to type and alcoholic support, it must be balanced by *cépages* with more finesse, "nerve," and resistance to oxidation to counteract its tendency to rapid oxidation and heaviness.

The requirements of the AOC were therefore modified to their present form in 1968. Permitted *cépages* are Grenache, Cinsault, Clairette blanche and rose, Picpoul, Calitor, Bourboulenc, Mourvèdre, Syrah, and Carignan. A minimum of 15% Cinsault is now required; none of the others, including Grenache, may now exceed 60% (formerly 65%). Carignan remains restricted to no more than 10%. (Required percentages regulate an estate's plantings, not the composition of a given *cuvée* of wine.)

Syrah and Mourvèdre are included in the list for the first time. Acknowledging their excellence for red wines, some growers are convinced that they must be used very sparingly in Tavel lest the wine be too dark and otherwise too strongly marked by their "varietal" character. Production of Tavel is limited to 42 hectoliters of wine per hectare of land.

Multiple Terroirs

As in the rest of the southern Rhône, Tavel estates take two forms. A few are of the single or château type. The majority are dispersed or village estates. Trinquevedel, with its 18th-century château, is one of only four single estates at Tavel. All are found east of the village, and all are on or adjoining a zone of "Astian"-stage sandy soil similar to that found on the east side of Châteauneuf-du-Pape, notably at Château Rayas. Prieuré de Montézargues lies on the south side and Château de Trinquevedel on the north side of the same rise, called locally "La Montagne Noire." Château d'Acquéria is off to the northeast among the rolling sandhills; Château de Manissy is just across the road to the northwest. The latter is already in the commune of Roquemaure on the only parcels of land outside Tavel itself to have been included in the 1936 delimitation of the area of appellation.

Calcareous slopes are found to either side of the sand in this zone, which actually begins a bit north of the village and west of the northern plateau, widening considerably as it extends south and east. For this reason I shall call it the central-eastern zone. Two additional zones with different *terroirs* can be distinguished. North of the village, stretching into and shared with neighboring Lirac, is the plateau of Vallongue, whose vineyards were reconstituted after phylloxera only since World War II. This is covered, as are similar "terrasses" at Châteauneuf-du-Pape, with alpine quartzite cobblestones over varying amounts of clay and sand. These are exposed as "earth" on the sides of the plateau. Last, again as at Châteauneuf, an area of even more recently dewooded and replanted broad slopes extends west of the village and is strewn with whitish rocks of "compact" local limestone over red clay.

Dispersed estates have parcels scattered in some or all of these zones, and to have a "complete" Tavel, they assemble their wine from the different terroirs.

Individual Wines

Multiple juices, multiple *cépages,* and multiple *terroirs* are the factors that make Tavel a special type among rosés. These same factors become variables that can distinguish the wine of one Tavel owner from another, for example, a soil balance inclining to sand, cobblestones or limestone rocks, or the precise mixture of *cépages.*

Three additional variables can cause style differences: whether a wine is cold-fermented, whether it undergoes malolactic fermentation, and whether it is aged in either vat or wood before bottling. Those who value a Tavel most for its youthful properties tend to cold-ferment, to block the malolactic from occurring, and to bottle early. Increasingly the matter of the malolactic is the most crucial factor. Blocking the malolactic in effect retains youth in the bottled wine by preserving a fresh nose and high acid level even if it is not drunk literally in its first year. Allowing the malolactic fermentation to take place makes a rounder and more "finished" wine to start with, one which will evolve, to my mind beneficially, in bottle. (Nevertheless, the oenologist who counsels many of the estates that block the malolactic points out that malic acid itself can provide support for longevity.)

All these variables will be noted to the extent possible in the commentary on individual producer's wines that follows. The wines are grouped according to the juices from which they are assembled.

Producers (arranged by composition)

Abbreviations particular to this chapter:

CE = central eastern zone	A = juice from direct pressing
N = northern zone	B = juice from maceration
W = western zone	C = juice from *marc*

Other abbreviations are found in the master list at the beginning of this book. Addresses of producers are 30126 Tavel, unless otherwise indicated.

JUICE A

Domaine de Lanzac, Norbert de Lanzac

Particularities under the late M. Raoul de Lanzac included late harvest, high alcohol, oak aging (the latter practice has now been abandoned).

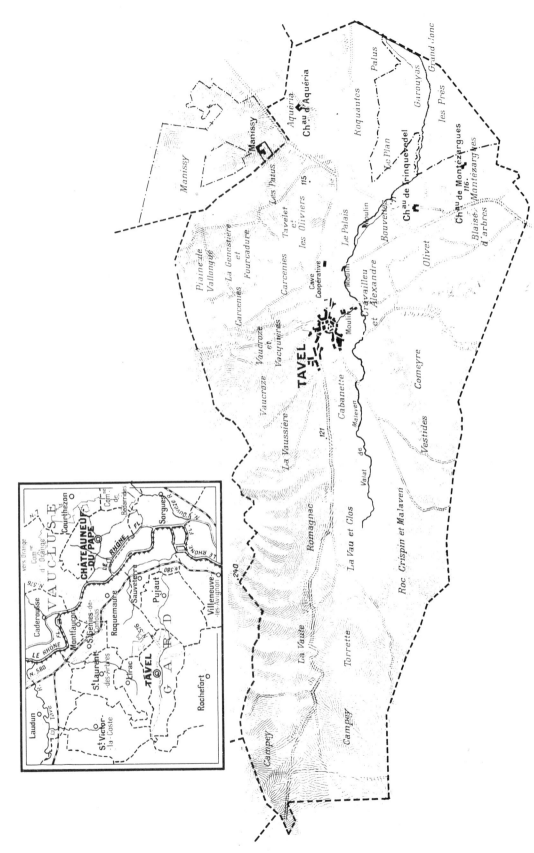

Tavel. Reprinted with permission of *Revue du vin de France* from *Atlas de la France Vinicole L. Larmat.* Copyright 1943, Louis Larmat, Paris.

5 ha, parcels in qrts Vallongue (N); Vestides (W); Bouvette (CE). "No sand." 54% GR, 27% CS, 9.5% CR, plus CT, BR, SY, MV. Lirac, and CDR from 5 ha at Lirac.

Domaine des Lauzes, Beccaria-Boband-Bouin

M. Beccaria sells his Carignan and plateau wine in bulk, and bottles only the production of his western parcels, covered with limestone rocks called *lauzes,* for greater delicacy and harmony.

12 ha, of which 11 are in qrts Vestides, Romagnac (W); and 1 in Vallongue (N). 60% GR, plus CS, CT, and a very little MV and CR. ❧ Other particularities include very light pressing and avoidance of malolactic fermentation.

Adolphe Roudil

Only about ¼ of this small estate's production is bottled.

5 ha, qrts Vaucroze et Vacquières, Roquautes (CE); La Vau et Clos, Malaven, Romagnac (W). 50% GR, some 85 years old, plus CS, CR, CT, PL. ❧ Wine rests 8 to 16 months in vat before bottling.

Seigneur de Vaucroze, SCA Leveque (Claude et Jean Leveque)

Estate has been in the hands of the same family since before the revolution. The late M. Gabriel Leveque was proud of making the "clearest" (lightest-colored) Tavel. He also aged the wine a long time in vat before bottling, a minimum of two years being continued by his sons. High alcohol. The best case for this style is made by restaurant "L'Auberge de Tavel," which serves Vaucroze on its "tasting" menu with dessert.

31 ha, principal parcels in qrts Vallongue (N); Vaucroze et Vacquières (CE); Torrette (W); Cravailleu, Cabanette (CE and W). 12 ha of CDR rosé from Lirac.

Domaine de Tourtouil, Edouard Lefèvre

Fairly strong flavor, minerally, and appley.

20 ha, parcels in Vallongue (N); Vestides (W); Vaucroze, Olivet, Manissy (CE). 60% GR, 15% CS, 10% CR, plus CT, SY, MV, a little PL. Vines average 40 years old. ❧ M. Lefèvre uses direct pressing because he prefers young, unaggressive Tavel. No malolactic fermentation.

Domaine du Vieux Relais, Félix Roudil et ses Enfants

Round, almost candyish fruit in a wine whose slightly buttery to vanilla nose comes from 6 months to 1 year in oak casks.

15 ha, in qrts Vallongue (N); Codoyeres, Palais, Blaise d'Arbres (CE); Vestides, Romagnac (W). 50% GR, plus CR, CS, MV, SY, BR, PL, CT. 2 ha of CDR from Rochefort-du-Gard (40% SY). Grandson Jean-Marie Bastide also owns 5–ha Tavel estate **Domaine St.-Ferréol.**

JUICE B + JUICE C

H **Château d'Acquéria,** SC Jean Olivier

Imported into the U.S. since the end of prohibition, the wine combines rich flavor, full body, and finesse.

50 ha surrounds the 18th century château in qrt Acquéria, originally called "Puy Sablonnier" —sandy mountain (CE). 45% GR, 14% CT, 18% CS, 8% MV, 4% CR, the rest diverse. 2.5 ha Lirac (GR, MV, CS) in production. ‵ Present owner M. Paul de Bez continues practice of oak fermentation and aging in oak, though the latter lasts a shorter time than formerly, and the malolactic fermentation is now avoided.

Association des Producteurs "Les Vignerons de Tavel"

Technically advanced cooperative makes 15,000 hl of Tavel intended for youthful drinking. Nevertheless, I find the wine full-flavored and tannic enough for development.

Founded 1937. 72.24% AOC. 140 members from Tavel and Rochefort-du-Gard (CDR). ‵ Particularities include cold maceration of the different *cépages* together, and both settling and centrifugation of the juice before cold fermentation.

H **Canto-Perdrix**, Méjean-Taulier

Wine is generally well structured, fruity with flowers and spices, round, long.

32 ha, parcels in Vallongue (N); Vaucroze (CE); Romagnac and La Vau et Clos (W). 60% GR, 15% CS, 5% CR, plus PL, CT, BR, MV, SY 4 ha. Lirac **Les Queyrades**. ‵ Usually rests 7 to 8 months in vat, 1984 sold early. No malolactic.

Domaine des Carabiniers, GFA du Domaine des Carabiniers, Roquemaure

For details, see Lirac.

Domaine du Corne-Loup, Jacques Lafond

Strong flavor and body, minerally and somewhat dark.

20 ha, parcels in qrts Campey, Torette, Vestides (W); Vaucroze (CE); Vallongue (N). 50% GR, 20% CS, 10% SY, plus CT, BR, CR. ‵ Some B2 by partial crushing. Tries to avoid malolactic fermentation.

Henri de Lanzac

M. de Lanzac regards his first *cuves* as the best because he harvests his old vines first. Also prefers the flavor of dark-colored Tavel. His own bottling (not commercialized) is dark, grenadine colored, and is a full, rich, solid mouthful of wine.

12 ha in qrts Roc Crispin and Malaven (W); Vaucroze et Vacquières, Palais, Olivet and Chemin du Roi (CE). 5 ha GR, 2.7 ha CS, 2 ha CT, .5 ha CR, plus diverse, including BR, SY, and field-blended PL. ‵ Its character is reasonably if not completely represented in the version bottled at the domaine and commercialized by the Châteauneuf-du-Pape *négociant* firm Les Grandes Serres, presented under the name **Henri de Montlauzy**.

H **Domaine Maby La Forcadière**, GAEC Domaine Maby

M. Armand Maby, former mayor of Tavel, advocates drinking Tavel young, and bottles his without malolactic fermentation and "sur lies" for leafy, yeasty nose.

60% of 50 ha is cobblestone covered. Principal parcels in Vallongue (N); Cravailleu, Olivet (CE). 50% GR, 18% CS, 5% MV and SY, plus CT, PL, BR, Calitor, CR. 30 ha **La Fermade** in Lirac. Now 60% MV, the red Lirac is aged in vat, oak casks and bottle before sale. M. Maby maintains a library of pure *cépage* wines from his Lirac property.

Also 20 ha of CDR from Lirac and Roquemaure. ☙ B2 by partial crushing. Cold maceration and fermentation.

H **Château de Manissy,** Les Perès de la Sainte Famille

A more than usually floral wine labeled "Tête de Cuvée" is produced "like virgin olive oil" from just the first juice to be "saignée." The monks also maintain a library of old vintages, from which I was once privileged to taste a perfectly intact 1957.

20 ha in qrt Manissy near the 18th century château (CE and N). GR "dominates," plus CS, CT, SY, MV, BR, PL, CR. ☙ Crushed directly above the maceration vats to avoid pumping, oak-aged.

H **Le Palais,** Charles Odoyer (no longer made)

Defying all technical preconceptions, the wine is rich, round with fruit and honey, even honeycomb—a flavor that one will then notice in other Tavels.

1.3 ha, qrts Palais, Blaise d'Arbres (CE); Vallongue (N). 50% GR, 20% CS, 30% CT, PL, CR. Old vines. ☙ Retired schoolteacher Odoyer harvested, macerated, fermented, and aged his Tavel in wood, the latter for about 1 year. It was then bottled unfined and unfiltered, principally for individual clients.

H **Prieuré de Montézargues,** GAFF Allauzen

Wine was bought from this estate, formerly a monastery, for the papal cellars in the 14th century. To my taste, great improvement in balance and freshness has followed recent modernizations and switch from direct pressing to maceration and "saignée."

30 ha adjacent to Château de Trinquevedel (CE). 55% GR, 20% CS, 6% CR, 8% CT, plus PL, BR, MV, SY. ☙ Cold fermentation, malolactic fermentation is avoided.

Domaine J.P. Lafond "Roc Epine," Jean-Pierre and Pascal Lafond

More delicate, perhaps not as dark as similar "Corne-Loup."

35 ha, parcels in Vallongue (N); La Vau et Clos, Vestides, Campey (W); Olivet (CE). 60% GR, 15% CS, 10% CR, 10% SY. 5 ha of Lirac and 4 ha (30% SY) of CDR from Lirac. ☙ Some B2 by partial crushing. Seeks to avoid malolactic fermentation.

Domaine des Trois Logis, Charmasson-Plantevin

Combining fairly high alcohol with no malolactic fermentation gives this wine a roundness unusual for the early drinking style.

20 ha, qrts Vallongue (N); Vaucroze, Manissy (CE); Comeyre, Vestides, La Vau et Clos, Romagnac (W). 60% GR, 30% CS, plus BR, CT, PL, SY, CR. ☙ Wine usually rests in vat 8 to 10 months before bottling.

H **Domaine Le Vieux Moulin,** GAEC Les Fils de Gabriel Roudil

M. Gabriel Roudil's father was a leader in obtaining judicial delimitation of the Tavel appellation. Slightly dark, the wine balances fruit and body, roundness and nerve; develops well.

46 ha, parcels in Vallongue (N); Vaucroze et Vacquières, Bouvette (CE); Vestides (W). 55% GR, 25% CS, plus about equal parts CT, CR, BR, PL. 3 ha of Lirac (GR, CS, SY) and 4.5 ha of CDR from Lirac (GR, CS, MV). **Réserve de Cravaillous** is a second

Tavel label. 🙠 Some Tavel for Europe used to be wood aged; now up to 1 year in vat before bottling.

JUICE A + JUICE B + JUICE C

H **Domaine de la Genestière,** Andrée Bernard

The late M. Georges Bernard aimed for moderate alcohol; the wine is now made in the same way by his *caviste* of the last 15 years. Generally fine wine, balanced between fruit and nerve, "stony."

28 ha, parcels in Vallongue (N); Vestides (W). 50% GR, 20% CS, 30% CT, PL, and CR. 11 ha of Lirac from the plateau of Vallongue. **Domaine de Longval** is a second Tavel label. 🙠 Juice is fined before fermentation. Wine rests 6 months or so in vat before bottling. Lirac gets 3 years oak age.

H **Château de Trinquevedel,** SCEA du Château de Trinquevedel
(François et Gérard Demoulin)

M. Demoulin worked closely with local French government research station (INRA), believes his wine benefits from a "certain" aging. I agree. It often needs advance opening due to dissolved CO_2. Delicate peach color and flavor too, with hint of nuts.

30 ha adjacent to Prieuré de Montézargues (CE). 44% GR, 20% CS, 17% CT, 6% CR, 4% SY, 3% MV, 5% BR, 1% Calitor. 🙠 Some B2. Juice fined, cold fermentation. In certain years a "Cuvée Speciale" for extra aging is made from the wines that take the longest to complete fermentation.

--------- *CRU:* LIRAC ---------

Thanks to the efforts of the proprietors of two historic estates omitted or excluded from appellation Tavel, appellation Lirac achieved a judicial delimitation in 1945. One of these, M. Mayer of Château Clary, made sure that the new AOC was given to all three colors of wines.

Modern red Lirac represents the other fork in the road of evolution from the tradition in La Côte du Rhône of making "clairet" wine. One can trace this route easily in the historic documents. Throughout the region, which included Tavel and all the communes now in AOC Lirac, the custom was to allow a 24-hour *cuvaison* for wine to be sold immediately (the ancestor of modern rosé), or a 4 to 6 day *cuvaison* for wine to be sold later (which would have produced a light red). Even then the "clairet" of Lirac was known for a little more firmness and color than that of Tavel. And the wine of Roquemaure, now the center of gravity of AOC Lirac, was given a longer *cuvaison* than the wines of either Tavel or Lirac village, the wine of Grenache (a *cépage* introduced about 1800) demanding 8 days (De Régis 1946).

Basic soil types are similar to Tavel, including cobblestone-covered plateaus, and compact limestone rock-covered slopes. Sandy subsoils predominate, and there are some wind-formed erosion soils.

Lirac reds and rosés must be produced from plantations with a minimum of 40% Grenache and a maximum of 60% of the ensemble of Grenache, Cinsault, Mourvèdre, and Syrah. The rest can include Clairette, Bourboulenc, Ugni blanc, Maccabéo, Picpoul, Calitor, and Carignan, as long as the latter does not exceed 10%. Whites must come from a minimum 33% Clairette, plus no more than 25% of any one of Bourboulenc, Ugni blanc, Maccabéo, Grenache, Picpoul, and Calitor. An additional technical particularity of Lirac rosé is that it may not be produced by direct pressing (juice A). Lirac is grown at a normal maximum of 35 hectoliters of wine per hectare of land and must achieve an 11.5% natural alcohol minimum.

Full productive and commercial advantage of Lirac's own AOC was not taken until replanting and extension of the vineyards followed the arrival of several important families of repatriated French from North Africa. This adds another localized technical particularity to some red Liracs, for a number of these "repatriés" employ the method of *lessivage* (continous pumping over) that was commonly used in Algeria. The purpose has less to do with the making of light-bodied red wine, which is traditional and expressive of the *terroirs* at Lirac, than it does with the making of a wine that is ready to drink when bottled.

Producers (arranged alphabetically)

Addresses are 30 (Gard), unless otherwise noted.

H **Château d'Acquéria,** SC Jean Olivier, Tavel

> For details, see Tavel.

Château de Bouchassy, Degoul et Fils, Roquemaure

Lirac red, white, rosé. **The Degouls reserve for their bottle only the wines that please them, and sell off in bulk the years (like 1983 and 1980) that do not. The primary material is excellent in red Lirac, warm, plummy and resinous, but the bottled wine sometimes shows the effects of too long a time in vat. No such problem affects the distinguished rosé, and the white too can be fine.**

18 ha of AOC Lirac all in Roquemaure, slopes. 60% GR, 5% each CS, MV, SY, plus CT and BR. 5 ha CDR also in Roquemaure, on the cobble-covered plateau near Cantegril-Verda. ‰ OT2, 8 to 10 days. Vaslin press. ‰ 2 years in vat, 1 to 2 years in bottle before sale.

Domaine des Carabiniers, GFA du Domaine des Carabiniers (Christian Leperchois), Roquemaure

CDR red and white, Lirac red, and Tavel. **Young M. Leperchois makes wine by traditional principles in a well-organized new *cave*. His clean, firm Lirac is a good illustration of how to base a *vin de garde* on tight structure rather than heaviness. Fine, even lean Tavel definitely merits being open a bit before serving.**

8 ha of AOC Lirac in Roquemaure, generally slopes near the Forest of Clary. 60% GR, 20% MV, plus CS and diverse. 4 ha of Tavel in qrts Vaucroze (CE) and Roc Crispin (W) are 60% GR, 10% SY, and 30% CS, CT, and CR. 12 ha of CDR at Roquemaure. Red *cépages:* 50% GR, 15% SY, 15% CS, and 5% CR; white *cépages:* 40% CT, 20% BR, 10% UN, plus MR and RS. ‰ Red is OT2, 8 to 10 days. Vaslin press. Tavel is B + C,

undergoes malolactic. 🐛 Red spends 2 to 3 years in oak casks. Tavel is 12 to 18 months in vat before bottling.

Domaine de Castel Oualou, Mme. Marie Pons-Mure, Roquemaure

Lirac red, white, and rosé. **Sound wines that seem to lack aromatic intensity of the first order.**

54 ha single estate all in Roquemaure. 25% each GR, CS, SY, 25% diverse. The name "Oualou" is Arabic for "there is no," so title means "no castle," which is why French regulations require an X to be printed through its picture on the label. 🐛 See Domaine des Causses & St.-Eynes for vinification.

Domaine des Causses & Saint-Eynes and **Domaine les Garrigues,** J.C. Assemat, Roquemaure

Lirac red, white, and rosé. **The method here yields reds that are virtually mature as soon as finished. More aromatic than most is the Causses "Syrah Dominante." Rosé is 90% Cinsault.**

"Causses" is 30 ha at St.-Laurent, 30% CS, 30% GR, 30% SY, plus MV and whites. "Garrigues" is 29 ha at Roquemaure, 20% CS, 20% GR, 10% whites, and the rest SY. 🐛 15 day CL with continuous pumping over *(lessivage)* for all reds but "Rouge d'Eté" (OT1). Rosé "par saignée." M. Assemat vinifies both his wine and that of his mother-in-law Mme. Marie Pons-Mure's Domaine de Castel Oualou (see) by the same methods in the latter's facilities. 🐛 Some reds receive 3 to 6 months in wood.

H **Domaine du Château Saint-Roch,** Antoine Verda et Fils, Roquemaure

Lirac red, white, and rosé. **Consistent high quality in all wines. Crisp, leafy to nutty, mineral white, especially full in 1984. Usual composition of peach fruit lozenge, floral rosé is to be drawn 50% from vats of all the *cépages* except Syrah, 50% all the free run juice of a vat of Grenache, Cinsault, Mourvèdre. Leafy, fresh, regular red with significant Cinsault avoided dryness in 1983. Ripe peaches and truffles typify reserve "Cuvée Ancienne Viguerie" for which the percentage of Grenache is increased and wood age extended (1979 rivals 1970 for being best I have tasted).**

42 ha, dispersed nearby. 40% GR, 20% CS, 12% SY, 12% MV, plus diverse *cépages* including CT, BR, GR blanc. Also own CDR **Domaine Cantegril-Verda** at Roquemaure, 60% GR, 25% CS, 5% SY, and diverse. Châteauneuf-du-Pape **"Cuvée Princes d'Orange"** in qrts mostly S has been GR, CT; SY, CS, and MV will be planted. 🐛 OT2, 6 days. *Cépages* vinified separately. Rosé "par saignée." White settled, must-fined, fermented cool, no malolactic. 🐛 Red Lirac spends 6 to 18 months in oak casks.

Château de Clary, Famille Mayer, Roquemaure

Lirac red and rosé. **At present the quality of the wine may not be up to the fame of the estate, though the firm constitution and truffle fragrance show its potential for class. The widow, daughter, and grand-daughters of the late M. Marius Mayer, one of the founders of the appellation Lirac, manage the estate. They believe the very first barrels of wine to be branded CDR came from here, and that the estate was also where the phylloxera epidemic started in France. Clary is one of three estates, with Manissy and Acquéria, into which the domaine of the viscount of St.-Priest was divided after execution of the incumbent viscount during the Revolution. Like** the others Clary would have continued to be included in AOC Tavel if the proprietor at the moment of delimitation, also owner of a sausage factory, had been interested in joining his colleagues in the necessary judicial proceeding.

49 ha in vine (besides 174 ha "Forêt de Clary"). Red *cépages:* GR, CS, MV, and a little CR. White are GR, CT, BR. 🐛 Formerly ST, now CL (first 1/5 of each vat is left with stems). 4 to 7 days (1985 rapid). 🐛 6 months in oak casks. The wine has been bottled and commercialized with the name of the estate by several *négociants,* including DuPeloux of Courthézon (Vaucluse) who were soon (1985) to bottle theirs "au domaine."

H Domaine du Devoy, J. and M. Lombardo, St.-Laurent-des-Arbres

Lirac red, white, rosé. **Excellent, tightly constructed reds without thickness, cedary and floral, develop tar and truffles. Normally there are a little more than 25% each Grenache and Cinsault, a little less than 25% each Mourvèdre and Syrah. Extra intense 1980 had 29% Mourvèdre.**

40 ha in vine on single estate just over ridge NW of St.-Roch. 4 ha GR, 10 ha CS, 7 ha MV, 4 ha SY, 3 ha blancs. 🐛 OT2 with some destemming, 10 days. *Cépages* vinified separately, Vaslin press; rosé "par saignée." 🐛 Wine rests 1 year in vat, no wood.

Domaine Duseigneur, Jean Duseigneur, St.-Laurent-des-Arbres

CDR; CDR Laudun; Lirac red, white, and rosé. **Definitely light, the Lirac reds can at their best (e.g., 1978) combine elegance with aromatic intensity and complexity. Pure Bourboulenc white; clean peach vanilla rosé was 70% Cinsault in 1984. M. Duseigneur is president of the official tasting commission for the AOC.**

13.5 ha of AOC Lirac, all slope, 40% GR, 25% SY, 20% CS, 10% MV, 5% BR. 4.5 ha of CDR and CDR Laudun at St.-Victor-la-Coste, 50% SY, 40% GR, 10% CT. 🐛 CL or OT2 depending on year and health of grapes. 8 days for Lirac, Vaslin press, rosé "par saignée." *Cave* is arranged so that one man can conduct the vinification. 🐛 Lirac red spends several months in oak casks.

Domaine de la Genestière, Andrée Bernard, Tavel

For details, see Tavel.

Domaine des Jonciers, Pierre Roussel, Tavel

Lirac red, rosé, white. **The cave is in Tavel, but the land is AOC Lirac. M. Roussel started to estate bottle a portion of his production in 1982. Available to taste in 1985 were a clean, fresh, 1984 Lirac rosé and a pure Bourboulenc 1984 Lirac white with paler color and more delicate nose than usual for that grape. 1983 red Lirac seemed vegetal, although spice lingered on the palate.**

32 ha on the plateau of Vallongue had to be cleared of woods when M. Roussel started here after 6 generations of his family had been *vignerons* in Algeria. 55% GR, 20% SY, 15% CS, 7% MV, 3% BR. 🐛 ST with destemming of GR and MV. 7 days, Vaslin press. Malolactic for rosé, not for white. 🐛 Reds spend 14 to 15 months in underground vats.

Domaine de Lanzac, Norbert de Lanzac, Tavel

For details, see Tavel.

H **Domaine Maby La Fermade,** GAEC Domaine Maby, Tavel

> For details, see Tavel.

H **Les Queyrades,** Méjean-Taulier, Tavel

> For details, see Tavel Canto-Perdrix.

Domaine Rousseau, Louis Rousseau, Les Charmettes, Laudun

CDR Laudun; Lirac red and rosé. **Fruity, slightly dusty regular Lirac is smooth and mature when bottled. To it a 1983 Lirac "Réserve Innocent VI" added some spice, vanilla, and chewiness from 40% Mourvèdre.**

> 24 ha of AOC Lirac is dispersed in Lirac, St.-Laurent-des-Arbres, and Roquemaure, 40% GR, 30% MV, 20% CS, 10% SY. 3.42 ha of CDR Laudun is 50% GR, plus CS droit, UN, CT, and young vine SY. ❧ CL with continuous pumping over *(lessivage)* is conducted at Domaine de La Tour, St.-Laurent-des-Arbres, formerly owned by M. Rousseau's brother-in-law, Charles Pons-Mure. Rosé "par saignée." ❧ No wood.

Domaine Roger Sabon, GAEC Roger Sabon et ses Fils, Châteauneuf-du-Pape (Vaucluse)

> For details, see Châteauneuf-du-Pape.

Chateau de Saint-Maurice d'Ardoise, André Valat, Ardoise, Laudun

> For details, see Laudun.

Château de Ségriès, Le Comte de Régis, Lirac

Lirac red, white, rosé. **The Comte de Régis is one of the founders of the Lirac appellation, author of the dossier that successfully made the case for it after Ségriès was excluded from Tavel (old labels show it as "Tavel" from "Lirac près de Tavel"). Son François de Régis now conducts the estate. The raw material in both red and white wine may be the best of Lirac—the latter surprisingly Graves-like when tasted young. The bottled wines, however, reflect too long a stay in vat for my taste.**

> Single estate with 20 ha in vine on east- and west-facing slopes either side of a little N-S valley. 50% GR, 20% CS, 20% SY, 10% diverse, including CR, CT, MV, UN, BR, Maccabéo. ❧ ST with optional destemming, 6 days average, Vaslin press, rosé "par saignée" (pale color preferred). ❧ Reds sometimes age several years in vat.

Philippe Testut, Lirac

Lirac red, white, rosé. **A producer to watch. Rosé shows great promise, peach-rose color and aroma, benefits from aeration. Red smells as if it has been in wood when it hasn't, tannic enough for M. Testut to consider destemming.**

> 10 ha of which almost 4 are ⅓ GR blanc, ⅓ CT, and ⅓ UN. Rest is 80% GR, 5% MV, 15% CS. M. Testut also has a property in AOC Chablis. ❧ ST, 8 to 12 days, rosé "par saignée." ❧ No wood now, but first Lirac (1977) was aged in wood "a long time."

Le Vieux Moulin, GAEC Les Fils de Gabriel Roudil, Tavel

> For details, see Tavel.

The following are cooperatives of this zone:

Cave Coopérative des Vins du Cru de Lirac, St.-Laurent-des-Arbres
Founded 1931. 52.02% AOC. Lirac, of which cave is the largest single supplier, from Lirac, St.-Geniès-de-Comolas, St.-Laurent-des-Arbres.

Cave Coopérative des Vignerons de Roquemaure
Founded 1929. 25.83% AOC. Lirac from Roquemaure, St.-Geniès-de-Comolas. CDR adds Montfaucon, Pujaut, Sauveterre.
CDR red and white; *CDR red "Cuvée Clement V": *assemblage* from selected qrts of Roquemaure is given 4 months in oak casks; Lirac red and rosé; Lirac red "Cuvée St.-Valentin": 1982 Lirac analog of "Clement V" was in cask in 1985.

─────── **CDR SOUTH OF TAVEL** ───────

Addresses of producers are 30 (Gard).

Le Caveau du Château de Domazan

Headquartered and with a tasting room in the Château, this is a proprietors' group formed for the purpose of commercializing wines made and bottled by its members, all from Domazan. The estates and proprietors are:

Château de Domazan, Christian Chaudérac
The only wine that can use the name of the Château because M. Chaudérac owns it.
Domaine du Mas d'Eole, Serge Gallon
Domaine Reynaud, Louis Reynaud (see)
Domaine des Roches d'Arnaud, Jean-Paul Arnaud
Domaine de Sarrazin, Daniel Charre

Domaine Reynaud, Louis Reynaud, Domazan

CDR red and rosé. **Firm red, even a little hard, with cherry fruit and vanilla butter that apparently came from Mourvèdre component in unwooded 1981.**
41 ha, all in Domazan, includes 3 ha of the only compact limestone rocks ("Barrémien") in Domazan. Rest plateau and sandy slopes. 50% GR, 30% SY, plus CS, MV, CR. ஃ ST, Vaslin press. ஃ Wine may spend sometimes up to 4 years in vat; some may spend 6 months in new oak *pièces* in the Caveau du Château de Domazan (see).

Mas des Seraphin, Jacques Mathieu, Domazan

CDR red and white. **Fragrant, round, plum-skin fruited, peppery red with just the right tannic interest for substance. Very good 1984, his first bottling; unassembled vats of 1985 showed lots of promise (especially Mourvèdre). Floral white has green apple flavor of dominant Bourboulenc.**
33-ha dispersed estate in Domazan and a little in Estézargues. 40% GR, 25% SY (moving toward 1/3), 10% CR, 10% MV, the rest CS. 1.5 ha of white are BR, CT, and

*Asterisk signifies recommended wines.

MR. ᐓ Red is CM for all the *primeur,* some GR, the CR and CS; OT2 partly destemmed for some GR, SY and MV. White is settled, must-fined, fermented cool, no malolactic. ᐓ For his own bottling the wine ages in vat. *Négociant* Georges Duboeuf (Romanèche-Thorins) buys *primeur* here and also commercializes the regular red with name of the estate.

Domaine du Cabanon, Achille Payan, Saze

CDR red. **Generally with a whole-berry, peppery nose, the wine is sometimes candyish, tending toward reduction and something of a tannic finish. I was favorably impressed (1985) by a sweet, resinous, tender 1983.**

14 ha on clay-lime slopes at Saze. 50% GR, plus CS, CR, SY. ᐓ Wine assembled from some CM (half the GR, CR, SY), 10 to 12 days, and some OT2, 5 to 6 days. Vaslin press. ᐓ Aged in enamel-lined vats for 1 year.

Domaine de la Charité, Valentin et Coste, Saze

CDR red, white, rosé. **Luscious rosé, fairly big floral white has between peaches and pear in mouth. Red has some of same flowers as white, attributed by M. Coste to Syrah planted on same cobble-covered, red earth parcel as Bourboulenc.**

22.5 ha in production. 50% GR, 25% CS, 15% SY, rest CR. 15–20 year average age. White are UN and BR. ᐓ CM, 7 to 8 days, Vaslin press. Rosé is made in the Tavel fashion, including juice C. ᐓ Red rests in vat 1 year.

H **Domaine des Moulins,** André Payan, Saze

CDR red. **M. Payan, a professional taster, makes a very consistent light-bodied red with real character, cedar-berry nose, tendency to a little yeastiness, slightly tarry. I preferred concentration of the 1984 to both pleasant spice of 1983 and slightly cooked fruit of 1985.**

40 ha, 2/3 at Saze, 1/3 on Domazan part of plateau shared between the two. 35% GR, 35% SY, 15% CS, plus CR, MV, CN, BR, CT. ᐓ CL, except OT2 for *primeur.* ᐓ Wine rests 1 year in vat before his bottling. It is also bought and bottled with the name of the estate by *négociant* George Duboeuf (Romanèche-Thorins).

The following are cooperatives of this zone:

Cave Coopérative d'Estézargues
80% AOC. CDR from Estézargues.
CDR red.

Cave Coopérative Les Coteaux de Fournès
Founded 1955. 45.12% AOC.

Les Vignerons du Castelas, Rochefort-du-Gard
Founded 1953. 60.3% AOC. CDR from Rochefort-du-Gard (half), Pujaut, and Saze. Recently installed facilities to allow longer fermentation of CDR reds (OT1).
CDR white and rosé; *CDR red (10% MV).

Cave Coopérative de St.-Hilaire-d'Ozilhan
Founded 1929. 64.29% AOC.

—— CDR-VILLAGES ——

Laudun

The communes of Laudun are Laudun, Tresques, and St.-Victor-la-Coste. One of the original 1953 Villages (then *appellations communales*), Laudun had been given a judicial delimitation in 1947. Addresses of producers are 30 (Gard), unless otherwise noted.

H **Faraud et Fils**, Palus, St.-Victor-la-Coste

CDR-Villages Laudun red. **M. Faraud, president of the St.-Victor growers and a restorer of romanesque chapels, lives next door to the Pelaquiés. For now he makes only reds, with great depth of fruit, a floral to truffle nose, and well-married wood-smoothness without wood taste. 1983 perhaps spicier and chewier than perfectly balanced 1981. Unassembled 1984s were less fat, 1985 more attractive as soon as finished.**

12 ha in AOC Laudun, dispersed. 45% GR, 20% each SY and CS, 10% MV, some CR and CT. 🐛 OT2, 8 to 10 days, Vaslin press. 🐛 Wine for estate-bottling gets 6 to 12 months in wood.

H **Domaine Pelaquié**, GAEC Emmanuel et Luc Pelaquié, Palus, St.-Victor-la-Coste

CDR-Villages Laudun red and white. **The young Pelaquiés gave up a legend about their wine when they abandoned their grandfather's 40–day maceration and years of oak age for reds, and wood fermentation for whites. The reality is an improvement in the white, clean, nervy but with a Châteauneuf white roundness, hints of stones, pears, and bananas from old-vine Clairette harvested "golden." The red tends toward concentrated berry and plum fruit, tight structure, leafy and floral fragrances, smoke, truffles, and seawater. I prefer full fruit and aromatics of 1984 to more raisined 1983. 1980 in my U.S. cellar (1986) is still developing.**

55 ha in vine, dispersed, biggest parcel on slope near the house. 50% GR, plus CS, SY, MV, CR, CT, BR, UN, Calitor, a very little RS. VN planted. 🐛 OT2, 15 days, hydraulic press. Avoid malolactic for white. 🐛 No wood.

Château de Saint-Maurice d'Ardoise, André Valat, Ardoise, Laudun

CDR-Villages Laudun red and rosé; Lirac. **The wines here are sound, very smoothly finished and *marchand* (commercial) at the outset because of the vinification. A Syrah-dominant *cuvée* sold in the U.S. under "Domaine de Mont Jupiter" label seems overwooded.**

67-ha single estate in Laudun. 3 ha of AOC Lirac form part of the estate just over the line in St.-Laurent-des-Arbres. 65% GR, 15% SY, 15% CS, 5% MV, CN and whites. 🐛 CL with "semi-continuous" pumping over. 🐛 Some wood for part of every assembled red, proportion and duration in wood at demand of client. M. Valat's biggest French buyer for Villages Laudun is Nicolas.

Domaine Rousseau, Louis Rousseau, Les Charmettes, Laudun

For details, see Lirac.

The following are cooperatives of this zone:

Cave des Vignerons de Laudun
    Founded 1925. 24.98% AOC.
    CDR-Villages Laudun red and white.

Cave des Vignerons des Quatre Chemins, Qrt Le Serre de Bernon, Laudun
    Founded 1958 specifically to specialize in AOC wine. 66.26% AOC. CDR principally from Laudun, Bagnols, Cavillargues, Sabran, St.-Marcel-de-Careiret, St.-Victor, Tresques.
    CDR "Serre de Bernon" red, white, rosé; CDR "Baronnie de Sabran" red, white, rosé (superior selection); *CDR-Villages Laudun "Les Quatre Chemins" white; CDR-Villages Laudun "Les Quatre Chemins" red.

Cave des Vignerons de Saint-Victor-la-Coste
    Founded 1925. 33.37% AOC. CDR from St.-Victor and St.-Paul-les-Fonts (most), plus Connaux, Laudun, Pouzilhac.
    CDR red; CDR rosé (GR and CT rose); *CDR white (CT dominant, UN, GR blanc); CDR-Villages Laudun rosé (pure GR); CDR-Villages Laudun red.

Chusclan (1)

The communes of Chusclan are Chusclan, Bagnols-sur-Cèze, Codolet, Orsan, and Saint-Etienne-des-Sorts. Like Laudun delimited in 1947, Chusclan was one of the original 1953 *appellations communales* for its rosé. The red was accorded Villages standing in 1971. Addresses of producers are 30 (Gard), unless otherwise noted.

H Château d'Orsan, Joseph Brunel, Orsan

CDR red. **Tasted at the estate these wines are dark, rich, plummy, peppery, and round in the Chusclan style, although not declared as Villages. They are bottled with the name of the estate by several *négociants,* including Vachet of Savoie and Les Grandes Serres of Châteauneuf-du-Pape (the latter's 1983 is a good representation). M. Brunel is brother of the owner of Château La Gardine at Châteauneuf-du-Pape.**
    32-ha single estate at Orsan. 50% GR (25-year-old vines), 25% CR (20-year-old vines), 25% SY (10-year-old vines). ❧ OT2, 8 days, Vaslin press. ❧ Practice is to bottle beginning January after the harvest.

Domaine de Signac, Castay et Johannet, Bagnols-sur-Cèze

CDR red, white, rosé. **Reds tend to be round, spicy, fairly light, sometimes lose freshness by being overly long in vat. Surprisingly this seems to hurt the white less.**
    37-ha single estate in Bagnols and Orsan. 45% GR, 15% SY, 15% CS, 15% CR, plus CN, CT rose. ❧ OT1 in part destemmed, 4–8 days. ❧ No wood. Up to 3 years in vat.

Cave des Vignerons de Chusclan

Remarkable investment in modern equipment and history of serious direction yield clean, well-made wines. Of two CDR-Villages Chusclan rosés, I usually prefer

crisper "Seigneurie de Gicon," which includes Cinsault, to the sometimes pure Grenache, correspondingly supple "Cuvée de Marcoule." Chusclan reds contain more Syrah than does CDR "Prieuré St.-Julien." There again I prefer "Gicon" with its cassis Syrah presence to somewhat overfinished "Cuvée du Père Bridayne."

Founded 1939. 46.8% AOC. 125 members from Chusclan, Bagnols, Saint-Etienne, Orsan and Vénéjan. ❧ Reds are assembled from ST (more in Chusclan) and CM (more in CDR). *Cépages* are fermented apart, some of each by each method. Rosé, for which Chusclan communale AOC was first granted (1953), is "par saignée" with use of some juice C as at Tavel. Rosé and white are centrifuged before cool fermentation. ❧ "Cuvée du Père Bridayne" receives wood age. All wines are millipore-filtered before bottling.

Other cooperatives in this zone are:

Cave Coopérative de Codolet

Founded 1928. 20% AOC. CDR from Codolet.

Cave des Vignerons d'Orsan

Founded 1929. 39.45% AOC. CDR almost entirely from Orsan.

CDR red, white, rosé; *CDR "Troisième Age" red; CDR-Villages red and rosé (not labeled Chusclan).

7

Northern Gard and Southern Ardèche

THIS GROUP OF WINES lies to the northwest of the southern and central group, off sometimes heavier soils, in a generally cooler, moister climate. The harvest begins about a week later than in the south-central sector. As a general rule, sites farther west have less mistral and more influence of the Cévennes mountains.

Again there has been historical recognition of the *terroir*'s vocation for bigger reds and excellent whites. Earlier in this century Galet (1962) put the area's wines in the second rank, after those of La Côte du Rhône, because "they were harvested later, with more color and body than the preceding." In fact some of the regional reds, those of Sabran for instance, are a bit obdurate in their youth, which can come as a surprise in wines that are not really heavy. At one time the *négociants* (after blending wines again) sought out the wines of the Bagnols area "whose acidity assures good holding power under hot conditions" (Chabaud 1967). The ranking and a blending-wine perspective should not obscure the positive structural implications of these descriptions.

———— CDR-VILLAGES OF THE NORTHERN GARD ————

Chusclan (2)

The climate difference referred to above suggests that producers from the northern part of Bagnols-sur-Cèze and from Saint-Etienne-des-Sorts should be listed here (Le Plâtre et Sarfati 1983). For a complete list of Chusclan communes, see Chusclan (1) entry in "CDR-Villages of Southern and Central Gard." Addresses of producers are 30 (Gard).

Domaine Le Haut Castel, Augustin Arène, Bagnols-sur-Cèze

CDR red, white, rosé. **Famous in the history of the region for their quality, the whites remain the domaine's extraordinary wines, in my opinion. My first introduction was a 1958, still green-tinted, delicate, floral and fresh in 1977. The red benefits from old-vine Carignan. Rosés can be disappointing.**

25-ha almost single estate all on south-facing slopes in Bagnols, overlooking the Cèze. At one time had more CR (average age 50 years) than the 2 GRs, plus SY, CS, CT, BR, PL, UN. ⟨❧ ST, 5 to 6 days, hydraulic press. ⟨❧ Red spends 1 year in cask.

H **Domaine de Lindas,** Jean-Claude Chinieu, Bagnols-sur-Cèze

CDR red, white, rosé; CDR-Villages Chusclan. **M. Chinieu, probably the only private grower to estate-bottle Chusclan, recently had to reduce the size of his vineyard.**

One hopes the quality can be maintained, for the 1980 (rounder, more buttery) and 1981 (more tannic) were both very fine, full of cedar, pepper, green olive, and resinous herbs (both are aging well as of 1986 in my U.S. cellar). To my taste 1984 augurs better for the continuity than drier 1983. Pure Clairette white is a sleeper, long and lemony.

10 ha at Bagnols, of which 6 are GR, 3 SY, and 1 CT. ❧ Harvested in hand-carried cases, OT1, with SY crushed by weight on bottom of each vat, 12 to 15 days. ❧ Wine rests in vat, is bottled early (after 8 months).

The cooperatives of this zone are:

Société Coopérative Agricole des Vignerons de Bagnols-sur-Cèze
Founded 1923. 27.7% AOC. CDR 90% from Bagnols.

Cave des Vignerons de Saint-Etienne-des-Sorts
Founded 1929. 51.51% AOC. CDR from St.-Etienne and Vénéjan.

Saint-Gervais

The sole commune is Saint-Gervais. Addresses of producers are 30 (Gard).

H **Domaine Sainte-Anne,** GAEC Domaine Ste.-Anne (Guy Steinmaier et Fils), Les Cellettes, St.-Gervais

CDR red, white, and rosé (beginning 1985); CDR-Villages red and white; CDR-Villages St.-Gervais red. **Often the best single CDR-Villages red, it is made to be aged in bottle, and when it has a fault, it is excess tannin.** My favorite *cuvée* combines older-vine Grenache, almost pungent, with a strong dose of Mourvèdre flowers, plums, and vanilla. It appeared in U.S. as CDR-Villages 1979, CDR 1980, and CDR-Villages "Cuvée Notre Dame des Cellettes" 1981. M. Steinmaier has now stabilized his labeling and produces plain CDR-Villages for early release, CDR-Villages St.-Gervais with the most Mourvèdre, and CDR-Villages "Cuvée Notre Dame des Cellettes" with about 70% Grenache. St.-Gervais 1983 (70% Mourvèdre) is my nominee for Ste.-Anne's greatest wine yet. In white, CDR 1986 contained Marsanne; Villages that is pure Roussanne is labeled Notre Dame.

26 ha planted in area formerly green-oak scrub, on rock-strewn plateau above the slopes of St.-Gervais. Red cépages: 60% GR, 20% SY, 10% MV, 10% CS. ha white: CT, BR, RS, MR, VN. ❧ Harvested in hand-carried cases. OT1, 10 to 12 days, Vaslin press. ❧ The wine rests in vat, in principle is bottled early.

The cooperative is:

Les Vignerons de Saint-Gervais
Founded 1925. About 33% AOC. CDR mainly from St.-Gervais, Bagnols, St.-Michel-d'Euzet.
CDR red; CDR rose; *CDR white (GR blanc, CT, BR); *CDR-Villages St.-Gervais red.

CDR OF THE NORTHERN GARD
AND SOUTHERN ARDÈCHE

Producers are arranged S to N, W to E. Addresses of the following producers are 30 (Gard).

Domaine du Marjolet, Bernard Pontaud, Gaujac

CDR red, white, rosé. **A maker who started bottling in 1978 I am watching especially for the quality of the white, which seems to gain some fat, and hazelnuts more than almond among its flowers, by including Grenache blanc with Ugni blanc and Bourboulenc. 1984 rosé and 1982 red also very attractive.**

25 ha of CDR, 50% GR, 20% SY, 10% CS, plus CR, MV, UN, BR, GR blanc. ❧ OT2 for about half; the rest, especially SY and MV, are CL except for *primeur,* which is OT1, harvested in hand-carried cases. Vaslin press. No malolactic for the white. ❧ No wood.

H **Domaine de la Réméjeanne,** François Klein, Cadignac-Sabran

CDR red and white. **From highest elevation in the Sabran group come firm, aromatic reds, with strong dose of Syrah, going from strength to strength as the vines mature. Red 1982, a marvel of dark, perfectly but not overly ripe fruit with butter and truffles, replaced the still youthful, more vanillaed 1980 as my favorite. 1984 promises to join this line of superior even-numbered years (back to 1978). Ugni blanc and Bourboulenc make a floral, bitter-almond white, first bottled in the 1983.**

M. Klein began at Réméjeanne in 1961 after repatriation from Morocco. Now has 20 ha of CDR facing east on terraced slopes, with an additional ha recently planted. 36% GR, 20% SY, 16% CS, 11% CR, 6% CN, 7% CT, 2% BR, 2% UN. ❧ OT2 with some destemming, 4 to 7 days, vertical press. ❧ Red ages about 12 to 18 months in vat.

Domaine de Lascamp, GAEC Imbert Père et Fils, Cadignac-Sabran

CDR red and rosé. **Descendants of a family resident here since 1674, the Imberts began to bottle their own wine in 1979. Some ups and downs of quality since, but there is good promise in these mostly firm, cassis to plum, often vanilla to almond smelling reds.**

35 ha, all in Sabran, 2/3 at Cadignac, 1/3 on plateau of Sabran. 50% GR, 25% CS, a little less than 20% SY, plus CT, CR. ❧ Formerly OT2 with some ST (especially SY). Began mechanical harvesting, CL vinification in 1983. 8 days, Vaslin press; rosé "par saignée." ❧ No wood, up to 1 year in vat.

H **Château de Boussargues,** Malabre Constant, Colombier-Sabran

CDR red, white, rosé. **Mme. Malabre began to bottle in 1980. Lighter bodied than the other Sabrans, tending to cassis, spice, pepper, the reds have begun to reveal a good capacity for development in bottle (e.g., 1981 tasted in 1985). 1983 the most complex aroma so far. The stunning wine, though, is usually the pure Ugni blanc, violet-flowered white. A very fruity, bone-dry rosé is produced only in certain years.**

DOMAINE DE LINDAS

CHUSCLAN
COTES DU RHONE
APPELLATION COTES DU RHONE CHUSCLAN CONTROLÉE

MIS EN BOUTEILLE AU DOMAINE PAR

J.-Claude Chinieu   75 cl

Propriétaire - Récoltant à Bagnols-sur-Cèze (Gard) France

Imported by :
AHD Associates, Inc., Grosse Pointe, MI

Domaine Sainte-Anne
~~~
Saint-Gervais
Côtes du Rhône Villages
APPELLATION CÔTES-DU-RHÔNE VILLAGES CONTRÔLÉE

Mis en bouteille au Domaine   75cl

G.A.E.C. DOMAINE SAINTE-ANNE "LES CELLETTES" SAINT-GERVAIS (GARD)
PRODUCT OF FRANCE

1983

Domaine de la Réméjeanne

CÔTES du RHÔNE
Appellation Côtes-du-Rhône Contrôlée

75 cl France

FRANCOIS KLEIN . PROPRIETAIRE·RECOLTANT . CADIGNAC . 30200 . SABRAN

GECEBEL PUBLICITE ENTRAIGUES

CHATEAU DE BOUSSARGUES

Côtes-du-Rhône
APPELLATION CÔTES DU RHÔNE CONTRÔLÉE

Mis en bouteille au château

FRANCE   MALABRE CONSTANT - SABRAN - GARD   37,5 cl

L'IMPRIMEUR, BAGNOLS-SUR-CÈZE

VIN DE FRANCE

Vieux Manoir du Frigoulas

Côtes du Rhône Villages
APPELLATION CÔTES DU RHÔNE-VILLAGES CONTRÔLÉE

ROBERT ALAIN ET FILS, PROPRIÉTAIRES RÉCOLTANTS
à St ALEXANDRE 30130

75 cl

Mis en bouteille par S.A.R.L. ROBERT Alain et Fils · 30130 St Alexandre

Domaine de Bruthel

COTES~DU~RHONE
Appellation Côtes-du-Rhône Contrôlée

e 75G ml   MIS EN BOUTEILLE AU DOMAINE

DE SERESIN PERE & FILS DOMAINE DE BRUTHEL 30200 SABRAN · FRANCE

DOMAINE DE L'OLIVET

Mis en bouteilles au Domaine

1982
75 cl
PRODUCE
OF
FRANCE

COTES-DU-RHONE
APPELLATION COTES-DU-RHONE CONTROLÉE

RODOLPHE-GOOSSENS, PROPRIÉTAIRE-RÉCOLTANT
BOURG-St-ANDÉOL (ARDÈCHE) FRANCE

CHATEAU ROCHECOLOMBE

PROPRIETAIRE-RECOLTANT A BOURG-SAINT-ANDÉOL (ARDÈCHE)

G. HERBERIGS

Récolte   1978

75 cl ## COTES DU RHONE
APPELLATION COTES DU RHONE CONTROLÉE

MIS EN BOUTEILLES AU CHATEAU   PRODUCE OF FRANCE

25-ha single estate surrounds a storybook, genuine 12th-century castle. 4–5 ha GR, 5 ha CS, 3 ha SY, 2.75 ha CT, 1.5 ha CN, 1.25 ha each of UN, PL, CR. 🕹 OT2, 6 to 8 days, Vaslin press. No malolactic for the white. 🕹 Red spends about 1 year in vat.

Domaine Moulin du Pourpré, Francis Simon, Colombier-Sabran

CDR red and rosé. **Vanilla in these reds seems to be a regional characteristic, over a plum, sour cherry (1983) or sweet cherry (1981) fruit (M. Simon's outstanding wines). They have good depth, pleasant chewiness, sometimes floral, sometimes resinous-spicy overtones.**

21 ha at Colombier. 40% GR, 10% SY, 15% CS, 25% CR, plus MV, CN, CT rose. Average age of vines is 50 years. 🕹 OT1 in open cement fermenter, submerged cap method is unusual for southern Rhône; 8 to 12 days. 🕹 Reds aged 12 to 18 months in vat (closed).

H **Domaine de Bruthel**, De Seresin Père et Fils, Colombier-Sabran

CDR red, white, rosé. **The Sabran tendency to backbone has been accentuated in these reds, perhaps because heretofore de Seresins have had no Cinsault. Young M. de Seresin now identifies his wood-aged wines by putting them in "Rhodanienne" bottles, and makes a distinct** cuvée **for the purpose with more Mourvèdre and Carignan, less Syrah, and longer** cuvaison. **In his 1979, 1980, 1981 I preferred the unwooded versions, but the new formula made a much less dry, more aromatic wooded 1982. Floral, leafy, stony white at 65% Ugni blanc shows the nobility of this grape in north Gard.**

24 ha at Sabran and Bagnols. 40% GR noir, 20% SY, plus MV, CR, CN, UN, CT, BR, GR blanc. 15% CS has been added from rented land. 🕹 OT2, cépages vinified separately, Vaslin press. No malolactic for white. 🕹 Some wines age 8 to 16 months in vat; that for "Rhodanienne" bottle is given 1 year in oak casks.

Domaine de l'Amandier, Urbain Pagès, Carmes-Sabran

CDR red and rosé. **Wines that require time in the bottle to open beyond initial hardness and sometimes vegetal, dusty tannin. Rare for this region is that Syrah is dominant in most** cuvées. **Precise comment is difficult because M. Pagès tends not to assemble his wines, but to bottle separately those that have won medals. Among these I have been pleased by a 1979 bronze medal winner and a 1981 silver, both 70% Syrah, 20% Grenache, 10% Cinsault; and by an 80% Syrah/20% Cinsault 1982 silver. Round, full-flavored rosés.**

30 ha divided between Carmes and Gaujac. The CDR portion is 50% SY, 25% GR, 25% CS, plus UN. Average age of vines is 14 years. 🕹 ST, 8 to 10 days, Vaslin press. Rosé "par saignée." 🕹 No wood aging, but also rare for the region is a stock that once reached 100,000 bottles maturing in the barn.

Domaine Saint-Nabor, Mme. Castor et Fils, Cornillon

CDR red, white, rosé. **At the western edge of the Côtes du Rhône, the Castors produce a crisp, stony white with the distinctive aroma of 25% Picpoul. Minerals show in the rosé and red, too; the latter, while light, is very fragrant (honeysuckle, perhaps).**

40 ha in vine on soil that is more calcareous than at St.-Gervais. 65% GR, 15% SY,

plus CR, CS, GR blanc, PL, CT. ❧ Began harvesting mechanically in 1984. CL, 6 to 7 days (8 for SY). *Cépages* vinified separately; rosé "par saignée." No malolactic in either rosé or white. ❧ Reds are aged 2 years in vat.

Château de la Chartreuse de Valbonne, Saint-Paulet-de-Caisson

CDR red. **An American donor, Dr. Justin Abbott, made possible the purchase of this former Carthusian monastery by a Protestant society for the care of lepers, and now also of former mental patients returning to society. Vines were restored to the monastery vineyards only in 1977, but forested microclimate and siliceous soil already give the 35% Syrah reds much truer Syrah nose and taste than many in the south.**

4.5 ha of CDR in St.-Michel-d'Euzet. 4 ha GR, 1 ha SY, .5 ha young-vine CS. ❧ OT1, in part using restored monastery stone vats, 10 days, hydraulic press. ❧ No wood.

Domaine des Riots, Alain et Fernand Riot, St.-Michel-d'Euzet

CDR red, white, rosé. **To the formerly pure Ugni blanc white, rich and enormously floral, the Riots added 10% Clairette for roundness in the 1984. Their other extraordinary wine to my mind is the Mourvèdre-based *cuvée* of red: 100% in 1980 and 1982, 50% in 1983.**

36-ha almost single estate lies just west of St.-Gervais. 11.5 ha GR, 8.5 ha CS, 4 ha SY, 4 ha CR, 3.5 ha MV, 2 ha UN (facing east on white clay), 2 ha CT. ❧ Switch to mechanical harvesting in 1984 changed vinification from OT2 to CL. Cold weather blocked the malolactic in white 1984. ❧ Part of the red spends "a little" time in cask.

Domaine de Roquebrune, Pierre Rique, Saint-Alexandre

CDR red, rosé, white. **"Cuvée du Vieux Chêne" is M. Rique's label for a small-barrel-aged red. I found the 1983 of this wine dry compared to either the rounder, resinous, buttery unwooded 1983 or a leaner but fruitier, more aromatic unwooded 1984. "Vieux Chêne" 1981 made a more harmonious case for wood treatment. White 1985 seemed strongly marked by its 20% Bourboulenc component.**

20 ha in vine at St.-Alexandre and Pont-Saint-Esprit, with mostly a northward exposure. 60% GR, 25% CS, 10% SY, plus CT, BR, CR. ❧ Most ST, 3 to 4 days, assembled with part CM, 10 to 12 days; rosé "par saignée." ❧ "Vieux Chêne" aged 1 year in small oak *pièces*.

H Vieux Manoir du Frigoulas, Alain Robert et Fils, St.-Alexandre

CDR red, white, rosé; CDR-Villages red, white. **The 5-*cépages* Robert white is often the best of CDR. 1979 in my U.S. cellar was still fresh in 1986. Yeasty, floral, peach, plum, mineral 1984 rosé contained Mourvèdre. Top of the line "Cuvée St.-Vincent" red is distinguished from "Grande Cuvée" by more Mourvèdre, no Carignan; has been declared Villages since 1983. The difference between the two is more of class and complexity than longevity, in which both score well (e.g., 1980s are still young in 1986).**

50-ha dispersed estate overlooking Rhône NE of St.-Gervais. 25 ha GR noir and 1.5 blanc, 5 ha CS, 4 ha SY, 2.5 ha MV, 4 ha CR, 2.5 ha PL gris and .5 ha blanc, 1.3 ha UN, 2.7 ha CT, 1.5 ha BR. Whites are planted on the cool clay-lime soils. ❧ OT1, 6–7 days and more crushed for early drinking "Cuvée Réservée," 12 days and fewer crushed for

"Grande Cuvée" and "Cuvée St.-Vincent." Rosé "par saignée." No malolactic in either rosé or white CDR. Will be done in white Villayes. 🐌 No wood.

Addresses of the following producers are 07 (Ardèche).

Domaine du Roure, Yves Terrasse, St.-Marcel-d'Ardèche

CDR red. **Deep berry fruit, initially masked by tannin in light, somewhat hard wines that are typical of their sector. Neither rough nor heavy, they still require time to come around. Well-structured 1981 was perhaps bettered in the series tasted in 1985 by riper 1982 and 1979.**

12-ha dispersed estate in St.-Marcel, most on cobble-sand-covered, clay-lime, southeast-facing slopes. 50% GR, 2 ha CS, 1 ha CR, .5 ha SY, .5 ha CT and a little MV. 🐌 OT2, 8 to 10 days. 🐌 No wood, several years in vat.

H **Domaine de l'Olivet,** Rodolphe Goossens, Bourg-St.-Andéol

CDR red, rosé, white. **Composition of the regular red here includes 40% Clairette to offset 15% Carignan. Fine, liquid, truffly, with hints of tobacco and meat fat, in the 1982 it was surpassed by a very successful pure Syrah, not astringent, almost black, with such true-to-type savors as tar, black pepper, and cinnamon. Equally surprising is full-flavored, round, almost Chardonnay-like pure Clairette white.**

9 ha in vine on slopes below and within sight of brother-in-law's Château Rochecolombe. 40% GR, 25% CT rose and blanche, 15% CR, 10–15% SY. 🐌 OT2, 8 days, *cépages* fermented separately, hand-operated vertical press. White, made from both CTs, is wood-fermented. 🐌 Red is aged in small oak *pièces* (some new).

H **Château Rochecolombe,** Gilbert Herberigs, Bourg-St.-Andéol

CDR red, white. **M. Herberigs stresses cleanliness of operation, tends to be very picky about the wines he selects for bottle (no 1977). Clean and fluid (even in 1982), they give hints of butter and truffles, and display a distinctive regional fruit—perhaps elderberry.**

20-ha single estate in Bourg. 50% GR, rest is 1/2 CT/CS, 1/2 SY. The château, on a Roman foundation, dates partly from the 16th century, partly from the 19th. 🐌 ST, 5 to 8 days, Vaslin press. 🐌 Wine ages 2 years in enamel-lined metal vats.

The following are cooperatives of this zone:

Cave Coopérative de Gaujac (Gard)
    Founded 1928. 26.71% AOC.

Cave Coopérative de Vénéjean (Gard)
    Founded 1929. 36.57% AOC. CDR from Vénéjean, Saint-Nazaire.
    *CDR rosé; *CDR red.

Cave Coopérative de Pont-Saint-Esprit (Gard)
    Founded 1926. 20.39% AOC.

Société Coopérative Vinicole de Bourg-Saint-Andéol (Ardèche)
    Founded 1929. 25.97% AOC. CDR from Bourg (most), St.-Marcel-d'Ardèche. CDT from Donzère, La-Garde-Adhémar, Pierrelatte.

SOUTHERN SUBREGIONS AND PRODUCERS

THE LEFT BANK

Every year in July, Vacqueyras (Vaucluse) hosts a wine festival for the 17 named Côtes-du-Rhône Villages. Photo courtesy of Robert Burns.

1983 **1983**

Cuvée Prestige

Châteauneuf du Pape

APPELLATION CHATEAUNEUF-DU-PAPE CONTRÔLÉE

Roger Sabon 75 cl

G.A.E.C. Domaine ROGER SABON & FILS
RÉCOLTANTS à CHATEAUNEUF-DU-PAPE 84230 FRANCE

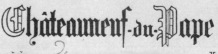

Châteauneuf-du-Pape

75 cl

Domaine du

Vieux Télégraphe

APPELLATION CHATEAUNEUF-DU-PAPE CONTROLÉE

MIS EN BOUTEILLE AU DOMAINE

GAEC H. BRUNIER ET FILS, PROPRIÉTAIRES-RÉCOLTANTS
ROUTE DE CHATEAUNEUF-DU-PAPE 84370 BEDARRIDES FRANCE

DOMAINE FONT DE MICHELLE

Châteauneuf-du-Pape

Appellation Châteauneuf-du-Pape Contrôlée

N° 01778   MISE EN BOUTEILLE AU DOMAINE   75 cl

LES FILS D'ETIENNE GONNET PROPRIETAIRES RECOLTANTS., BEDARRIDES (Vse) FRANCE

Clos Saint-Jean

Châteauneuf-du-Pape

APPELLATION CHATEAUNEUF-DU-PAPE CONTRÔLÉE

MISE EN BOUTEILLE PAR MME GUY MAUREL ET FILS
PROPRIÉTAIRES-RÉCOLTANTS CHATEAUNEUF-DU-PAPE 84230
TÉLÉPHONE (90) 83.71.33
PRODUCE OF FRANCE   75d

1981 CUVÉE VIGNERONNE **1981**

Châteauneuf du Pape

Appellation Châteauneuf du Pape Contrôlée

MIS EN BOUTEILLE A LA PROPRIETE   75 cl e

HENRI BOIRON, PROPRIETAIRE RECOLTANT A CHATEAUNEUF DU PAPE, FRANCE

CÔTES DU RHONE
APPELLATION CÔTES DU RHÔNE CONTRÔLÉE

CHÂTEAU DU
BOIS DE LA GARDE

MIS EN BOUTEILLE A LA PROPRIÉTÉ

C. MOUSSET - PROPRIÉTAIRE A SORGUES - VAUCLUSE - FRANCE

La Vieille Ferme

Côtes du Ventoux

APPELLATION COTES DU VENTOUX CONTRÔLÉE

Récolte 1983

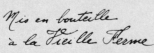

*Mis en bouteille
à la Vieille Ferme*

750 ml   Alc. 12.5% by vol

LA VIEILLE FERME s.a NÉGOCIANT A ORANGE (Vse) FRANCE

Cru de Coudoulet

COTES-DU-RHONE
APPELLATION COTES-DU-RHONE CONTROLÉE

Sté FERMIÈRE DES VIGNOBLES PIERRE PERRIN
AU CHATEAU DE BEAUCASTEL COURTHEZON (Vse)
MIS EN BOUTEILLE DU CHATEAU

TABLE WINE - PRODUCT OF FRANCE - SHIPPED BY

750 ml.
BORDEAUX   Robert Haas Selections   Alc. 12.9 % by vol.
BEAUNE

IMPORTED BY VINEYARD BRANDS - CHESTER VI

8

Southern Vaucluse

CLIMATES ON THE LEFT BANK tend to become cooler as one moves both north and east. The mistral is strongest in the center of the valley (the Rhône "corridor"), and is less influential farther east because of the wind shadow formed by the south-east to north-west angle of the Alpine foothills. The Southern Vaucluse is the warmest part of the left bank, and harvests at just about the same time as the Southern and Central Gard. It is the one area of the Vaucluse, because of Châteauneuf-du-Pape, to have had a large, virtually monocultural vineyard, famous like that of La Côte du Rhône before phylloxera.

CRU: CHÂTEAUNEUF-DU-PAPE

Zones of Production

The area of appellation Châteauneuf-du-Pape is an undulating plateau that runs along the left (east) bank of the Rhône from Orange with its still functional Roman theater in the northwest to Sorgues (north of Avignon) in the southeast. The plateau rises at its highest point to about 120 meters, which is enough to dominate that part of the Rhône valley.

In the 14th century the popes left war-torn Italy and at the instigation of the king of France settled in Avignon, which conveniently belonged to its bishop. This also placed them near some possessions, formerly known as the Marquisat of Provence, that they had acquired as spoils of war from the king of France following the victory of his forces over the Albigensian heretics. From the defeated counts of Toulouse, the kingdom of France got Languedoc, and the popes got the Comtat Venaissin. As a summer residence in the Comtat, the popes chose the now-ruined château still perched at the top of the village of Châteauneuf, which also belonged to the bishop of Avignon. So, later on, the town (not the castle) came to be spoken of as "of the Pope," more specifically, "Châteauneuf-Calcernier [for its lime kilns] dite du Pape." It is also worth noting that the *château neuf* (new castle) and the town were both known as such before the popes chose to summer there and refurbish the castle. Apparently it was new by comparison to the Château de l'Hers, downhill next to the Rhône (LeRoy 1961).

From their summer place the popes had a magnificent view. One can look east across the Ouvèze River to the broad expanse of the Comtat all the way to the Mont Ventoux, which Petrarch climbed when he too lived in Avignon. Down the Rhône, one sees the papal palace in Avignon and even the Alpilles beyond, where the traveler may have visited the ruins of Glanum or Les Baux. West is the Rhône and old Languedoc. The grounds of the château are a marvelous place to picnic, next to a patch of yellow-flowered broom or startling red poppies, perhaps after a walk among the vines in the clos where the popes had their vineyard.

Ascent to the château from the village, Châteauneuf-du-Pape (Vaucluse). Photo courtesy of Rosalind Srb.

Palace of the Popes (14th century), Avignon (Vaucluse). Photo courtesy of Rosalind Srb.

The château is still a focal point in the life of Châteauneuf. Its now-restored basement is where, on April 25, the Saint Mark's day tasting of Châteauneuf-du-Pape wines is held. In the morning, separate juries for new, old, and white wines do their solemn and sometimes animated best to rank the wines presented anonymously for their consideration. All have previously passed through a preliminary screening. Winners are announced that evening during a festive meal. Festivity also reigns when Châteauneuf-du-Pape's wine fraternity, the Echansonnerie des Papes, meets in the basement of the château to induct new members and otherwise promote the consumption of Châteauneuf-du-Pape on a grand scale. Concerts and art exhibits are given in the château during summer.

The Châteauneuf-du-Pape appellation was delimited by the courts under the system of laws on origin that preceded AOC. At the time, grapes from "alien" areas were being vinified in town and sold as the Châteauneuf-du-Pape then attractive to *négociants* for resale as "Burgundy." Reasoning that a wine good enough to be bought for that purpose must be good enough to sail under its own colors, the growers took steps to protect its authenticity. They elected lawyer Baron LeRoy de Boiseaumarié their leader in 1923, created their own rules of quality control—substantially those in the present AOC—and brought a lawsuit before the court of Orange not long afterward. Experts were

Looking east from the château at Châteauneuf-du-Pape. Within the walls *(clos)* was the papal vineyard, in the middle distance is the clear outline of a plateau (La Crau), and in the distance is the Mont-Ventoux. Photo courtesy of Rosalind Srb.

appointed by the court to delimit the boundary and other conditions historically attached to the appellation. In their report (1929) the experts said that, faithful to "loyal, local and constant usage," their criterion in tracing the boundary was following the limits of the plateau. Elevation, they said, was the primary quality factor, then presence of the classic soil formation. Heavy soil along the river was definitely excluded.

As a result appellation Châteauneuf-du-Pape is like that of St.-Emilion in covering an area larger than the named commune itself. It includes the parts of the adjoining communes of Orange, Courthézon, Bédarrides, and Sorgues that share the same plateau. Atop the plateau lie the classic *cailloux roulés* of Châteauneuf, rounded quartzite "pebbles"—really cobblestones—of Alpine origin. The plateau has five levels of elevation that mark its erosion by floods of the ancient Rhône. The largest of the cobblestones are found on the highest level, as at Mont-Redon and on the adjacent parcels of Domaine de Cabrières, and then again on the lowest (e.g., Chante-Perdrix). The combination of the reflected light and heat from the stones and exposure to the mistral makes the grapes from the plateaus high in sugar and low in acidity. There are fewer cobblestones and more "earth" on the sloped sides of the plateaus and in the little valleys in between. The bedrock is a limey sandstone locally called *safre*.

The cobbles rest on a soil of sedimentary origin from the miocene geological epoch, a mixture by turns predominantly gravel, sand, or clay. Here the *terroirs* begin to differ. South of the village of Châteauneuf, between the road to Sorgues and the Rhône, is a low-lying zone where gravel predominates. East of the village, along the roads to Bédarrides and Courthézon, sand often predominates. There are even pockets of pure sand from the "Astian" stage, as at Tavel. North of the village, to either side of the road to Orange, the *terroir* is mainly calcareous clay.

On the broad slopes northwest of the village, north of the road to Roquemaure, a different bedrock appears. It is a compact limestone of the Barrémian stage which lies very close to the surface. As a result the slopes of this zone are strewn with jagged flattish chunks and shards of this local rock, what little soil there is being a reddish clay.

Wherever possible the comments to follow indicate the zones (S, E, N, and NW) in which the estates or their parcels are found. Some very rough generalizations about these zones are that lighter and shorter-lived wines come from south of the village, an area of very well drained soil, protected from the mistral. From the north, off clay-lime soil fully exposed to the mistral, come bigger, harder, longer-lived wines. The eastern wines, where there is more sand and eastward exposures, seem to combine fullness with finesse and aromatic complexity. Skeletal soil in the NW may promote a certain leanness and intense aroma.

AOC Regulations

The regulations on productivity of appellation Châteauneuf-du-Pape are the strictest in France. No more than 35 hectoliters of wine per hectare can ever receive the appellation, and in some years less. If more than 20% above the annual limit is produced, not only the excess, but all the wine loses its right to any *appellation contrôlée*. Five percent of the grapes, and in some years more, must be culled out at harvest to make an ordinary wine, called the *râpé*, out of substandard grapes. A Châteauneuf-du-Pape can be red or white, and must achieve a minimum of 12.5% natural alcohol. No chaptalization is allowed.

On the other hand, the appellation allows the grower a choice of numbers and proportions among the 13 permitted *cépages*. Since the creation of the appellation, and especially since World War II, a great effort has been made to restore the traditional diversity of *cépages* to Châteauneuf-du-Pape. These two factors lead to variation of *encépagement* among the estates, particularly in the choice of *cépages* with which to balance Grenache. At first Syrah was the most favored for this purpose. Now there are signs of a turn toward Mourvèdre. This in fact was the desire of the Committee of Experts appointed by the judiciary in 1924 to define the appellation. Some growers feel that in the Châteauneuf climate the results with Syrah are a bit blatant and common. The Mourvèdre is thought to have more class and be truer to the *terroir*.

Châteauneuf-du-Pape. Reprinted with permission of *Revue du vin de France* from *Atlas de la France Vinicole L. Larmat*. Copyright 1943, Louis Larmat, Paris.

Styles

Since Châteauneuf-du-Pape is the largest *cru* of the Rhône valley, and the one with the highest proportion of privately produced wine in the total of its production, it is useful to distinguish styles of estate wines within the basic type. I see these styles as elegant, classic, and robust. The description of the styles, as well as the attempted placement of wines within these categories, is based on tasting the wines, and never by simple inference from winemaking method or any other single factor.

The balance in an elegant wine favors finesse. It is a wine of moderate alcohol (for a Châteauneuf) in which there is no trace of thick or aggressive tannin. Instead the texture is said to be *coulant* (flowing) or *désaltérant* (thirst-quenching). These wines are often accessible in their youth. This and their light body should not lead to the conclusion that as a category elegant wines will not age. Especially because Grenache tannin can be oxidative, a distinction should be made between tannin and total structure. Even a light wine can be more or less concentrated and tightly structured *(bien charpenté)* for the long haul.

A certain tannicity begins to be a factor in classic wines, although they are lean rather than thick or heavy. The category represents something of a compound or spectrum of wines that at one end are more elegant and at the other more robust. I could say they are medium bodied, but what I really mean by classic is a wine that performs an aesthetic balancing act between somewhat opposing qualities. It flows and has body, has muscle with grace, has both reserve and depth, and is at once generous and restrained. Usually less forthcoming in their youth, among the classic wines are to be found the longest-lived Châteauneuf-du-Papes.

With robust wines the balance definitely tips in favor of body. Big and burly *(costaud)*, the wines frankly assert their tannin and are usually high in alcohol. Especially when young they seem "chewy" or thick with tannin, with minerals, and with fruit that is almost crammed into the wine. Among the robust wines are some that are definitely difficult to drink in their youth and thus require aging. As with elegant wines, however, it is important to distinguish tannin alone from structure. If the tannin in a robust wine is oxidative, it does not necessarily signify long life.

Producers (arranged by style)

Abbreviations particular to this chapter:

N = northern zone	E = eastern zone
S = southern zone	NW = northwestern zone

For other abbreviations, see the master list at the beginning of this book. All addresses are 84230 Châteauneuf-du-Pape, unless otherwise indicated.

ELEGANT STYLE

Domaine Paul Autard, GAEC Hoirie Paul Autard, Courthézon

An impressive set of wines were tasted from cask during my 1985 visit to this estate, when it had been bottling only a small part of its production for 6 years.

Young winemaker M. Jean-Paul Autard does not believe in thick, heavy Châteauneuf, but gives up no intensity while achieving a fruit that stands up to wood age. 20–30% Syrah showed in the strong blackberry of the still yeasty "semi-macération" 1984; more Grenache was expressed in the cedary "semi-macération" 1983 and supple assembled 1982; while an assembled 1980 was moving on to tar and truffles. The version of 1980 already in bottle was not as exciting as these.

11.5 ha of Châteauneuf-du-Pape are planted on cobble and sand-covered, east-facing slopes above the qrt de l'Etang(E). 60% GR, 10% each of SY, MV, MD, and CS (with a few CT, RS, and GR blanc). 12 ha of CDR, also at Courthézon, are planted 70% to GR, 15% CS and CN, 10% SY, plus diverse white *cépages*. ❧ 60% produced by OT2, with about 30% whole berries, 7 to 10 days. 40% is OT1("semi-macération") harvested in cases, uncrushed, 8 to 12 days. Pneumatic press. The two wines are assembled for bottle in proportions determined by the character of the year. ❧ A vaulted, underground *cave* houses oak casks in which the wine spends 1 to 4 years.

Comte de Lauze, SCEA Jean Comte de Lauze; SCEA du Chantadu

Berryish-cassis fruit, especially concentrated in 1981, develops spices and truffles with age. 1979 was a bigger wine than some, still developing in my U.S. cellar (1985). Distinguished, pale, light-green white, tropical fruit aroma. A 1985 tasted in the U.S. under the "Comte d'Argelas" label was interestingly smokey, seemed tighter-structured and more mineral than formerly.

20 ha of Châteauneuf-du-Pape, dispersed. 65% GR noir et blanc, 20% SY, 5% CS, 5% MV, 3% CN, plus diverse. 16 ha of CDR from Orange and Sorgues. For the name of his domaine M. Joseph Jean uses a code name by which he was known during the resistance. ❧ OT2, grapes broken by force of pump to vats only, 10 to 12 days, pneumatic press. ❧ Diatomaceous earth filtered before up to 2 years aging in oak casks and *pièces*.

Domaine Durieu, Paul Durieu

Perhaps because Syrah and Counoise show slightly too much, one can sometimes smell stems with the pepper in this blackberry-fruited wine. As well, there can be vanilla and smoke, as in the definitely ripe but balanced 1982. A floral note was struck in both the 1984 Châteauneuf and the CDR-Villages.

21 ha of Châteauneuf-du-Pape, most in the qrts of Farguerol and Pied de Baud (N), of which 2.1 ha is SY, 1.5 ha is MV, 1 ha is CN and the rest, except for a new plantation of RS, is GR. M. Durieu, who is mayor of Camaret, also owns 30 ha of CDR on the Plan de Dieu at Camaret and Travaillan. 6 ha of CDV at Mormoiron and Saumane are recently purchased. ❧ OT2 sees about 50% of the grapes arrive intact at the vat, 10 to 12 days, Vaslin press. ❧ Wine spends about 1 to 2 years in oak casks.

Château de la Gardine, SCA du Château de la Gardine (Gaston Brunel et Fils)

La Gardine is a very good illustration of the factors other than vinification that determine style—in this case the predominance of skeletal soil(Barrémian). The wine is compact and finely structured, to my taste resembling the best reds of the Gard department. Its reputation among wine brokers is for a consistent quality that makes it a good bet no matter the year. Thus a light and spicy 1975 was nevertheless clean and intense. 1980 achieved more alcohol than is normally La Gardine's style (13.8%), will likely be a *vin de garde*. 1983 retained typical elegance, remaining fluid and cool, while adding extra ripeness and aromatic intensity.

54 ha in vine, NW. 65% GR, 25% SY, 5% MV, plus RS, BR, and diverse. La Gardine also produces a CDR-Villages on the slopes at Roaix and Rasteau (Vaucluse). ✌ OT2, with crushing by force of the pump only, optional destemming, 10 to 12 days, Vaslin press. ✌ In principle a single wine is assembled here. Wine spends 3½ years in oak casks, 6 months in bottle before sale. 90% of La Gardine's production is now estate-bottled.

Domaine le Grand Coulet, André Drapéry, Sorgues

M. Drapéry bottled from 1964–72, then reverted to bulk sale (a lot to B & G), resumed bottling again in 1981. I miss the contribution of wood age to Châteauneuf typicity in this currently light-bodied, spicy wine.

20-ha single estate in Sorgues (S). ✌ OT2, 20 days, Vaslin press. ✌ 2 years in vat, no wood age.

Château Maucoil, SCV Domaine Pierre Quiot, Orange

Maucoil participates in what for me is the house style of all the Domaine Quiot wines. It is *marchand*, pleasant, smooth, well finished, but with the high relief of personality evened out in favor of wood patina. Nevertheless the 1984 showed a distinct floral nose and whiff of lozenge fruit and *terroir* I did not remember from Maucoil, and flowers and spices were also present in the somewhat rounder 1983.

16 ha on mostly cobblestone-covered soil in qrts Maucoil, Mont-Redon, Cabrières (N) and Bosquets (also N but nearer the village). 80% GR, plus CS, CL, MV. ✌ Vinification was formerly ST with a week's cuvaison, but since 1982 has been CL, 12 days; hydraulic press. ✌ 6 to 12 months in oak casks.

Other "Domaines Quiot" (all vinified at Maucoil):

Châteauneuf-du Pape **Quiot Saint-Pierre**

15 ha, mostly clay, in qrts Palestor, Bois Lauzon, Cabrières (N) and Bois de Boursan (S).

Gigondas **Pradets**

14 ha (plateau) planted to GR, MV, CL, CS, SY. Red and rosé.

CDR **Patriciens**

6 ha at Orange, just below Maucoil. Almost 100% GR. Red and rosé.

H **Domaine de Nalys**, SCI Domaine de Nalys

Nalys makes more white Châteauneuf than any other domaine. It is consistently the best or nearly so: a lemony, leafy, floral, resinous green-gold wine that despite its rich softness develops well in bottle (1984 added an extra dimension of fresh acidity). Potential longevity—try the still fresh 1977 if it can be found—is probably why Nalys is cautious about the trend to cold fermentation and blocked malolactic for white Châteauneufs. Red Nalys has an equally strong personality in my view, and despite commentary to the contrary, a capacity for development in bottle along with initial attractiveness. It usually gives a whiff of pepper and stones to the nose, plus butter, banana, flowers, spice, vanilla and more-or-less tarry resin and licorice according to the year and *cuvée*. Several are made according to the style demands of important clients. The best in my experience (including deeply tannic 1978 and perfectly balanced 1981) is the *cuvée* called "Châtaignier," which reflects the proportion of *cépages* in the plantation and origin from old vines in the quartier of Nalys itself. Nevertheless a Lichine selection 1971, obtained from normal French commercial channels and tasted in fall of 1985, most recently demonstrated the aging potential of Nalys: well conserved and still improving when finished 24 hours after opening.

52 ha, with three principal groups of parcels in the neighboring qrts of Nalys, Bois Sénéchaux, and La Crau (E). Formerly belonged to the late Dr. Philippe Dufays, ex-physician, viti- and vinicultural experimentalist, and founder of the Châteauneuf-du-Pape wine fraternity, l'Echansonnerie des Papes. All 13 grape varieties, with at present, 55% GR, 13% SY, 6.25% GR blanc, 5.5% CT, 3.55% BR, 3.45% CS, 2.4% MD (saved from disappearance by Dr. Dufays), 3.5% diverse field-blended, 1.6% CN, 2% VA, 1.5% MV, 1.3% RS, 0.5% PC, and 0.2% TR and PL. ❧ The present oenologist of the domaine, M. Pélissier, joins the late doctor in preferring the name *méthode à l'ancienne* to carbonic maceration for their technique, in which intitial crushing occurs only by the weight of the bunches in transport and in filling of the vat. 10 days; pneumatic press, even more definitive for elegance than vinification in M. Pélissier's opinion. ❧ Filtration through diatomaceous earth when finished. 3 months to 2 years in oak casks.

Clos de l'Oratoire des Papes, Léonce Amouroux

Sometimes very floral, sometimes dominated by the wood finish, as in disappointingly short 1984 bought in the U.S.

60 ha adjacent to La Gardine (NW). Red *cépages:* 80% GR, 20% SY, MV, and CS. White *cépages:* 40% GR blanc, 30% BR, 30% CT. ❧ OT1, but some—especially SY—destemmed, 7 to 14 days. *Cépages* fermented apart, pneumatic press. Press wine is used for Châteauneuf according to the character of the year. ❧ 1 year in vat and 1 year in oak casks. The rest of the wine's stay in small barrels is determined by the demand for the wine to be bottled.

Quiot Saint-Pierre, SCV Domaine Pierre Quiot, Orange

See Château Maucoil

Domaine Saint-Préfert, Mme. Veuve Camille Serres

Mme. Serres believes that St.-Préfert may have been the first in the postwar period to have commercialized white Châteauneuf-du-Pape. My sense is that the red wine, light-bodied and elegant in its inherent structure, is sometimes overwhelmed by the taste of wood.

The domaine conducts 25 ha of vineyard, all of which are in the qrt of Serres (S). Red *cépages:* 65% GR, 10% each of CS, MV, and SY, and 5% diverse. White *cépages:* GR blanc, CT, BR. ❧ Formerly ST, OT2 since 1984, 5 to 6 days (with the pulp of the white grapes added to the red must after the free run juice for white wine is drawn off from the press). ❧ After filtration through diatomaceous earth, the wine is lodged in oak casks for from 18 months to 4 years, as regulated by the demand for bottled wine. The St.-Préfert wines are commercialized by the *négociant* firm Les Grandes Serres of Châteauneuf-du-Pape.

Domaine de la Solitude, GAEC Lançon Père et Fils

I used to find the wine intensely floral and tarry, and while never heavy, fully Châteauneuf in savor (an excellent 1972, for example). Recent years (1980–82) seem light colored and less intense.

35 ha in the qrt of La Solitude (E). **1985 shows improvement.** Mostly sandy soil. Was 50% GR, 25% CS, 15% SY, 5% diverse. Now 10% CS, 20% SY, 15% MV. Some more than 100-year-old vines date from the first replantation at Châteauneuf after phylloxera. The estate has been in the same family (on Mme. Lançon's side) since 1652. In the family's possession are labels of "Vin de la Solitude" that adorned the first wines of Châteauneuf to be labeled. CDR **Château des Vallonnières** from Sabran (Gard) is vinified at Châteauneuf. ❧ Since 1954 the wine has been produced by pure or "integral" CM, 20 days, pneumatic press. ❧ Filtered through diatomaceous earth when finished to minimize racking. 16 to 18 months in large barrels, 10% 4 to 6 months in new oak pièces.

Domaine de Terre Ferme, SCEA du Domaine de Terre Ferme, Bédarrides

Until recently, grapes from the Terre Ferme estate were vinified by the *négociant* firm Cave Bérard Père et Fils, whose Châteauneuf-du-Pape could therefore contain, but was not limited, to Terre Ferme's wine. Following the death of Bérard Père in December 1983, the two affairs, property and *négociant* business, have been completely separated. The result, beginning with the 1985 harvest, is that the wines of Terre Ferme will now be sold in the embossed Châteauneuf-du-Pape bottle, which only proprietors may use.

It is too early to say exactly what the style and quality of this wine will be, though it will likely have continuity with the Cave Bérard Châteauneufs, both because they used to contain this property's wine and because Cave winemaker Garcia continues his work for the domaine. Of the two Cave red Châteauneufs that might be predictive, the "Carte d'Or" was usually the more elegant and floral, although with a recognizably "traditional," slightly oxidized, sour butter and animal nose. The "Cuvée Prestige" tended to be more robust, concentrated, earthy, and nuanced. M. Garcia's tentative *assemblage* of the new wines of 1985 resembled "Prestige."

55 ha, of which the greater portion is in the qrt Terre Ferme of Bédarrides (E). 26 ha GR, 3 ha CS, 4 ha SY, 3 ha MV, 9 ha GR blanc, 1 ha BR and CT. Additional CT, BR planted. ❧ The red wines are produced in part by ST (although with no pumping), in part by OT1, and then assembled—"the most important phase," according to owner M. Pierre Bérard. Techniques for the youthful-drinking-style white, of which Bérard is a leading exponent, include fining the must in order to ferment clear juice, low temperature fermentation, and avoidance of the malolactic fermentation. ❧ Bérard has been moving toward less time in oak casks for his reds, deploring the old tendency to bottle Châteauneuf "too late" and to drink it "too warm."

Domaine Trintignant, SCEA Jean Trintignant

On the whole the Trintignant reds seem light-bodied, very clean, if slightly reduced, and highly scented in a quite typical Châteauneuf range including raspberry, smoke, black pepper, cedar, and spices. I have some hesitation about the years since 1979, having found the 1981 and especially the 1980 already advanced in maturity by

1985, and the 1983 light in color. Grenache blanc, Clairette, Bourboulenc, Roussanne, and diverse field-blended *cépages* enter the light green-straw, youthful-drinking-style white.

35 dispersed ha represent the family estate of Mme. Paul Jean (née Trintignant), widow of a former president of the Châteauneuf-du-Pape Growers Federation. Since 1976 she has run the property herself. 25 ha GR, 3 ha SY, 2 ha CS, plus all the rest of the 13. CDR at Courthézon and Uchaux (Vaucluse). &? 40% of the red—more if the weather is cold—"habitual," i.e., ST, 8 to 10 days. 60%—less if the weather is cold—OT1, 15 to 21 days. The two vinifications are conducted separately and the wine assembled afterwards. Pneumatic and Vaslin presses. &? After stabilization by passage outdoors in the cold weather, the wine for estate bottling is aged in oak casks. "La Reviscoulado" is a label for Châteauneuf-du-Pape sold direct.

Domaine de Valori, "Domaines Meffre"

See **Château de Vaudieu**

Château de Vaudieu, Société Civile des Vignobles de Vaudieu ("Domaines Meffre")

My impression is that the wine usually has as much the character of the Meffre house style as it does of a Châteauneuf, but greater firmness and concentration can emerge in certain years (e.g., 1978).

75 ha near Domaine de Nalys and Château Rayas (E). Red *cépages:* 75% GR, 10% SY, 15% CS and MV. White *cépages:* 60% GR blanc, 40% RS, CT, PC. **Domaine de Valori** is an adjacent 15 ha Châteauneuf estate, vinified at Vaudieu. &? CL, part ST (the lower part of each vat, to facilitate drawing off the finished wine), 13 to 16 days, impulsion press. Only the "jus de goutte" is employed for the Châteauneuf. &? The wine spends about 1 year in oak casks. **Terres Blanches** is a second label. For other "Domaines Meffre" wines see Gigondas, Château Raspail.

CLASSIC STYLE

H **Domaine de Beaurenard,** Paul Coulon et Fils

Beaurenard often has the most pronounced aroma of whole berry fermentation among the Châteauneufs, perhaps from the layering of crushed and whole berries in the vat. So delicious is the wine when young that one may be tempted not to let it develop in bottle, which it does very well, steadily taking on a more characteristic Châteauneuf nose with age. A 1967 gained while being open during a 1980 tasting, and a 1974 was in full form beside a 1976 with lots in reserve when the two were tasted in 1982. There is almost always more tannin in Beaurenard than is apparent. 1980 showed excellent balance, and a nicely fat 1984 combined raspberry, cassis, and cedar.

32 ha of which about half is in one parcel in qrt Beaurenard (NW) that seems responsible for an especially floral GR. Plantation is 68% GR, 10% SY, 9% MV, 11% CS, 2% CT. 45 ha of CDR at Rasteau (most) and Séguret was formerly known as "La Ferme Pisan." Production from this property allows M. Coulon to satisfy his clients who demand wine for immediate consumption, without bottling a *cuvée* of Châteauneuf for this purpose. At Rasteau M. Coulon also maintains an extensive and most interesting wine and wine-making museum. &? OT1 with lightly crushed bunches and about 1/3 uncrushed alternately layered in the vats, 2 weeks *cuvaison,* horizontal press. &? Finished

wine is filtered through diatomaceous earth before being lodged in oak barrels, first casks and then *pièces,* for about a year.

H Château de Beaucastel, Société Fermière des Vignobles de Pierre Perrin, Courthézon

The animal, fungal, tarry nose of an evolved Beaucastel often aligns its character with the great reds of the Côte de Nuits, especially from Gevrey-Chambertin. Probably the longest lived Châteauneuf-du-Pape of all, it tends to be more reduced and enclosed than harsh when young. From there the wine opens slowly and magnificently, with wines I have tasted back to 1929 still seeming to be in the process of development. Notable recent wines have included the vast 1970 and 1973, more elegant 1972, 1979 (which I preferred for its superbly balanced richness to the more austere 1978), and the similarly full and well-balanced if more compact 1981. 1984 shows great promise, with the Mourvèdre at 30% equaling Grenache in the *assemblage*. White Beaucastel, in recent years reaching 90% Roussanne, is also a keeper. The malolactic is done, and since 1980 about 1/3 has been aged before *assemblage* in new oak barrels.

Formerly known as Domaine de Beaucastel. Approximately 70 ha in qtr Coudoulet (N), conducted according to organic farming principles. 50% GR, MV raised to 20% by late owner Jacques Perrin with cuttings from Domaine Tempier at Bandol. Also SY, CS, GR blanc, RS, and a few of all 13. 30-ha H CDR **Cru du Coudoulet** in Courthézon, just across highway from Beaucastel. GR, MV, SY, CS. Since 1982, the produce of CDR **Chemin des Mulets,** adjacent, has been sold to Jean-Pierre Perrin's "La Vielle Ferme." ❧ François Perrin carries on the form of CL vinification unique to Beaucastel among the Châteauneufs. Since 1964, the whole crop, destemmed but not crushed, has been heated as the grapes are pumped toward the vats, for better extraction of color and tannin and to kill the harmful enzyme polyphenoloxidase. They are then quickly cooled and fermented at a low temperature for 15 days. Cépages are fermented apart, pneumatic press. Free-run and press wines are finished apart before incorporation. ❧ After resting in *cuve* for clarification, the wine is aged in oak casks until the optimum moment by taste (12 to 18 months), then racked back into enamel-lined vats to hold until bottling.

Domaine de Cabrières, SCEA du Domaine de Cabrières (Louis Arnaud et ses enfants)

From being almost fatiguingly robust, Cabrières has made steady progress toward a more liquid and balanced, indeed classic, structure. Better control of temperature, less time in wood where need be, and clean handling of clean wine have produced the results without sacrifice of the "sacredness" of long *cuvaison*. The evidence includes a truffly, almost Corton-like 1977 that shows (1985) no signs of fatigue, a rich but definitely not premature 1982, and a floral, peppery 1983 that is actually fresh. About 8% of Cabrières's production is now in white.

40 ha, the major part of which is in qrt Cabrières (N) adjacent to Mont-Redon. 90% of Cabrières's land is cobble-covered. 50% GR, 10% each of CS, SY and MV; 20% CT, CN, and BR. INAO propagated MV from Cabrières, some of the oldest at Châteauneuf. 20 ha elsewhere in Châteauneuf produce wine sold in bulk, not as Cabrières. ❧ OT2, 1 month *cuvaison*. Almost the full panoply of progressive methods for making fresh whites is employed: immediate pressing without crushing, settling under CO_2 at low tempera-

ture, fining of the must, fermentation at low temperature, blocked malolactic, cold-stabilization, and sterile filtration. ❧ Red wine is filtered through diatomaceous earth before being aged 1 to 3 years in oak casks. No racking. **"Les Silex," "La Cuvée des Tonneliers,"** and **"Grand Devès"** are additional Cabrières labels.

H **Les Cailloux,** Lucien Brunel et Fils

A certain number of "late harvest" Grenaches contribute to the distinctive nose of Cailloux, still evident in the very well balanced 1980 tasted in 1985, perhaps masked by tannin in the 1983. The quality orientation of the Brunels was well illustrated by the severe *triage* which allowed them to make an excellent wine in 1975. Best I have tasted was a 1974 labeled "Tête de Cuvée."

19 ha dispersed. Principal parcels N and S. 70% GR, 10% each CS, MV, SY. ❧ OT2. Formerly about 2/3 of the grapes entered the vat whole. Present tendency is toward more nearly 1/3, to increase acidity. ❧ Average 2 years in oak casks. Wine is bottled in the facilities of the proprietors' union "Reflets du Châteauneuf-du-Pape."

Clos du Calvaire, SCEA du Domaine du Père Pape (Maurice Mayard)

M. Mayard, well known as a *courtier* (broker) specializing in the best Châteauneuf, succeeded his father as proprietor of the family vineyards in 1976. Dark, full, and rich without heaviness, Calvaire's fruit lies between black raspberry and black cherry. Sometimes showing fairly pronounced reduction scents at the start, the bouquet opens toward *garrigues,* butter, vanilla and truffles. The real successes so far have seemed to me the 1980 and 1982 (notable in a difficult year). When tasted in 1985 from both barrel and an early bottling, the 1984 bid fair to join the roster. A first attempt at white was made in 1984.

Conducts 23 ha, of which a major portion is on the NE-facing slope of La Crau just below that portion of Nalys (E). 75% GR, 10% CS, 10% SY, with a little MV, VA, and 5 ha of CT rose and blanche, GR blanc, RS, BR. ❧ Blends OT2 for the major part, 10 to 15 days in stainless steel, with CM for 1/2 the SY, Vaslin press. ❧ Following malolactic fermentation, the wine is filtered through diatomaceous earth, then lodged in a separate aging *cave* for 6 months or so in vat before another 6 to 12 months in oak casks.

Domaine des Chanssaud, Roger Jaume et Fils, Orange

Formerly a mineral-dry and heavy wine, a new *cave de vinification* dating from 1981 has occasioned a shorter *cuvaison* and better balance in the recent wines. As with other Châteauneufs of the northern tier, the reduction scents tend more to barnyard than to truffle.

28–30 ha, including Châteauneuf-du-Pape in the qrt Cabrières on slopes below Mont-Redon (N), and CDR. 75–80% GR, plus CS, MV, and some field-blended SY and CT. ❧ OT2, 7 to 8 days; first press (hydraulic) incorporated. ❧ 12 to 18 months in oak casks.

Domaine Chante-Cigale, GAEC du Domaine Chante-Cigale (Sabon-Favier)

For me the wine has usually been typified by uncomplicated purity of flavor. An exceptional balance between fruit and wood was struck in the 1978 and 1979, the latter of which M. Noël Sabon indicates is "to keep." The trend continued in a 1980

notable for finesse and an extra nuance of *terroir*. Son-in-law M. Favier now makes the wine.

28 ha, 80% GR, 5–6% each of SY, MV, and CS. M. Favier has a CDR vineyard at Travaillan (Vaucluse) whose wine is vinified at Châteauneuf. ❧ ST, 21 days. ❧ Wine is withdrawn from cask by taste (around 3 years) and lodged again in vats before bottling.

H Les Clefs d'Or, Domaine Jean Deydier et Fils

A wine of remarkably clean outline, depth, and concentration of fruit without thickness. It has floral, spicy and resinous nuances, often developing the scent of truffles with age—as in the 1977, which proved to be a *vin de garde* in that difficult year. 1980 is also one of my favorites for balance, with 1979 perhaps the best all around in my tasting experience at this estate.

21 ha, with one big parcel of 14 ha in the qrts Pielon and Terre Blanche (N). Another parcel of 6 ha on the plateau of La Crau near Nalys (E). 70% GR. VA and MV together outweigh SY in the rest. 2 ha of 100–year-old vines at La Crau. 12 ha of CDR from Mondragon (Vaucluse). 60% GR, 20% CS, plus MV and CT rose. ❧ OT2 with optional destemming (up to 1/4). 25–30% of the grapes arrive intact at the vats. *Cuvaison* up to 3 weeks. Press wine optionally incorporated. Clefs d'Or began making a cool fermented white from GR blanc, BR, and CT in 1981. ❧ Red spends 3 years in vat and oak cask to avoid fining and filtering.

Domaine du Clos-du-Roi, Guy Mousset

See **Château des Fines Roches**

Réserve des Diacres, Henri Chausse

On the whole a tender wine with red fruit savor and a pleasantly stinky nose, ranging from *garrigues* to barnyard and truffles.

Exploits 10 ha in 42 parcels, of which the principal ones are in the qrts Vaudieu and Boucou (E) and Bois Dauphin (N). 80–85% GR, 5% CS, 5% MV, 5% diverse including SY. Average age of vines is 60 years. ❧ OT2, 21 days. The first press (hydraulic press) is incorporated, immediately if the *vin de goutte* is not finished. ❧ 1 year of aging, of which 6 months are in wood.

Domaine de Farguerol, Joseph Révoltier et Fils

A lighter bodied *cuvée,* selected from the whole property, is presented under the Vieux Chemin label. Under the Farguerol label is a heftier wine, with much more Syrah, strictly from that part of the property. M. Révoltier is a past president of the proprietors' union "Prestige et Tradition," where his wine is bottled.

22 ha now in vine will rise to 27. Before its expansion by acquisition of the Farguerol property (N) from Dr. Dufays, estate was known as Vieux Chemin for a parcel near Vaudieu (E). ❧ Formerly ST, now OT2 with about 50% of the grapes intact. 15 to 21 days, impulsion press. ❧ About 1 year in wood.

H Château des Fines Roches, Catherine Barrot-Mousset

Fines Roches seems to have gained both substance and floral elegance from its present vinification, while remaining the roundest and most complete Châteauneuf of the Mousset group, probably because of its proportion of old vines. Truffle and animal scents develop with age, as in the very distinguished 1979. 1981 and 1983 also excellent, with 1984 promising more grace than the latter.

45 ha located between Fortia and La Nerthe, just across the road from La Solitude (E). 70% GR, 10% SY, 10% CS, 5% MV, plus MD, CN. 2.5 ha of white just planted: GR, CT, BR, RS. M. Barrot, in charge of the vineyard, worked closely with the late Dr. Philippe Dufays. 𝒆𝒂 A very advanced vinification facility, of the type that allows the bunches as they arrive at the top of each stainless steel vat to be crushed or destemmed or not as desired, was first used at Fines Roches in 1976. It now belongs to a proprietors' vinification cooperative SICA "La Grenade," and in it the wines of all the Mousset family domaines, among others, are vinified. Vinification of Fines Roches is OT1, with about 1/3 of the grapes entering the vat intact, especially the last to arrive. 10 to 14 days, Vaslin press. 𝒆𝒂 The Mousset Châteauneufs receive 3 to 6 months in oak casks. A particularity of the Mousset domaines is that each makes only one *cuvée*, which therefore represents an "assemblage totale" of that property's production.

Other "Domaines Mousset," all commercialized by the *négociant* firm Louis Mousset of Châteauneuf-du-Pape, are:

Châteauneuf-du-Pape **Domaine de la Font-du-Roi,** Jacques Mousset
  Distinctively buttery, perhaps next best after Fines Roches. 24 ha in qrt Font-du-Loup (E). 70% GR, 10% SY, 7% MD, 3% CS.
Châteauneuf-du-Pape **Domaine du Clos-du-Roi,** Guy Mousset
  25 ha (S). 85% GR, CS, PL.
Châteauneuf-du-Pape **Clos Saint Michel,** Guy Mousset
  10 ha (S). 90% GR, and SY.
H CDR **Château du Bois de la Garde,** Catherine Barrot-Mousset
  60 ha at Sorgues. GR, CS, MV, Oeillade, CN, and 70-year-old CR (which made up 30% of the 1984). Many of the accessory *cépages* are field-blended.
CDR **Domaine du Grand Vaucroze,** Guy Mousset
  12 ha at Sorgues. GR, CS, CR, young-vine SY.
CDR **Château du Prieuré,** Guy Mousset
  45 ha at Sorgues. GR, CS, CR, SY.
CDR **Domaine de Tout-Vent,** Jacques Mousset
  20 ha at Sorgues. GR, CS, MV, CT, PL, and SY (16–17% of the 1984).

H **Château de la Font du Loup,** Jean Roch Mélia, proprietor, Courthézon; Charles Mélia, producer

M. Charles Mélia is the proprietor's grandson. He says his real vocation is "making perfume." In part he is referring to the intense aroma of his wine, which is distinctly floral with usually a blackberry fruit (especially 1979) and a fine but notable tannin, as in the scarcely evolved 1981. 1980 here was outstanding, attractive early, yet holding well in 1986.

Single estate with 14½ ha in production, qrt Font du Loup (E). Partly on sandy slopes that face northeast toward the town of Courthézon and partly, behind and above the château, on the cobble-covered plateau not far from Vieux Télégraphe. 9 ha GR, 1½ ha CS, 1½ ha MV, 1½ ha SY, and 1 ha whites, including 50% GR and 50% evenly divided among BR, CT, and RS. Average age of the vines from which the estate-bottled wine is produced is 40 years. 𝒆𝒂 OT1, obtained by passing 2/3 of the bunches through a crusher which rests directly over the vats, while leaving the other 1/3 uncrushed. 10 to 12 days. 🥢 Before *assemblage*, the press wine spends 1 year in oak casks. A remodeled cellar will eventually have space to allow more of the wine to spend, probably, a shorter average time in wood.

Domaine de la Font-du-Roi, Jacques Mousset

See Château des Fines Roches

H **Château Fortia,** Baron Le Roy de Boiseaumarié

M. Henri Le Roy, the present baron, sometimes seems excessively modest about the wine of Fortia, which I find consistently one of the best. It is especially notable for the nuanced, almost Côte-de-Nuits bouquet it develops with age. Probably the best 1969 of all Châteauneufs. Perfect balance in 1978.

30 ha just east of the village off the road to Bédarrides. Estate of the late Baron Pierre Le Roy de Boiseaumarié, in effect founder of *appellation d'origine Châteauneuf-du-Pape.* 70% GR, 12–15% SY, 3% MV, 1.5% CN, a very little CS, and 6% of white, mostly on a patch of calcareous soil. 🥢 ST, partially destemmed (around 25–30%), about 21 days. 🥢 20 to 24 months in wood.

Château de la Grande Gardiole, Courthézon

The property belongs to M. André Rey, who also owns Château St.-André at Gigondas. None of M. Rey's wines are estate-bottled, and this one is distributed with the name of the domaine by the Burgundian *négociant* firm of Mommessin. In my experience the wine is a roundly fruity and pleasant, if not first intensity, Châteauneuf that, in the past, has seemed overwooded when tasted from the bottled version.

60 ha just south of Beaucastel (N). 70% GR, 20% SY, 10% CS. 60 ha of Châteauneuf-du-Pape **"La Chartreuse"** at Bédarrides, Château St.-André at Gigondas, CDR at Violès, Rasteau, and Vacqueyras (Vaucluse), CDV at Serres (Vaucluse). 🥢 ST conducted at Château St.-André. 15 days average. Press wine is not incorporated. 🥢 Until 1980 aged in oak and chestnut at Grande Gardiole as demanded by the client. *Elevage* is now the buyer's responsibility. **Château de St.-André** is a second label for Châteauneuf-du-Pape from the Courthézon property commercialized by the *négociant* firm Cave St.-Pierre of Châteauneuf-du-Pape.

H **Domaine du Grand Tinel,** Elie Jeune

My impression is that the Tinel wines divide into two groups, with those since 1980 on a superior level of quality. The 1975–1979 tend toward a baked or even dried fruit, probably peach, with spices and a hint of wood as a separate flavor. 1979 is probably the richest of these. Beginning with the 1980, the wines feature deeper, darker fruit, probably cassis, with cool resins of provençal herbs, and hints of smoke, truffles, tar, and the stony *terroir*. 1981, 1983, and 1984 are probably the most compact and resinous, 1980 and 1982 more round and plummy.

70 dispersed ha in AOC Châteauneuf-du-Pape include 35-ha La Petite Gardiole (N). 70% GR, 30% SY, MV, CS, CN, MD, BR, CT, and GR blanc. 5 ha of CDR at Courthézon. 🥢 OT2, perhaps 1/4 whole berries to start. SY and CN are fermented apart, other *cépages* are fermented by *quartier*. *Cuvaison* averages 3 weeks, Vaslin press.

🐚 Kept in vats until spring, passed through a diatomaceous earth filter, then lodged in oak casks 2 to 3 years. **"Cave St.-Paul"** is a second label for Châteauneuf-du-Pape.

H **Domaine du Haut des Terres Blanches**, GAEC Domaine du Haut des Terres Blanches (Rémy Diffonty et Fils)

M. Diffonty's *cave* is one of the few in Châteauneuf where one can taste old wines. Until 1983, he usually assembled a *vin de garde* with Grenache and 20% to 25% Mourvèdre, and occasionally a lighter *cuvée* with less Mourvèdre, plus Cinsault and Clairette. The former, which I have tasted repeatedly in vintages back to 1957, is big and firm without thickness, very well defined and balanced. The bouquet shows marked development in the direction of tar and truffles with each year of barrel and eventual bottle age, the wine retaining an impression of sweetness even into old age. With less Mourvèdre at his disposal now, it is to be hoped that M. Diffonty will retain a "Mourvèdre" *cuvée* in his traditional style, alongside what would become a new "Syrah" *cuvée*. Unified 1985 nevertheless promising.

33 ha in production, largest parcel in qrt Pradelles (N). Until 1983, 55% GR, 20% MV, 14–15% CS, 8–9% SY, a few CT. An exchange of parcels with another property to make the estate less dispersed then augmented the GR proportion to 70%, diminished the MV to 5%. Since 1983, M. Diffonty has rented and made the wine of 10-ha Châteauneuf estate **Domaine de la Glacière** (NW), 80% GR, 8–10% CT, plus MV, VA, and newly planted SY. 🐚 OT1, maybe as few as 1/3 crushed, 14 to 21 days. In principle the qrts are fermented separately. Vaslin press. 🐚 When clear, put in oak casks for at least 3 years, often longer. **Domaine de la Bastide** and **"Réserve du Vatican"** are second Haut des Terres Blanches labels.

Clos du Mont-Olivet, GAEC du Clos Mont-Olivet (Les Fils de Joseph Sabon)

Mont-Olivet is distinctively fragrant of sour butter and pepper, which can be cayenne pepper in unassembled wine just from the Mont-Olivet qrt. For some reason recent vintages have seemed drier than the wines of my earlier experience, like the superb 1972.

24 ha, parcels in qrts of Mont-Olivet (E), Galimardes (S), Bois Dauphin, Palestor and Pied de Baud (N). Around 85% GR, with SY, CS, VA, MV, CT, and BR. Oldest vines date from before WWI. 🐚 OT1. *Cuvaison* "lasts as long as the harvest," which means that the first vats filled take 3 weeks and the last, 1 week. Hydraulic and Vaslin presses. 🐚 2 to 3 years in wood, after which the wine is bottled in the facilities of the proprietors' union "Reflets du Châteauneuf-du-Pape."

H **Domaine de Mont-Redon**, SA de Mont-Redon

Contemporary Mont-Redon seems at once leafy, floral, and peppery, a bit reduced at the start, stressing construction rather than thickness. Here, 1978 surpassed 1979, 1981 was in fine form in 1985, 1983 successfully avoided excessive dryness, and tightly constructed 1984 has deep berry fruit and the scent of lavender. White is made in the newer, fresher style by centrifuging the juice before a cold fermentation. Mont-Redon produces a limited quantity of very fine marc brandy.

Began with 2 ha, but now the largest property in Châteauneuf with 95 ha in vine. 60 are next to Domaine de Cabrières on the same high, cobble-covered plateau. Two of the present owners, M. Jean Abeille and M. Didier Fabre, are trained oenologists. Red *cépages:* 65% GR, 15% SY (some planted in 1929), 6% MV being augmented to reach 10%, 10% CS, and 4% diverse. White *cépages:* 40% GR blanc, 25% BR, 20% CT, 10% PL, 5% TR. 16 ha CDR at Roquemaure (Gard) is planted 70% GR, 20% CS, 10% SY. Wine is vinified at Mont-Redon. A newly purchased CDR property in Orange is adjacent to Mont-Redon, but not yet planted. ❧ OT2, around 1/3 destemmed. 14 to 21 days, pneumatic press. ❧ Finished red wine is centrifuged or filtered through diatomaceous earth so that clean wine is lodged in barrels by January. Most oak casks, but 1000 hl of 1986 will be 3 months in new oak *pièces.*

H Clos des Papes, Paul Avril

If there is any excess in Clos des Papes it is sometimes (deliberately) tannin. Nevertheless the increased Mourvèdre in the composition of this wine shows up in the years since 1979 as a finer, more compact structure, yielding a wine at once more solid and liquid, less dry and thick than formerly. The wine retains its tendency to ripe black cherry fruit from late-picked grapes, accompanied by a classic ensemble of fragrances, often nutmeg, licorice, and truffles. Recent standouts include a very long and well balanced 1980, smelling of cassis, leather, and butter; one of *the* successful 1983s, mature to the nose but not dry in 1985; and a very clean, spicy 1984, with hints of stones. Since 1981 the white has been made from five *cépages,* and has become one of Châteauneuf's most distinguished, combining the fresh fragrances of the youthful-drinking style with richness and body indicative of potential longevity.

32-ha dispersed estate. Parcel from which estate draws its name is inside the walls of the old papal vineyard, just northeast of the château. 70% GR, no CS as a matter of policy. M. Avril does not believe large-berried grapes can produce *vin de garde* (proportion of skins to juice is too small). MV has been augmented to around 20% of the red *cépages,* with about 8% SY, plus VA, MD, CN. White: 20% each of RS, BR, CT, PL, GR blanc. ❧ Modernized facility allows very gentle crush directly above vats for OT1. Partial destemming is possible but rare. 14 days, vertical press. Wine finishes in glass-lined vats. ❧ 12 to 18 months in oak casks in humidity and temperature controlled *cave.* The mistral would otherwise cause a loss of wine by evaporation, and M. Avril believes it prematurely "dries out" the flavor.

Domaine du Père Caboche, Jean-Pierre Boisson

Before the new installation the red wines were robust, but since, they have gained elegance, if sometimes seeming to lack fullness. Beginning in 1980, a *cuvée* "Elisabeth Chambellan" has been distinguished by production from centenarian vines and a higher percentage of the *cépages* other than Grenache. Clean, straightforward white is leafy-fresh, with a taste of pears in the 1984.

30 ha, more than half on the plateau of La Crau near Nalys and Vieux Télégraphe. M. Boisson is an ex-president of the Federation of Châteauneuf-du-Pape Syndicates of Growers. The family have been proprietors at Châteauneuf since 1650. 80% GR, 10% SY, 10% MV, CS, BR, CT, MD, and GR blanc. 6 ha of CDR at Courthézon and Sorgues. ❧ Formerly ST, but in 1974 Père Caboche pioneered the type of installation that eliminates pumping and permits any form of vinification desired when the grapes are delivered to the top of each vat. Now OT1, with GR lightly crushed, CS, SY, MV

not. *Cuvaison* averages 3 weeks in stainless steel vats that can be water-cooled or coil-heated at need. 🍇 Cold-stabilized (since 1978), the wine spends 2 years in oak casks, then 1 to 5 years in bottle before sale.

"Cuvée Princes d'Orange," Antoine Verda et Fils, Roquemaure (Gard).

See Lirac Domaine du Château Saint-Roch.

Château Rayas, Jacques Reynaud

The many particularities make this the most unusual wine of Châteauneuf-du-Pape, defined for me by its unique combination of concentration and finesse when tasted early on from the barrel. From bottle I have had reservations, sometimes from too strong a taste of aldehyde and oak, albeit delicious oak, and sometimes from the smell of the *cave*. These reservations extend to the tasting in the U.S. of some earlier Rayas and Pignan vintages. On the other hand, bottled 1981 Rayas seems clean, fine and tight in its structure, with tar and resins to the nose, while barrel-tasting in 1985 suggests Rayas may be one of those Châteauneufs where 1984 is preferable to 1983.

Only 13 of 50 ha in the qrts of Pignan and Rayas (E) are planted to vine. As for the rest, one walks the property from one patch of gently sloped vineyard to another through thick stands of umbrella pine *(pignan)*, allepo pine, and green and white oak. These woods make for a moderate microclimate, as does the northeastward exposure and a soil, almost pure sand, with only scattered cobbles. "For the moment," says M. Jacques Reynaud, son of the late M. Louis Reynaud and now manager of the property for the heirs, "the only red *cépage* at Rayas is Grenache, about 80%." CT, GR blanc, each 10%. A few of these enter the red wine as a result of field-blending. Some CS will be planted. **H CDR Château de la Fonsalette** at Lagarde-Paréol (Vaucluse), 150 ha, of which 12 are in vine: GR, CS, SY, Chardonnay, RS, GR blanc. Fonsalette is vinified at Rayas. **Fonsalette Cinsault, practically black in color, immensely floral and tarry, is the most extraordinary product of that *cépage* I have ever tasted.** 🍇 Late harvest followed by ST, 3 to 15 days. *Cépages* are fermented apart, pneumatic press. A portion of the white Rayas is barrel-fermented. 🍇 Red wine is both finished and aged in oak *double-pièces* for 2 to 3 years. **Clos Pignan** is the label of Rayas' second wine.

H Domaine Roger Sabon, GAEC Domaine Roger Sabon et Fils

In general the wines here are both round and firm, with a sour butter nose that develops cedar, pepper, and tar. In my experience the most distinguished wine of the estate has usually been a richly long and aromatic *cuvée* produced from old vineyards of Grenache field-blended with Mourvèdre, Syrah, and other diverse *cépages*. Beginning with the 1982, this wine has been regularly identified by the Sabon "Cuvée Prestige" label, although the 1981 was called "Cuvée Réservée." Now the latter designation is applied to a somewhat more aggressively tannic, Grenache-Syrah *cuvée*. The normal Sabon label without the name of a *cuvée* now indicates an *assemblage* primarily of Grenache and Cinsault.

12 ha, the greater part on the border of Châteauneuf and Courthézon (E). M. Roger Sabon, brother of Châteauneuf proprietors Joseph and Noël Sabon, was one of the founders of the proprietors' union "Reflets du Châteauneuf-du-Pape." He left in 1972 upon acquiring property outside Châteauneuf-du-Pape. 85% GR, plus SY, CS, MV,

CN, RS, BR, GR blanc, CT rose. 17 ha in Roquemaure (Gard) include 9 of CDR and Lirac. 85–90% GR, 5% SY, and CS. ℬ OT1, 40% of the grapes start out intact. Cuvaison averages 3 weeks. A cool-fermented white with no malolactic is about 30% CT. ℬ Finished red ages 18 months to 2 years in oak casks.

Domaine de la Roquette, Brunier Frères (was René Laugier)

Perhaps the red wine lacks a certain core, but it has improved in fragrance and balance in recent years. A very attractive white was produced in 1984. M. Laugier may be the only producer of Châteauneuf-du-Pape to have bottled the totality of his production. He was one of only three to make marc brandy. The *cave* is equipped with a tasting room capable of receiving even large groups of drop-in visitors.

30 ha, largest parcel in qrts La Roquette and Pielons (N). 6 ha SY, 3 ha MV, the rest GR, with CT, BR, RS, and PL recently augmented. ℬ Until 1986 ST, destemming optional, 10 to 14 days. Wine from the first two turns of a Vaslin press incorporated. ℬ 1 to 3 years in oak casks.

Clos St. Michel, Guy Mousset

See Château des Fines Roches

Domaine des Sénéchaux, SCEA Domaine des Sénéchaux Pierre Raynaud

A wine that to my taste formerly lacked the substance to balance its alcohol has improved greatly in the 1980s. Longer *cuvaison* and better control of temperature now reveal a sometimes almost startlingly cool resinous character, specifically pine, even down to the oil and flavor of pine nuts. This can be too much in the white (as in the 1983), but combined with more familiar butter, fungal and mineral over-tones in balanced reds like 1980 and especially 1981, it strikes a note of length and finesse.

29 ha of Châteauneuf-du-Pape, with the biggest parcel in qrt Bois Sénéchaux (E) is planted 70% GR, 10% CS, 5% SY, 5% MV, plus some of all 13. ℬ ST includes some destemming according to the year, 12–15 days. Now an impulsion press is employed, while the hydraulic press still serves for the white, which is cool-fermented and undergoes no malolactic. ℬ Clean wine (diatomaceous earth-filtered) is aged first in oak casks, then in reused *pièces,* for 12 to 18 months.

Domaine de La Serrière, Michel Bernard, Sommelongue, Orange

The red Châteauneuf has a very particular floral bouquet, perhaps from some very old Grenache vines in the qrt Bois Lauzon of Orange. It seems to be a wine that keeps well; 1979 tasted in 1985, for example, had retained almost the full force and freshness of a youthful wine. Freshness, spice, and stones characterize 1982 available in the U.S. The 1983 white (malolactic fermentation avoided) was fuller and finer to my taste than the 1984.

5 ha of Châteauneuf-du-Pape (N). 80% GR, 15% SY, plus MV, CT, BR. Bernard is also the owner of 19 ha of CDR in Orange and Sérignan (Vaucluse), 60% GR, 15% CS, 10% CT, 8% MV, 5% old-vine CR, and 2% PL. He has an additional 15 ha of CDT on the plateau of Donzère (Drôme), 10 ha of which is GR, 2.5 ha CS, and 2.5 ha SY. ℬ OT1, 14 days, Vaslin press. ℬ 1 to 2 years in oak casks. The wine is commercialized by Domaines Michel Bernard (see under "CDR in the Environs of Châteauneuf-du-Pape").

Domaine du Vieux Lazaret, GFA du Domaine Raymonde Quiot, proprietor; SA du Domaine du Vieux Lazaret, producer

This estate entered the market under its own name in 1979, having been until then one of the highest quality suppliers of Châteauneuf to *négociants,* including Jaboulet's "Les Cedres," for many years. Usually attractive at the outset, the red wines are tightly and finely rather than heavily structured, with butter, stones, cedar, and truffles showing what is in a Châteauneuf that has never seen wood. To my taste 1980, 1981, and 1983 Vieux Lazaret make the best case for this not very typical practice. White has been made since 1982. Pale straw and lively, it hints at flavors of pear, honey, and nuts.

75 ha, one group of parcels in qrt St.-Jean and Pied Redun (E), the rest S and NW. About 1/4 of the vines are more than 50 years old. Red *cépages,* eastern portion: 80% GR, 10–12% SY, around 5% MV. Remainder: 70% GR, 10% CS, 10% SY, 10% diverse. 5 ha of white: BR, CT, GR, with RS and PL. 12 ha of CDV at Caromb (Vaucluse), 90% GR, plus CR (was to plant SY 1985). ❧ ST, optional destemming, average *cuvaison* 3 weeks. About half the SY is vinified separately; Vaslin press. ❧ At present no capacity for wood age, but intent is for only a few months in wood even so, perhaps according to *cépages.*

H Domaine du Vieux Télégraphe, GAEC H. Brunier et Fils, Bédarrides

For a decade or more Henri Brunier has been on a quest to eliminate oxidation from Vieux Télégraphe, and that has obliged him to make the tannins finer. After 1978 he eliminated fermentation in cask, as well as pumping of the grapes from reception to fermenter. In 1982 he switched to a pneumatic press. Throughout he was gradually diminishing the time the wine spent aging in wood. Now his wine is not as just plain huge as it was, but the deep, concentrated, well-defined fruit it always had is more to the fore. It becomes ever clearer that Vieux Télégraphe is one of the great masterpieces of the aesthetic tension definitive of Châteauneuf-du-Pape—that between alcoholic warmth and richness and an ensemble of alcohol-volatilized fragrances that are fresh and cool, leafy, resinous, even mentholated. To this add flowers, essential oils, truffles, and hints of stones and seawater from the *terroir.* As of 1986, 1981 may be the best example of this more classic style. 1978 and 1972 (better balanced) are going strong in the older robust style. 1979 promises to live forever. 1980 had too much exaggerated flavor of cassis for me. Because of the year, 1982 is for early drinking. Almost thickly tannic 1983 is something of an unintended throwback to Brunier's old style whose success has surprised him. He prefers 1984, with its structure based on acidity. Superbly floral white is made in limited quantities.

Single estate with 35 ha in production in qrt of La Crau (E). Part on the plateau not far from that part of Nalys, some with fewer cobbles and more clay on the slope toward Bédarrides. Estate gets its name from the tower depicted on the label that was once a relay station in a turn-of-the-19th-century optical telegraph system. 75% GR, 8% CS, 10% SY, 5% MV; 2% GR blanc, CT, BR, and RS. Some 70-80-year-old vines. ❧ Beginning in 1979, new installation allows the bunches to arrive by gondola above each stainless steel vat and be passed through the crusher or not as desired. OT1, 30% whole berries (none are destemmed), 10 to 15 days. "Because the equipment is modern," says

M. Brunier, "we can return to the practices of 100 years ago." Was Vaslin; pneumatic press first used 1982. ≈ Formerly 18 to 24 months in oak casks, now 12.

Robust Style

Domaine Lucien Barrot (formerly Cuvée du Tastevin),
GAEC Lucien Barrot et Fils

M. Barrot prefers to bottle his wines, intensely and deeply fruity with a characteristic florality at the start, when they have achieved a proper "goût du vieux" (old taste) from long aging to maturity in barrel. For *amateurs* of this style I can say that the wines often have what it takes to stand up to this treatment, years like 1979 and 1981, for example, exhibiting excellent balance and an elaborate bouquet.

Exploits 20 ha of Châteauneuf-du-Pape, but bottles only the production of his own 14 ha of property, in qrts Terres Blanches, Coteau de l'Ange, Brusquières (N); Pignan, Font du Pape, Montpertuis, Boucou (E); Marines (S). 70 ares CS, 30 ares SY (plus 70 ares newly planted), a little MV and CT rose, and the rest GR. 80% of the vines are more than 60 years old. ≈ OT1, 21 days, Vaslin press. ≈ Minimum 2 to 3 years in oak casks, that is to say, the wine rests in wood until bottled. Bottling is done by the growers' union "Prestige et Tradition."

Domaine du Bois Dauphin, J. Marchand

Raspberry, leafy, spicy, peppery wine gains vanilla, licorice, even tobacco from small barrel aging (and some dried-outness too).

25 ha of Châteauneuf-du-Pape, dispersed, N and S. 80% GR, plus SY, CS, a little MV, CT, BR, RS. 5 ha of Lirac at St.-Laurent-des-Arbres; 5 ha of CDR "**Les Vallonières**" at Sabran (Gard) co-owned with Domaine de la Solitude. ≈ ST, 15 days. 1st press from hydraulic press is incorporated. ≈ 6 months to 2 years in oak casks. A special mark, "Bénitié," is used for a non-vintage *assemblage* that has been aged in *pièces*.

Bosquet des Papes, Maurice Boiron

A wine that perhaps stresses sturdiness more than nuance with its definitely wooded impression. Nevertheless, the tannins seem more lively than dry. The fruit in years like 1981 and 1983 tends toward warmth and ripeness, verging on late harvest, with hints of the barnyard and occasionally something baked, caramel or mocha, as well as minerals. 1982 had a commanding 14.6% alcohol, while 1984 is exceptional for the freshness of its aromas.

22 dispersed ha are conducted, with the principal parcels in qrts Mont-Redon, Brusquières, Cabrières, and Gardiole (N). 80% GR, 7% SY, 5% MV, 3% CS, 2% CT. ≈ Some OT1, some OT2, 20 days; Vaslin Press. White is made in the progressive style with settling, fining of the must, cool fermentation, and blocked malolactic. ≈ The wine spends 18 to 24 months in oak casks. Bottling is conducted at the proprietors' union, "Prestige et Tradition," of which M. Boiron is a past president.

Domaine du Caillou, Claude Pouizin, Courthézon

See Clos du Caillou in "CDR in the Environs of Châteauneuf-du-Pape."

H Domaine Chante-Perdrix, GAEC Chante-Perdrix, Nicolet Frères

Warm, chewy, enormous wine, with a grandiose, distinctive, almost decadent "late harvest" bouquet. The alcohol level is high enough to make it tiring to drink in summer. Lighter years like 1973 and 1980 are magnificently balanced.

18-ha single estate, qrt Condorcet (S). Susceptibility to drought caused by gravel subsoil occasionally obliges Nicolets to irrigate, permitted in extraordinarily dry years no more than twice before Aug. 15 in one growing season. 80% GR, 10% SY, and 10% MD make up the red *cépages*. 1 ha of CT, BR, PL, GR blanc. ❧ ST, 8 to 15 days, hydraulic press. First press incorporated. ❧ 3 years wood age in oak casks. The wine is bottled at the proprietors' union "Reflets du Châteauneuf-du-Pape."

H Domaine Font de Michelle, Les Fils d'Etienne Gonnet, Bédarrides

The Young Gonnets' first bottling was of the 1974. Don't be fooled by the more discrete handling of wood in recent years —the *wine* is hefty, frankly tannic, packed with cassis to blackberry fruit, and develops a truffle nose with age. Standouts include a magisterial 1978, in 1985 more and more resembling the greatness of a 1967, a truffle-cedar-blackberry 1980, and one of the very best balanced 1983s. In fact 1984 may be more tannic. The white is a pale green-gold, extremely fresh with a touch of *pétillance*. Usually bottled before malolactic, it may just be the most substantial and full-flavored of the youthful-drinking-style whites.

Now almost consolidated, 32 ha in production on the Bédarrides slopes and a little on the plateau of La Crau in front of Vieux Télégraphe (E). The father started this estate with 200 parcels. Red *cépages:* 70% GR, 10% CS, 10% SY, 10% MV. White: 50% GR, 25% BR, 25% CT. ❧ OT2, about 60% of each stainless steel vat crushed, almost none of the SY, 14 days. Tried CM for SY in 1984. *Cépages* are fermented apart. When completed, new installation will resemble Vieux Télégraphe's and so allow OT1. ❧ 24 to 36 months aging, of which from 6 to 12 months are in oak casks.

Domaine de Marcoux, GAEC Elie et Philippe Armenier

Blackberry fruit in a solid, spicy wine that develops tar and truffles. Older vintages in excellent condition, such as 1978 and a 1967 without browning tasted in 1985. The cool-fermented white, first made in 1982, by the 1984 had become genuinely distinguished, at once full and lively.

23 ha of Châteauneuf-du-Pape, with principal parcels in qrts Beaurenard (NW); La Crau (E); Esqueirons, Galimardes, and Serres (S). 70% GR, plus SY, CS, MV, CT, BR, GR blanc. Some 90-year-old vines. 2 ha CDR at Courthézon and Orange. ❧ A newly purchased *cave de vinification* in the countryside will require some changes to convert from ST to OT2. Vintages made in the old village *cave* and a portion of the recent wine OT1, 15 days. (In the village one can still see the traditional Châteauneuf vat carved into the bedrock.) Hydraulic press. ❧ Red aged in oak casks according to the character of the year (e.g., very little for 1982). **"L'Echaufette"** is a second label for the Châteauneuf.

Domaine de Montpertuis, Paul Jeune

There is a tendency to cherries in this wine for *amateurs* of the big, wooded, spicy style. Sometimes slightly hard or dry, it has real finesse and balance in the less

wooded 1977 and 1981. A fresh, leafy, floral white, at once mineral and honeyed in the finish, was made in 1984.

42 parcels make up the 25 ha of Châteauneuf-du-Pape, the principal ones in qrts Cabrières (N), Montpertuis and La Crau (E), and La Croze (S). 70% GR, 7–8% CT, plus CS, MV, SY, BR, and field-blended GR blanc. More than half the vines average 50 to 70 years old. ❧ OT2, 15 days (last vats to be filled) to 21 days (early vats to be filled); Vaslin press. ❧ Wine is aged 1 to 2 years in oak casks and *pièces*.

Château La Nerthe (formerly Château La Nerte), SCA Château La Nerthe (formerly Domaine de la Nerte)

For commentary, see Chapter 1.

Single estate with 58 ha in vine qrt La Nerthe (E). Formerly 85–90% GR, 5% for the ensemble of MV, CS, CN, 5% SY, 3% CT. ❧ ST, 12 days, Vaslin press. ❧ 3 years in oak casks.

Cave Perges, Lucette and Frédéric Nicolet

The son of one of the owners of Chante-Perdrix makes a heavily Grenache wine from vines that average 50 years old. It shows round and plum fruit, not thick, with lots of vanilla and only occasionally a hint of licorice. Where 1981 was a little dry, 1982 was actually balanced at 15% alcohol, 1983 a *vin de garde*.

4 ha, dispersed mostly S. GR and CS. ❧ OT2, crushing by force of pump only, 15 days. 1st juice from Vaslin press incorporated. ❧ 3 years in oak casks and *pièces*. Wine is bottled at the growers' union "Reflets du Châteauneuf-du-Pape."

H **Domaine des Relagnes,** Henri Boiron

A wine that used to be almost undrinkably thick achieved a balance in 1979 it has never lost since, even in the extra-alcoholic 1982. Plum, black and even sour cherry fruit yields butter, cedar, and eventual noble tar and truffles to the nose. Long and liquid, the 1983 avoided the dryness that mars some others, but I rank 1981 higher for concentration and nuance, to which that special 1979 adds even more opulence and cleanness.

14 ha dispersed estate has its biggest parcels in qrts Charbonnières and La Crau (E), Esqueirons (NW). 85% GR, plus more MV than SY, a few CS, and some field-blended white *cépages*. Vines average 55 years old, some planted 1908. ❧ OT2 (was ST until 1978), about 15 days; Vaslin press. ❧ The wine ages about 18 months in oak casks. "Cuvée Vigneronne" is another label for this wine.

H **Clos Saint-Jean,** Mme. Guy Maurel et Fils

The special quality of discretion and painstaking care about the accomplishments of the Maurels is symbolized, at least through 1985, by the absence of even a modest sign on the gate to say where the *caves* of this important estate were located. Once there, one will find a source of wines which, no matter how deeply and darkly red fruited, powerful and tannic, have been held in cask and bottle to be sold only when they have achieved perfect balance by taste. This more than bigness or age for its own sake is the great prize in wines that smell of roses and a slightly sour lavender and vanilla wood with, eventually, noble Côte-de-Nuits style tar, leather, and

truffles; and that play off their power and warmth against cool cedar and the resins of herbs in the stony *garrigues* soil. 1980 seems a marvel of florality and balance, the late M. Maurel's 1978 spicier, 1974 still full of strength. In the series tasted, only the 1976 may have had aldehyde hints in 1985 of being past its peak.

32 dispersed ha are conducted. The majority is along the route de Bédarrides (E) between Terre Ferme and Fines Roches. Also E is some in the Boix de la Nerthe, and there is some in qrt Pied de Baud (N). 70% GR, 15% SY, plus CS, MV, CT, and diverse field-blended *cépages*. 60% of the vines are more than 30 years old. &. OT2, 20 to 25 days, Vaslin press. &. Wine is aged 2 to 4 years in oak casks according to the character of the year, then longer if necessary in the bottle (1974 was not sold until 1983). The Maurel sons are augmenting the proportion of St.-Jean sold in bottle, which had become of "secondary importance" to their father.

Pierre Usseglio

Sometimes a ripe, peachy character, with the suppleness to balance the tannic finish (1979), sometimes a more baked, prune impression makes the tannin seem woodier (1980). Because the time in wood is regulated, as is the old custom, by the demand for bottled wine, a 1978 tasted from the bottle in 1982 had spent 3 1/2 years in cask.

18 ha of Châteauneuf-du-Pape dispersed in all the zones are exploited. Of these, 5 ha are M. Usseglio's own property. Average age of vines in the share-cropped portion exceeds 50 years. 80% GR, 20% field-blended MV, CN, CS, and SY for the red *cépages;* CT, BR, and young vines of RS and GR blanc are the whites. &. OT1, 14 to 21 days, hydraulic press. &. Wine spends a minimum of 2 years in oak casks.

Cuvée du Vatican, Diffonty et Fils

These are distinctly high alcohol wines, by tradition and choice of late harvest date. Recent changes in vinification, temperature control, press and wood have added other dimensions to their substance. Also M. Félicien Diffonty, the mayor of Châteauneuf-du-Pape, says he takes a more direct hand in care of the wine than formerly. Whatever the reasons, there is more aroma, depth and complexity of fruit than formerly, with the result that the 1982, with a startling 15.7% alcohol, is better balanced to my taste than either a spicier but also drier 1983 (15%), or a thinner, greener 1981 (13.7%). Earlier I had preferred lighter years like 1973 and 1975.

17 dispersed ha of Châteauneuf, in qrts Roumiguières, La Crau, Mont de Vies (E); Bois Lauzon, Tresquoa (N); Barbe d'Asne (S). 75% GR, 10% SY, plus CS, CN, MV, and 3–5% CT blanche and rose. &. OT2 since 1979, 3 to 4 weeks cuvaison, impulsion press since 1979. &. Time spent in oak casks is now "less" than the former 3 years, and the stock of casks has been refreshed.

Jean Versino

Big, full-bodied, sometimes chewy wine with sour butter, vanilla, licorice nose. More finesse than usual in a 1980 that retained a hint of dissolved CO_2. Grapes from qrt Pied de Baud (N) were included for the first time in Versino's 1982, and seemed to contribute (in 1983) added pepperiness.

4.4 ha, dispersed. 70% GR, plus MV, SY, CN and diverse field-blended *cépages*. &. M. Versino may be the last to prefer harvesting in the traditional wooden "cornus" (horn-shaped buckets) to plastic cases, but to avoid oxidation he no longer tamps the bunches down as was the old custom. OT1, 8 to 12 days, hydraulic press. &. 2½ to 3 years in oak casks (*foudres* and *demi-muids*). The wine is fined but not filtered before bottling.

Domaine de la Vieille Julienne, Arnaud-Daumen, Orange

Big, somewhat hard wine that from the start has a "rancid," slightly barnyard nose like others in the northern tier, on top of black raspberry. Wood at first adds vanilla, then the long stay in cask to my taste dries out the fruit, deliberately, of course, given the conception of "old" wine as wine that has been aged to full maturity before bottling.

Exploits 8 ha of Châteauneuf-du-Pape, dispersed, but all in the qrt Cabrières (N). 70% GR, 10% SY, 10% MV, plus CS, CN, CT. CDR in Orange. &. OT2, 10 to 15 days, hydraulic press. &. 3 to 4 years, sometimes longer, in oak casks (in 1983, some 1972 was still in barrel).

The cooperative of this zone is:

Les Vignerons du Cellier des Princes, Courthézon

Founded 1925. 42.38% AOC, which is produced in the facility named "Le Cellier des Princes," separate from the original *cave* now used for VDT. Châteauneuf-du-Pape, mostly from Courthézon, Bédarrides, and Orange, represents a little less than 10% of that AOC's production, enough to make the Cellier the largest single supplier. CDR communes add Jonquières and Sarrians.

CDR red, rosé, white; Châteauneuf-du-Pape.

Châteauneuf-du-Pape *Négociants:*

Cave Bérard Père et Fils, Négociant, Bédarrides

When Bérard Père was alive, Cave Berard were vinifiers, especially of Châteauneuf-du-Pape from Bérard's properties, as well as buyers and blenders of finished wines from other producers. Châteauneuf-du-Pape under the Bérard label could contain but was not limited to Bérard's proprietary wines. Now the property and production of its wines, under the name Domaine Terre Ferme, have been separated from the *négociant* business. The latter, in the hands of a society called Cave Bérard, no longer vinifies. The Cave Bérard Rhône Valley wines are red Châteauneuf-du-Pape "Carte d'Or" and "Cuvée Prestige," Gigondas, Crozes-Hermitage, CDR-Villages and CDR "Rascassas;" white Châteauneuf-du-Pape, CDR-Villages; and rosés from Tavel and Lirac.

Du Peloux & Cie., Négociants-éleveurs, Courthézon

A small, serious *négociant* firm founded after World War II by M. Paul Dupeloux and carried on by his family. Its line features wines of the Rhône valley and Provence, including six *crus*, CDR-Villages, CDR-Vacqueyras, and the following wines with the labels of particular domaines:

Châteauneuf-du-Pape

APPELLATION CHATEAUNEUF-DU-PAPE CONTRÔLÉE

DOMAINE DE BEAURENARD

MISE AU DOMAINE

Paul COULON

PROPRIÉTAIRE-RÉCOLTANT, 84230 CHATEAUNEUF-DU-PAPE (FRANCE)

PRODUCE OF FRANCE

73 cl

LES CLES D'OR

Châteauneuf-du-Pape

APPELLATION CHATEAUNEUF-DU-PAPE CONTROLÉE

S. C. E. A.

Domaine Jean Deydier et Fils

PROPRIETAIRES RECOLTANTS A CHATEAUNEUF-DU-PAPE (Vse) FRANCE

MIS EN BOUTEILLE AU DOMAINE

75 cl

Château de Beaucastel

APPELLATION CHATEAUNEUF-DU-PAPE CONTROLÉE

Sté FERMIÈRE DES VIGNOBLES PIERRE PERRIN

AU CHÂTEAU DE BEAUCASTEL COURTHEZON (Vse)   73 cl

ESTATE BOTTLED   MISE AU CHATEAU

CHATEAUNEUF-DU-PAPE

Tête de Cru

1974

CHATEAU-FORTIA

PROPRIÉTÉ DU BARON LE ROY DE BOISEAUMARIÉ

S. A. R. L.

CHATEAU FORTIA - 84 CHATEAUNEUF-DU-PAPE   73 cl

GRANDS VINS 1977   DE FRANCE 1977

Châteauneuf-du-Pape

"Domaine du Haut des Terres Blanches"

APPELLATION CHATEAUNEUF-DU-PAPE CONTRÔLÉE

MISE EN BOUTEILLES AU DOMAINE

GAEC DOMAINE DU HAUT DES TERRES BLANCHES

DIFFONTY RÉMY & Fils, Propriétaires-Récoltants à Châteauneuf-du-Pape - 84230 - France   75 cl

---

Domaine du Grand Tinel

CHATEAUNEUF DU PAPE

APPELLATION CHATEAUNEUF-DU-PAPE CONTROLEE

Mis en bouteille au domaine

E. JEUNE PROPRIETAIRE - RECOLTANT CHATEAUNEUF-DU-PAPE (Vse) FRANCE   75 cl

---

MISE EN BOUTEILLES AU DOMAINE

Châteauneuf-du-Pape

APPELLATION CHATEAUNEUF-DU-PAPE CONTROLÉE

DOMAINE DE MONT-REDON

PROPRIÉTAIRE RÉCOLTANT

S.A. D'EXPLOIT. DU DOMAINE DE MONT-REDON A CHATEAUNEUF-DU-PAPE (VAUCLUSE) FRANCE

Alcool 13°7   PRODUCT OF FRANCE   73 cl

CLOS DES PAPES

CHATEAUNEUF-DU-PAPE

APPELLATION CHATEAUNEUF-DU-PAPE CONTRÔLÉE

Propriété PAUL AVRIL à
CHATEAUNEUF DU PAPE -Vse   Les AVRIL premiers Consuls et Trésoriers
de Châteauneuf du Pape de 1756 à 1790

MIS EN BOUTEILLE A LA PROPRIÉTÉ   75cl

Châteauneuf-du-Pape:

Domaine de la Crau, Jean Marquis, Courthézon
  9 ha qrt La Crau (E). GR, CS. ST, 15 to 21 days.

Domaine du Cristia, Alain Grangeon, Courthézon
  8 ha, qrt Cristia (E). GR, SY, CS, MV, MD. OT, 8 to 15 days.

Gigondas:

Domaine du Pesquier, Raymonde Boutière, Gigondas
  For details, see Gigondas.

Lirac:

Château de Clary, Famille Mayer, Roquemaure
  For details, see Lirac.

CDR:

Domaine Emile Charavin, Rasteau

Domaine de la Damase, Serge Latour, Violès
  For details, see "CDR of the Lower Ouvèze and Plan de Dieu."

Domaine de l'Escaravaille, Ferran, Roaix
  Vineyard at Rasteau.

Les Grandes Serres

This *négociant* firm commercializes a line of wines from all over France, including Châteauneuf-du-Pape, Gigondas, Tavel, Lirac, Beaumes-de-Venise, CDR-Cairanne, CDR-Rasteau, and CDR and CDV from the Rhône valley. Among these are the following wines from particular domaines:

Châteauneuf-du-Pape:

Domaine St.-Préfert
  For details, see Châteauneuf-du-Pape.

Lirac:

Domaine Magdebor, André Poussot, Lirac

Tavel and CDR:

Domaine de Montlauzy, Henri de Lanzac (de Montlauzy)
  For details see Tavel, Henri de Lanzac.

CDR:

Château d'Orsan, Joseph Brunel, Orsan
  For details, see Chusclan.

Louis Mousset, Négociant-éleveur

In addition to distributing the wines of the "Domaines Mousset" (see Château des Fines Roches), the Louis Mousset firm commercializes a number of other proprietors' wines, often estate bottled. Among these are:

Châteauneuf-du-Pape:

"Cuvée du Majoral," SCEA Domaine Juliette Avril

Domaine de Marcoux, GAEC Elie et Philippe Armenier
For details, see Domaine de Marcoux.

"La Pontificale," GIE La Pontificale
Wine is assembled from the production of several private proprietors.

"Cuvée Vigneronne," Henri Boiron
For details see **Domaine des Relagnes**

Gigondas:

Domaine de Saint-Cosme, Henri Barruol
For details, see Gigondas.

CDR:

Domaine de la Beaume, Max Aubert, Ste.-Cécile-les-Vignes
For details see Cairanne, Domaine de la Présidente.

Domaine de la Patrasse, SCEA du Domaine de la Patrasse, Orange
An estate just north of the border with AOC Châteauneuf-du-Pape. GR, CS, a very little SY.

Père Anselme, Négociant-éleveur

This *négociant* house, whose corporate name is Brotte et Armenier, was founded in 1931 by Charles Brotte, father of the present head, M. Jean-Pierre Brotte. The firm takes its name from an ancestor of the founder, known as "Père" in the village of Châteauneuf for his venerable age and wisdom. It markets a line of regional AOC wines from the Rhône valley and Provence, as well as 9 of the *crus* of the CDR, CDR-Villages, CDR-St.-Gervais, CDR-Séguret, CDR-Vacqueyras, and CDR-Valréas. The most particular wines come from three domaine labeled bottles:

Châteauneuf-du-Pape:

Domaine François Laget
Domaine de la Petite Bastide, Rémy Diffonty,
For details see **Domaine du Haut des Terres Blanches.**

CDR:

Domaine de la Tour Paradis, Chabot, Aiguèze (Gard)

An additional Châteauneuf-du-Pape, "Les Eglantiers," is always a wine selected from a different small proprietor each year.

Caves Saint-Pierre, Négociant-éleveur

Caves Saint-Pierre, founded in 1898 by Henri Bouachon, commercializes four main lines of wine. "Saint-Pierre" is the mark of their basic CDR in red, rosé, and white. A second line features "Côtes" and "Coteaux" wines from around the south of France. "Grandes Appellations" are 7 of the crus of the CDR, plus CDR-Villages, CDR-Cairanne, and

CDR-Vacqueyras. Most particular of all is the line of "Domaines and Châteaux" labeled wines that include one proprietary wine of the Bouachon family. These are:

Châteauneuf-du-Pape:

Roger Bouachon

Domaine des Cigalons, Emile Raymonde, Courthézon
    E. 75% GR, 25% SY and MV.

Domaine Condorcet, Bouche-Audibert
    15 ha qrt Condorcet (S). 7 ha GR, 5 ha SY, 2.5 ha PL, .5 ha CS. This domaine is cited as the first in the Vaucluse to have planted SY (1860).

Domaine des Pontifes, Allemand
    One of this domaine's parcels is within the walls of the former papal vineyard surrounding the château.

Château Saint-André, André Rey, Gigondas
    For details see **Château de la Grande Gardiole.**

Gigondas:

Domaine St.-François-Xavier, André Gras, Gigondas
    For details, see Gigondas.

Tavel:

Domaine J.P. Lafont [sic] **"Montolivet,"** J.P. Lafont [sic], Tavel
    For details see Tavel, Domaine J.P. Lafond "Roc Epine."

Domaine Magdebor, André Poussot, Tavel

CDR-Villages:

Domaine Courtois, Mme Christiane Courtois, Vinsobres
    30 ha, 78% GR, 12.5% SY, 7% CR, 2.5% CT. CL.

CDR:

Château d'Aigueville, GAEC du Château d'Aigueville, Uchaux
    For details see "CDR of the Massif d'Uchaux."

Château de Bastet, C. Aubert, Sabran (Gard)

Domaine des Boumianes, Lucien Meger, Domazan (Gard)
    25 ha.

Domaine du Grand Prébois, Louis Biscarrat, Orange (Vaucluse)
    25 ha single estate.

Domaine Saint-Antoine, Isnard, Sablet

Château Saint-Pierre, Requin, Montfavet (Vaucluse)

CDT:

Domaine la Tour St.-Rémy, "Le Terroir St.-Rémy," proprietor at Baume-de-Transit
    For details, see CDT.

CDV:

Domaine Troussel, GAEC du Domaine Troussel, Carpentras
    For details, see CDV.

─────── CDR SOUTH OF CHÂTEAUNEUF-DU-PAPE ───────

The Côtes du Rhône south of Châteauneuf-du-Pape are found on similar plateaus to that of Châteauneuf-du-Pape itself. Producers are arranged by movement S to N. Addresses of producers are 84 (Vaucluse).

Chartreuse de Bonpas, Jean-Olphe Galliard, Caumont-sur-Durance

CDR red and white. **This domaine, housed in a former Carthusian monastery, is the farthest south in the CDR on the left bank of the Rhône. M. Jérôme Casalis, son-in-law of the late M. Galliard, is now in charge. The wine's type will become clearer as the vines mature, but it is already being made in an attractive, drinkable style. Of wines available to taste in 1985, by far the most interesting was the red CDR 1984: intensely fruity and smelling of resins, essential herb oils, and pepper. Also a cut above the ordinary was a nutty, grassy, lemon-buttery pure Clairette CDR blanc.**

20 ha in vine on the southern end of same plateau and its flanks as Châteauneuf-de-Gadagne. Red *cépages:* 60% GR, 20% CS, 10% CR, 10% MV. Average age of vines 15 years. White CT is planted on SW-facing slope of an old quarry. ❧ OT2, 4 to 6 days in stainless steel. *Cépages* are vinified separately; Vaslin press. White is settled, must fined, no malolactic. ❧ Wine rests 6 to 7 months in stainless steel vats before bottling within the year.

H **Domaine de la Chapelle,** Marcel and Claude Boussier, Châteauneuf-de-Gadagne

CDR red and rosé. **The estate takes its name from the chapel adjoining the *chai* built, as was the *cave,* in the 18th century when the property belonged to the Jesuits. The special wine here is a very low productivity, old-vine "réserve" from a cobblestone-covered parcel that represents about one-third of the property. Usually a brilliant dark ruby, definitely robust, it remains balanced even though normally in excess of 14% alcohol, because supported by concentrated fruit and a nuanced bouquet that becomes increasingly burgundian with age. A 1970 tasted at table in 1985 was still going strong.**

12–14 ha in production on a plateau that resembles the situation and soil of the *other* Châteauneuf (du-Pape) except that it is crossed by rows of trees planted as wind breaks. 40% GR (some more than 90 years old), 40% CS, SY, MV, UN, and CT. ❧ CL, 4 to 6 days, Vaslin press, most not incorporated. ❧ After a year in vat, the wine spends a minimum of 1 year in cask (2 to 3 years for the "réserve").

Domaine Deforge, J. Deforge, Châteauneuf-de-Gadagne

CDR red. **Madame Deforge, widow of the late jockey, made her first wine here in 1982, and very respectable it is. Showing in 1985 lots of clean cedary Grenache, it avoids the wood taste and dryness that for my taste mar the 1983. Best wine tasted on that occasion was a fine, ripe, resinous 1979.**

30-ha single estate on the plateau. 60% GR, 25% CS, 2 ha SY, 1 ha MD, plus MV, CT rose and blanche, GR blanc. 12 ha are old vines, rest have been planted since Deforge bought the property in 1966. ❧ 1/3 of the production was machine harvested for the first time in 1985. CL, 6 days, continuous press. ❧ Wine is given 4 months minimum in oak casks.

Domaine Frédéri Mitan, Frédéri Mitan, Vedène

CDR red and rosé. **I have not tasted enough to comment on these wines, but must mention an estate whose owner is mayor of Vedène, a provençal musician, and son of a provençal poet.**

Conducts 7 ha in vine all in Vedène, on the northern end of the same plateau as Châteauneuf-de-Gadagne. 60% GR, plus CS, MV, SY (in that order). ❧ Vinification depending on the year, sometimes CL, 5 days *(primeur)* to 8 days, sometimes OT. Vaslin press; rosé "par saignée." ❧ Red is aged 1 year in oak casks.

Domaine du Grand Plantier, Daussant Père et Fils, Vedène

CDR red and rosé. **M. Daussant describes rosé as "his specialty," and it is the wine of note here: fairly dark, fragrant, clean, fresh, savory of red fruits and fresh apples. The reds seem less satisfactory, slightly too reduced to start, slightly burny in the finish—except for a nicely fluid, peaches and cedar 1979.**

8 ha of CDR all at Vedène. 50% GR, 20–25% CS, 15% MV, 10% SY, plus BR. Some 86-year-old vines. ❧ ST, 4 days, hydraulic press. ❧ No wood.

The following are cooperatives of this zone:

Cave Coopérative Vinicole, Morières-les-Avignon
Founded 1929. 52.29% AOC. CDR from Morières (2/3), Jonquerettes, St.-Saturnin-les-Avignon, Vedène.
CDR red and rosé; *CDR blanc de blancs (GR, CT, RS).

Cave des Vignerons du Duché de Gadagne, Châteauneuf-de-Gadagne
Founded 1929. 33.13% AOC. CDR from Châteauneuf-de-Gadagne (majority), Caumont-sur-Durance, Jonquerettes, St.-Saturnin-les-Avignon, Vedène.

— CDR IN THE ENVIRONS OF CHÂTEAUNEUF-DU-PAPE —

The environs of Châteauneuf-du-Pape are defined as the same communes within which AOC Châteauneuf-du-Pape has been delimited. Producers continue to be arranged in rough S to N order of the communes. Addresses of producers are 84 (Vaucluse).

Domaine de Tout Vent, Jacques Mousset, Sorgues
See Châteauneuf-du-Pape, Château des Fines Roches.

Château du Prieuré, Guy Mousset, Sorgues
See Châteauneuf-du-Pape, Château des Fines Roches.

H **Château du Bois de la Garde,** Catherine Barrot-Mousset, Sorgues
See Châteauneuf-du-Pape, Château des Fines Roches.

Domaine du Grand-Vaucroze, Guy Mousset, Sorgues
See Châteauneuf-du-Pape, Château des Fines Roches.

Clos du Caillou, Claude Pouizin, Courthézon

CDR red, white, rosé; Châteauneuf-du-Pape. **Among wines available to taste in 1985, I preferred the red CDR "Bouquet des Garrigues" 1982, for its deeper fruit, tighter construction, and better balance with the wood, over both 1982 Châteauneuf-du-Pape and 1983 CDR Clos du Caillou itself. The Châteauneuf seemed cleaner and finer when tasted in the bottling available from the Cellier de l'Enclave des Papes (see Valréas).**

The only reason the Clos du Caillou vineyard, on a classic cobblestone-covered plateau surrounded by AOC Châteauneuf-du-Pape, is not one, is that a former owner would not allow the visit of the court-appointed experts who delimited the appellation. Its 22 ha are today planted 1 ha SY, .5 ha RS, .8 ha GR blanc, and the rest GR. **"Bouquet des Garrigues"** comes from 25 ha near "Cru du Coudoulet," 2 ha SY, 2.2 ha CT, 1.5 ha CS, 1 ha CR, the rest GR. Châteauneuf-du-Pape "mise en bouteilles au **Domaine du Caillou"** is 7.42 ha dispersed in the qrts Cassanets, Guigasse and Bédines (E), .2 ha SY, .2 ha CS, .4 ha MV, .15 ha MD, the rest GR. ❧ ST, 8 to 10 days (Clos), 12 to 14 days (Bouquet and Châteauneuf). Hydraulic press; rosé "par saignée." ❧ 1 to 3 years in oak casks in a completely underground, vaulted cellar.

H **Cru du Coudoulet,** Société Fermière Pierre Perrin, Courthézon

See Châteauneuf-du-Pape, Château de Beaucastel.

Domaine de l'Enclos, Charles Bonvin, Courthézon

CDR red. **Wines tasted at the estate from vat and M. Bonvin's own bottling (unfined and unfiltered) are moderately tannic and full of character, somewhat resembling that of neighboring Châteauneuf-du-Pape in their butter, spice, and, in the 1980, floral finish. The 1982 sold under this label in the U.S., while of good quality, seems less intense, perhaps from the year.**

15-ha walled, single estate, cobble-covered, once belonged to the château that is now the city hall of Courthézon. 70% GR, plus CT, MV, SY, CS. All vines are more than 50 years old. ❧ OT2, 3 week *cuvaison*; hydraulic press. ❧ After *assemblage* the wine is sent to Burgundy for conditioning, bottling, and commercialization by the *négociant* firm Calvet.

Domaines Michel Bernard, Orange

The Domaines Michel Bernard are actually a sort of cooperative (SICA) of private growers, formed in 1980 for the purpose of bottling, and in some cases commercializing, wines that are produced and aged by the individual members. These numbered 24 by 1984. When commercialized by the SICA, the wines are given the names of their private domaines of origin, but owners' names are replaced by the collective formula Domaines Michel Bernard. Thus these wines are legitimately said to be "mise en bouteille au domaine," but they are not all from properties owned by M. Bernard. Some of the Domaines in the group with the names of their owners follow. Regrettably, a complete list was not given by M. Bernard.

Châteauneuf-du-Pape and CDR:

Domaine de la Serrière, Michel Bernard, Orange

For details, see Châteauneuf-du-Pape.

Châteauneuf-du-Pape:

Domaine de la Guérine, Aimé Arnaud, Orange

    Vineyard in the qrt Cabrières (N). Large majority old-vine GR. ST, long *cuvaison.* Aged in oak casks.

Domaine des Trois Plantiers, Mme. Jean Avril, Châteauneuf-du-Pape

    Approximately 30 ha of which 20 are N. 75% GR, plus CS, SY, MV, CT, BR. Was CL assembled with a little CM. Now OT2 3 years in cask.

Domaine de la Vialle, Mme. Bernard, Orange

    Vineyard near Château de Beaucastel (N). Almost 100% GR. ST, 2 years wood.

Tavel:

Domaine des Franquizons, André Poussot, Tavel

Les Patriciens, Orange

    See Châteauneuf-du-Pape, Château Maucoil

The cooperative of this zone is:

Les Vignerons du Cellier des Princes, Courthézon

    See Châteauneuf-du-Pape.

Négociant at Orange:

La Vieille Ferme, Négociant, Orange

A 1985 on-the-scene vertical tasting of every year of Vieille Ferme CDV since 1978 revealed a wine consistently solid while fluid in structure, expressive of each vintage's character, and at or near the top of all Ventoux known to this writer. On the same occasion, the Vieille Ferme CDR 1983 exhibited an ensemble of fruit flavors almost as black as its color—blackberry, black currant, black cherry—under a nose of broom flower, lavender, vanilla, and a hint of stony soil. A somewhat drier 1982 had even stronger vanilla and floral components.

    La Vieille Ferme is not the name of a property, but that of a highly specialized *négociant* business created by M. Jean-Pierre Perrin, of the family that owns Château de Beaucastel (AOC Châteauneuf-du-Pape). At present five wines are offered:

H CDV Red

    The Ventoux has become the workhorse of the Vieille Ferme line, accounting for about 90% of red wine sales. It is the wine that most continues to fulfill the original purpose of the Vieille Ferme *marque,* namely, to provide an alternative in a moderate alcohol, drinkable red to the Châteauneuf style of Rhône. The *assemblage* was therefore to contain plenty of *cépages* other than Grenache. At first M. Perrin sought out grapes and wines from the cooler alpine fringes of the CDR. When the cost of CDR threatened to make the price of Vieille Ferme unattractive, he turned to the CDV, particularly to the more elevated zones. Now his chief sources are the regions of Villes-sur-Auzon, Mazan, Le Barroux, Caromb, Bédoin, and the sector north of the Mont Ventoux served by the cooperative of Puyméras. 🍇 Perrin has a vinification facility at Jonquières (Vaucluse) where he makes about 20% of the CDV blend from purchased grapes (CL, 8 days). *Assemblage* for the 1984 contained 25% SY, 10% CS, 10% CR from Villes-sur-Auzon, 5% MV, and the rest GR. ❧ The CDV is not wood aged.

CDV Rosé

Pure CS, "par saignée," from Villes-sur-Auzon.

H CDR Red

M. Perrin returned to offering a CDR red in 1982. The Chemin des Mulets vineyard, planted to GR and 10% each of SY, CS, and MV, is the source of the wine. Formerly commercialized by Beaucastel, it is now sold to Vieille Ferme after being vinified at Beaucastel by the same methods as are employed for Beaucastel and CDR Cru du Coudoulet, and given 6 months wood age.

CDR white

Pure BR from the area of Laudun.

CDL White

The wine is pure Chardonnay, vinified at the cooperative of La Tour d'Aigues (Vaucluse).

9

The Ouvèze Valley

IN GENERAL the area begins to harvest about a week later than the southern Vaucluse, although some sectors harvest distinctly later because of elevation (Dentelles de Montmirail). There is somewhat less mistral in the narrower, northeast part of the valley (Séguret and Roaix).

—— CDR OF THE LOWER OUVÈZE AND PLAN DE DIEU ——

The Plan de Dieu is a broad, low plateau covered with mixed broken rocks and "rolled" stones, smaller than those on the high plateaus, over a light, well drained, hence drought-susceptible soil. It edges (e.g., at Jonquières) onto the ancient river bed of the Ouvèze, a deep gravel base. In general this makes for lighter-bodied reds than from the high plateaus or slopes.

While some vineyard sites on the Plan had medieval fame, virtual monoculture of the vine such as one now sees awaited earth-moving machines powerful enough to clear the land of its predominant juniper and green oak scrub *(garrigues)*. Hence this is one of the principal areas of new plantation since World War II to participate in the more than threefold increase in CDR production during that time.

The producers below are arranged roughly in SW to NE order, i.e., from those closest to Châteauneuf-du-Pape to those closest to Cairanne. Addresses of producers are 84 (Vaucluse).

H **Domaine Martin de Grangeneuve,** Hélène Martin et Fils, Jonquières

CDR red and white. **Taking advantage of a high percentage of old Carignan in the vineyard, Grangeneuve produces a *vin de garde* with about 50% Carignan, and won a gold medal at Paris for an 80% Carignan in 1980. Though hard, the tannin is fine, making such wines suitable for the experiments in small barrel aging M. Martin has been conducting with them and other *assemblages,* including an 80–95% Grenache, and an 80– 100% Syrah (the latter very true to character in 1982).**

60 ha in vine, all in Jonquières. Red *cépages:* 65% GR, 20% old-vine CR, rest is 12-year-old SY planted in the sandy areas. No MV because the gravel subsoil makes the soil too well drained. White: ⅓ each GR, CT, BR. ❧ OT1 in outdoor stainless vats. 8 to 10 days for earlier drinking, 12 to 15 for *vins de garde.* ❧ *Vins de garde* receive 1 year in oak *pièces,* others age in enamelled vats.

H **Domaine de la Berthète,** SCEA Cohendy-Gonnet, Camaret

CDR red, rosé, white. **Trained in oenology at Beaune, M. Cohendy fils is now in charge of the domaine. The white with its hints of nuts in the nose and the floral rosé are delicate and distinguished. The reds seem full of cherries, are refreshing and long, especially full-bodied and herb-scented in 1984.**

The domaine began with 6 ha in vine 25 years ago, now has 40, 30 in Camaret, 10 in Jonquières. Red cépages: 60% GR, 20% SY, 10% CS, 5% each MV and CR. To the few CTs and BRs have just been added a planting of GR blanc. 50% of the vines range in age from 13 to 35 years. ⁂ OT2, 3–4 days for SY, 10 to 20 for GR according to the *terroir*. Vaslin press. The white and rosé ("par saignée") juices are fined before fermentation, then fermented at a low temperature. ⁂ 2 years in vat, no wood.

H **Domaine du Vieux Chêne,** GAEC Jean-Claude and Dominique Bouche, Camaret

CDR red; VDP white and rosé. **Two *cuvées* of excellent CDR red are produced. "Cuvée des Capucines" is usually composed about 80% Grenache and 10% each of Syrah and Muscardin. Extremely aromatic in a leafy, herbal, floral direction, it is thought of as for early drinking, yet is compact and well structured enough to develop in bottle. "Cuvée de la Haie aux Grives" has 90% or more of selected Grenache plus Syrah. It is a bigger bodied, slightly less refined wine, definitely more interesting in its now unwooded form.**

30 ha, dispersed in the nearby communes of Camaret, Travaillan and Sérignan. Red *cépages:* 80% GR, 15% SY, 5% MD. White: 60% CT, 10% each GR, BR, RS, and VN. Some vines are 68 years old. About 50% of the production is in highly regarded VDP du Vaucluse, being from part of the property outside the AOC area. The red even has 10% SY. ⁂ OT1, 8 to 15 days, pneumatic press. ⁂ Formerly, "Cuvée de la Haie aux Grives" received 3 months small-barrel age. Now all aging done in vat.

Domaine de la Grangette St.-Joseph, Monique Tramier, Violès

CDR Red. **Good depth and concentration of fruit in these wines that finish smooth, even vanillaed, without seeing wood. Most impressive in my experience is probably the 1981, followed closely by 1978.**

The Plan de Dieu at Travaillan (Vaucluse), looking toward Gigondas.
Photo courtesy of Rosalind Srb.

Approximately 55-ha single estate in Violès and next-door Jonquières. 70% GR, 20% CR, plus MV, CS. Average age of vines 30 years, some date from 1920. ❧ ST, with optional destemming. 8 to 10 days, hydraulic press, optionally incorporated. ❧ Aged in vat 1 to 2 years. Before the estate began to sell its own wine in bottle, it was bottled and commercialized by the old *négociant* firm Ogier of Sorgues.

Domaine Saint-Pierre, J.C. Fauque, Violès

CDR red, white, rosé; Gigondas. **My notes indicate a preference here for the CDR wines tasted from vat or only after a short time in cask. From bottle the CDR seems to retain more fruit than does the Gigondas, which tends to hardness and astringency. Regrettably I have never tasted the latter before bottling.**

20 ha of CDR conducted in Violès and Sablet. 2.5 ha of Gigondas. 80% GR, plus SY and CR. ❧ ST, 10 to 15 days (shorter toward end of harvest). Hydraulic press. ❧ As of 1983 M. Fauque had enlarged the capacity of his cave for aging in oak casks, in which the wine spends 18 months.

Vignoble de la Jasse, Daniel Combe, Violès

CDR red. **Along with cherry fruit at the center, there is a characteristic taste of licorice that can sometimes be startling (1978) in wines that are otherwise somewhat blurred in outline, rich, soft, moderately chewy, and wood-smooth.**

9 ha of which 7 are at Travaillan, 2 at Violès, conducted without use of synthetic pesticides. GR, MV, CS. ❧ ST, 12 to 15 days. ❧ It is surprising when visiting such a small proprietor to find a vaulted cellar crammed with *demi-muid*-size oak casks, in which the wine spends a year. A minimum of SO₂ is employed. 1981 was the first wine ever filtered.

Domaine de la Damase, Joffre Latour et Fils, Violès

These are big, late-harvest, sometimes port-like wines, especially so in 1981. M. Serge Latour sometimes likes to keep the wine longer in wood than I prefer, especially as not all the wood in his cellar tastes good. Nevertheless, a wine with the depth of fruit to sustain this treatment can produce the epitome of this style, as was the deep black cherry, vanilla-licorice Grande Réserve 1980.

13 ha in vine at Violès, Travaillan and Jonquières. 70% GR, 20% old-vine CR, and 10% young CS. ❧ ST, 4 to 5 days, hydraulic press. ❧ Wine for their own bottling is aged in oak casks at their *cave*. The *négociant* firm DuPeloux of Courthézon also bottles and commercializes Damase with the name of the estate, and conducts their own *élevage* under cleaner conditions.

Domaine de Bel-Air, Gerald Boyer, Violès

CDR red. **As tasted from vat or in the estate's own bottling, this is a wine of some depth and richness that nevertheless retains nerve and liquidity. Berry to plum fruit, with pepper and vanilla (1984), a discrete hint of licorice (1983), and cedar (1982). A Bellicard-bottled version was not available for tasting at the estate.**

20-ha single estate in the qrt Bel-Air of Violès. 60% GR, 30% CR, 5% each SY and CS. M. Boyer is president of the Violès growers' syndicat. ❧ ST, 8 to 10 days. ❧ M. Boyer's own bottling is labeled **"Cuvée des Barons de Bel-Air."** For this he ages the wine 1 year in vat. Also after a year in vat, 90% of the estate's production is bought by the *négociant* firm Bellicard (Piot) of Avignon.

H Domaine de l'Espigouette, Edmond and Bernard Latour, Violès

CDR red, white, rosé. **A domaine that seems to be making steady progress toward finer wines with less of the exaggerated licorice that sometimes affects those from Violès. Son Bernard is now the winemaker for both his father and himself, but the wines from the two shares of the property are separately made and labeled. Perhaps Edmond's best ever is CDR 1981 red, full of dark red fruit savor, with hints of licorice and tobacco, wood smooth without wood taste until very slightly at the finish. Bernard is less apt to age in wood than his father, to excellent effect in the rich, clean, resinous, spicy 100% Grenache CDR "Cuvée Festival" 1982.**

12 ha dispersed, a little less than 70% GR, plus SY and MV belong to Edmond. 12 ha, of which more than half is on the Plan de Dieu, belong to Bernard. His SY and CS came into production in 1984. ☙ ST, 5 to 8 days (formerly 10–15). Hydraulic press, rosé "par saignée." White CDR through 1984 was in effect a "blush" wine from CS. ☙ The wines are now cold-stabilized. Some, especially Edmond's, are given a passage in oak casks.

Domaine des Favards, Jean-Paul Barbaud, Violès

CDR red and rosé; CDR Villages. **M. Barbaud's normal practice is, early on, to put a 90% Grenache–10% Cinsault, without wood age, into a Burgundy bottle. Later, he puts a Grenache-Syrah-Mourvèdre, aged in cask, into a "Rhodanienne" bottle. Of**

Vendange (grape harvest) on the Plan de Dieu. Photo courtesy of Robert Burns.

the two 1983s I preferred the nose of the former, more tender wine, but the flavor of the second—more structured but still lively, though a little musty. Then in 1985, the 1984 Grenache-Cinsault was to have been bottled second because its malolactic was slow to finish. At that time a 1981 bottled for a year was M. Barbaud's best show, retaining a clean aroma of fresh plums, with a subtle finish of vanilla and licorice, and no heaviness. Rosé is very attractive here.

29 ha of CDR in Violès, Camaret and Travaillan, of which 10 ha on the Plan de Dieu can be Villages. 80% GR, plus SY, CS, MV, and a little CR. ❧ OT2, 5 to 10 days (shorter at end of harvest); hydraulic press. ❧ 4 to 24 months in oak casks for the "later" bottled *cuvée*.

Bois des Dames; Abbaye de Prébayon, Violès

See Gigondas, Château Raspail.

Château la Courançonne, SCEA Château la Courançonne, Violès; "La Fiole du Chevalier d'Elbène," Meffre Frères et Fils, Séguret

The wine of Courançonne yields a pronounced, almost seedy red raspberry fruit that seems to show up in other reds of the Plan de Dieu. Some real freshness was retained in the very good 1982 by keeping it out of wood. The Fiole in both 1979 and 1980 gives a richer impression than other Ségurets; the 1980 tasted in 1985 was still in full form.

Courançonne is a single estate of 100 ha at Violès planted to GR, CS, SY. **Château de la Diffre** and "la Fiole" come from 100 ha at Séguret, mostly on slopes between Séguret and Crestet. Plantation there is 60% GR, 20% each SY and CS. ❧ ST, hydraulic press. ❧ Some wines are aged in oak casks. The Séguret is sold by the estate under the "La Fiole" label while, at least through 1983, the "Diffre" label was given exclusivity to a *négociant* who commercialized the wine. The Meffres started selling some of their own wine in bottle in 1980.

Domaine Le Grand Retour, H. Faurous et Fils (until 1984), Travaillan

CDR red and rosé. Up until now the red has been a drinkable commercial product if sometimes a little high in alcohol, with its share of the raspberry fruit that seems to characterize the Plan de Dieu. Somewhat petrolish and resinous to start, it ages out rather quickly to drier fruits, apricot or prune. The 1983 seemed already quite advanced in 1985. Estate has made something of a specialty of a fairly dark, full flavored rosé, definitely for drinking in its youth.

Until 1984 it was a single estate of 140 ha, all at Travaillan, 65% GR, 10% CS, 10% MV, and 15% SY, CT rose, and CN. The original name, which refers to the repatriation of the Faurous family to France from Algeria, will be retained for the third of the property belonging to M. Jean-Marc Faurous. Not yet definitively named are the thirds of M. Pierre Faurous and Mme. Pierre Roussel. The three have begun to work their land separately. ❧ Through 1985 one wine was still being made for separate commercialization by the various parties. 30 ha (now divided) are machine-harvested. CL, 20% with stems left on; Vaslin press. Rosé is made in the Tavel fashion, with maceration first, then using both free-run and press juice. The must is centrifuged, then cool fermented. ❧ No wood.

Château-Saint Jean; Domaine de Plan de Dieu, Travaillan

See Gigondas, Château Raspail.

Domaine Martin, SCEA Les Fils de Jules Martin (René et Yves Martin), Travaillan

CDR red, white, rosé; CDR-Villages red; VDN Rasteau. **Consistent quality in a style that stresses vinosity, tannin, and the effects of wood age more than fruit. Butter, smoke and with development, spices and truffles appear in the nose, while the finish is almost tingly. CDR 1982, a little more fruity, was the supplest and least concentrated I tasted, perhaps from its 25% Cinsault. 1980 (4 years in wood) and 1981 (3 years) both seemed more balanced than the 1983, bottled in May 1985 at U.S. client's insistence on that vintage.**

39 ha of CDR in Travaillan, Cairanne (both on the Plan de Dieu), Rasteau (slope), and Sérignan. 55% GR, plus CS, SY, MV, CT, and 5% CR. ᏋᎧ ST, 5 to 7 days, Vaslin press. Rosé "par saignée." ᏋᎧ Wine spends a minimum of 2 years in oak casks, more as determined by demand for bottled wine. The Martins have bottled for 30 years.

Domaine de la Meynarde, Travaillan

See Gigondas, Château Raspail.

H **La Vignonnerie Plan Deï,** J.M. Lobreau, Travaillan (For some wines, J.M. et S. Lobreau, Camaret)

CDR red and white; CDR-Villages red. **M. Lobreau continues to be the winemaker at Domaine de la Meynarde now that it belongs to Gabriel Meffre (see Gigondas, Château Raspail). These are the wines of his own estate. A CDR-Villages, made since 1983, is 50% Mourvèdre, 30% Grenache. CDR Plan Deï is 60% Grenache, 30% Mourvèdre, 10–15% Counoise. CDR Cabassole is pure old-vine Grenache from the *quartier* of that name in nearby Camaret. CDR Les Rouvières is a lighter bodied, somewhat smokey, pure Grenache, also from Camaret. All these were especially resinous in 1983, and had more flowers and red fruit in 1984, which will receive less wood. CDR La Vignonnerie is made for early drinking from 80–85% Grenache, plus Mourvèdre and Counoise. The line is completed by the lemon-anise flavored Plan Deï white, 70% Bourboulenc plus Clairette. Best wine I have had from here was the stunning 1982 Cabassole.**

20 ha of which 15 were formerly part of the Domaine de la Meynarde when it was part of the Seagram's empire. 15 ha of GR, plus MV, CN, CT, and BR. Average age of vines 20 to 25 years. ᏋᎧ CL with machine harvest, 15 days for the *vins de garde*. Fermentation of the white wine is finished in oak casks. ᏋᎧ Villages, Plan Deï, Cabassole, and Rouvières reds are aged in oak *pièces* for 6 to 18 months. The white is aged up to 9 months in casks. La Vignonnerie reds are not wood aged.

— THE DENTELLES DE MONTMIRAIL—*CRU:* GIGONDAS —

There is literary and archeological evidence of reputed Gallo-Roman viticulture here, and fame for the wines continued into medieval and Renaissance times (e.g., those from the Abbey of St.-André and the Prince of Orange's own vineyards). Nevertheless, the traditional agricultural economy of Gigondas was mixed, perhaps especially so during the 17th and 18th centuries. Not until 1956 and the freezing of the olive trees did the plantation of vine exceed *oliviers*, for example.

Vines had begun to attract more attention in the 19th century when Eugène Raspail's wines became known in the commerce for their "proportion of alcohol." After phylloxera there were some pioneers in bottle sale, Hilarion Roux and Amadieu, but even more important were a trade in wine grapes to private makers and sale of the principally Grenache wine to *négociants* for the eventual "doctoring" of Burgundy.

This probably accounts for the sense of the Gigondas *vignerons* that it is Grenache that made their fame. Stubborn as their wine, they recently succeeded in getting the INAO to raise the maximum permitted Grenache in the plantation of Gigondas to 80% from the 65% figure that had stood since Gigondas was promoted in 1971 from being one of the original CDR-Villages (then *communales*) to local AOC standing.

Some Gigondas growers say that while others may have to worry, Gigondas Grenache doesn't oxidize. An alternative hypothesis would be that a good many Gigondasians have developed a taste for the slight maderization that goes into making a wine in the "forme oxidative." (See Grenache under "Southern Climate and *Cépages*.") In any case a certain smell of slightly dried hay that may even be from the *terroir* appears very early in many Gigondases, and is harmonious with the "pre-aged" treatment of which Gigondas remains an important center.

The village of Gigondas (Vaucluse) and the Dentelles de Montmirail. While Vacqueyras and Sablet to either side belonged to the Comtat Venaissin, Gigondas was part of the Principality of Orange. Photo courtesy of Rosalind Srb.

The zones of production at Gigondas are "vertical." The cobblestone-covered plateau that traverses Vacqueyras from Sarrians culminates below the village of Gigondas on top of cliffs that overlook the Ouvèze and the much lower plateau of Sablet. Onto the Gigondas plateau incline the sandy-lime slopes, with a northwestern exposure. These descend from the Jurassic limestone peaks of the Dentelles de Montmirail mountain range—the interior of which with its "marne" soil makes up the third and highest zone, harvested much later than the rest.

Gigondas may be made in either red or rosé (the "saignée" of which from the vats may help to achieve the characteristically black color of the red). In addition to the 80% maximum of Grenache, the revised regulations demand that red Gigondas be based on plantation of at least 15% Syrah and/or Mourvèdre and no more than 10% of the other CDR *cépages* excluding Carignan. For rosé all *cépages* besides Grenache and again excluding Carignan must not exceed 25%.

Gigondas is grown at a normal maximum rate of 35 hectoliters of wine per hectare of land, and as at Châteauneuf-du-Pape, there is a requirement to cull out defective grapes to make *râpé,* between 3% and 20% of the crop as determined annually by the authorities. Minimum natural alcohol must be 12.5%. No chaptalization is allowed.

Gigondas is something like Cornas in being recognizable in a blind tasting from its brilliant dark color alone. And while Gigondas resembles Châteauneuf-du-Pape in scale, if anything it is an even bigger, somewhat sturdier and less complex wine. Within generally robust dimensions, then, it is nevertheless useful to place individual wines in the same style categories already defined in the discussion of Châteauneuf-du-Pape.

Producers (arranged by style)

Addresses of producers are 84190 Gigondas, unless otherwise noted.

ELEGANT STYLE

Domaine des Bosquets, Mme. Brechet
  See **Château Raspail.**

Domaine de Cassan, SCIA St. Christophe, Lafare
  See Beaumes-de-Venise.

Domaine de la Chapelle, Christian Meffre
  See **Château Raspail.**

Domaine de Daysse, Jacques Meffre
  See **Château Raspail.**

H **Domaine de Longue-Toque,** Serge Chapalain
Wine evolves from violets and raspberries with vanilla and resin, to apricots and truffles and, while never thick or heavy, has the very definition of a Gigondas nose. More substantial *cuvées* are held for later bottling here. Thus to my mind the last-bottled 1981 was the preferable wine, as was the 1983 that contained 70% Grenache, scheduled for September 1985 bottling.

COTES du RHONE

Appellation Côtes du Rhône Contrôlée

- Cabassole -
1983

J.M. et S. Lobreau
propriétaires à Camaret
Vaucluse - France
75 cl

Mise en bouteille
à la
Propriété

DOMAINE DE LA BERTHETE

PRODUCE OF FRANCE

Côtes du Rhône
APPELLATION CÔTES DU RHÔNE CONTRÔLÉE

1982

MIS EN BOUTEILLE AU DOMAINE
COHENDY-GONNET SCEA
PROPRIÉTAIRE RÉCOLTANT, CAMARET (VAUCLUSE)
FRANCE

e 75 cl

Côtes du Rhône
APPELLATION CÔTES DU RHÔNE CONTRÔLÉE

Domaine du Vieux Chêne

Mis en bouteille au domaine

G.A.E.C. Jean-Claude & Dominique Bouche

Propriétaires-Récoltants à Camaret (Vaucluse)

France
75 cl

DOMAINE DE LONGUE-TOQUE
GRAND VIN DES CÔTES DU RHÔNE

MIS EN BOUTEILLE AU DOMAINE
GIGONDAS
PRODUCT OF FRANCE
ALCOHOL 13% BY VOLUME
APPELLATION GIGONDAS CONTROLÉE
RED TABLE WINE
SERGE CHAPALAIN VIGNERON A GIGONDAS — VAUCLUSE, FRANCE
750 ml

L'OUSTAU FAUQUET

VIN DES COTES DU RHONE
GIGONDAS
APPELLATION GIGONDAS CONTROLÉE
75 cl

RECOLTE ET MIS EN BOUTEILLES PAR
G.A.E.C. ROGER COMBE & FILS, VIGNERONS A VACQUEYRAS VAUCLUSE

CRU DU PETIT MONTMIRAIL

FRANCE

Vin des Côtes du Rhône
DOMAINE
DU
PESQUIER
Gigondas

appellation Gigondas contrôlée
mis en bouteille au domaine
73 cl
Ce vin a été l'objet de tous les soins de
R. Boutière et Fils vignerons à Gigondas (V^{se})
— Téléphone (90) 65-86-14 —
France

DOMAINE DU TERME

GIGONDAS
APPELLATION GIGONDAS CONTROLÉE

R. GAUDIN. Viticulteur à GIGONDAS. Vaucluse

MIS EN BOUTEILLE AU DOMAINE
75 cl

PRODUIT DE FRANCE

Domaine Saint-Gayan

VIN DES CÔTES DU RHÔNE
Gigondas

APPELLATION GIGONDAS CONTROLÉE
75 cl
MISE EN BOUTEILLE A LA PROPRIÉTÉ
MEFFRE ROGER, PROPRIETAIRE, A GIGONDAS (V^{se}) FRANCE

23 ha dispersed (1/3 N and 2/3 S). 65% GR, 20% SY, 10% CS, 5% diverse including CT and MV. ❧ Wine is assembled from OT1, 17 to 18 days, for southern parcels, with CL, 10–12 days, for northern parcels. Vaslin press. ❧ Stabilized by outdoor storage during the winter. 6 to 12 months in wood. Neither fined nor filtered.

H L'Oustau Fauquet

See Vacqueyras, Domaine de la Fourmone.

Château Raspail (formerly Domaine du Colombier), Gabriel Meffre

In my experience Meffre's Gigondases are sound, correct, certainly not heavy, but lack distinctiveness—especially of aroma. From this point of view 1985 tasting of the 1983s suggests that Raspail may be emerging as a more substantial individualized wine.

Both an estate owner and a *négociant* on a grand scale, Gabriel Meffre's proprietorship began at Gigondas with Domaine de Daysse (see below). The wine called Raspail was formerly made and commercialized by M. Meffre as Domaine du Colombier. Another part into which the historic estate of 19th-century notable Eugène Raspail was divided, it was owned by M. Bernard Ay. Now M. Meffre owns Raspail's château—which was known from its *quartier* as the Château du Colombier before it became Château Raspail—and the wine of this estate, adjoining the château, is vinified there and so bears its name. At present it counts 17 ha (plateau), 65% GR, 25% SY, and 10% diverse *cépages*. ❧ CL, in part ST (the lower part of each vat); 12–14 days; impulsion press, but the press wine is not incorporated. The other Domaine Meffre Gigondases are vinified in a similar way, but at the headquarters of Ets. Gabriel Meffre just below the village of Gigondas. ❧ The Meffre Gigondases are aged about a year in oak casks. The "Domaines Meffre" wines are commercialized by the *négociant* firm Etablissements Gabriel Meffre, Gigondas.

Other "Domaines Meffres":

Gigondas:

Domaine des Bosquets, Mme. Brechet, née Meffre
  35 ha (slope). This also once belonged to Eugène Raspail.
Domaine de la Chapelle, Christian Meffre
  16 ha (slope).
Domaine de Daysse, Jacques Meffre
  20 ha (plateau).

Taken together these three properties are 80 % GR, 15% SY, and 5% diverse *cépages*.

Châteauneuf-du-Pape:

Château de Vaudieu
  For details, see Châteauneuf-du-Pape.

CDR:

Château de Ruth (Part of same exploitation with **Vignoble de Florette**), Ste.-Cécile-les-Vignes

115 ha. 70% GR, 15% SY, plus CS and CR. "Cuvée de Nicolas Beauharnais" receives 6 to 8 months wood age.

Domaine de la Meynarde, Travaillan
50 ha.

Château Saint-Jean (Exploited with **Domaine de Plan de Dieu**), Travaillan
220 ha. M. Meffre opened this and the following estate on the vast tableland (Plan de Dieu) below Gigondas to cultivation by removing the juniper and green oak *garrigues*, beginning in 1946, with American war-surplus earth-moving equipment.

Bois des Dames (Exploited with **Abbaye de Prébayon**), Violès
200 ha.

Château Saint-André, Pierre Veyrat (Mme. Françoise Veyrat),
Domaine de Saint André

The wines I have tasted from the late M. Veyrat's era (1970, for example) combined a nose in the "forme oxidative" style with elegant structure. To that non-agressivity is now added a fresher, leafy-floral aroma that makes St.-André one of the few candidates for being a "pretty" Gigondas, combining black cherry fruit (as in 1984), sometimes licorice (as in 1982), and a characteristic hint of bitterness in the finish. All the 1983 was sold off in bulk.

53 ha on the plateau just above the Ouvèze River. 80% GR, 10% MV, 5% each of CS and SY. 🍇 CL, 10 to 12 days; Vaslin press, but no press wine incorporated. 🍇 The wine spends 1 to 2 years in oak casks (only 8 months for the 1982). **Abbaye de St.-André, Clos de la Moutte,** and **Fons Caristie** are additional Gigondas labels.

Domaine Saint-François-Xavier, GAEC Domaine St.-François-Xavier,
André Gras et Fils

CDR; Gigondas. **Somewhat lightweight, raspberryish, leafy, spicy 1982s. In 1983, M. Gras was just about to embark upon estate-bottling.**

15-ha single estate of Gigondas (plateau near Pesquier). 70% GR, 10% each SY, CS, MV. 8 ha CDR from Vacqueyras. 80% GR, plus SY and a little CR. 🍇 OT2, 3 weeks *cuvaison;* hydraulic press; incorporates first press. 🍇 6 months in oak casks follow 1 year in vat.

CLASSIC STYLE

Pierre Amadieu, Gigondas

Gigondas red and rosé. **Amadieu is both a proprietor and *négociant-éleveur*. All the Gigondas is from his own property, and so is simply presented with his name and address on the label, as above. It makes an excellent case for mountain Gigondas, marked by Syrah: lean, structured, not thick, and usually with a spicy-peppery finish.**

125 ha in vine, of which only 6 are on the plateau. The rest is made up of the Domaines **Romane** and **Machotte,** mountain sites of 400m elevation. 60% GR, 35% SY, plus diverse *cépages* including MV, CS, CN, GR blanc, and CT. The vineyards are fertilized organically, until 1983 by his own flock of sheep. 🍇 ST, averaging 10 days, hydraulic press. Gigondas rosé "par saignée," surprisingly represents 10% of all Amadieu's Gigondas sales, and is composed of GR, CS, and CN. 🍇 The wines are filtered

through diatomaceous earth, then aged in oak casks according to the character of the year for an average of 2 years. Amadieu retains a remarkable aging cellar, which houses 160 *foudres,* in an abandoned railway tunnel NE of Nyons (Drôme), then returns the wine to Gigondas for bottling. Amadieu's Gigondas is commercialized by the *négociant* firm Les Celliers Amadieu of Gigondas.

Domaine Raspail-Ay (formerly Château Raspail), Dominique Ay

Gigondas red, and a very little rosé in certain years. **The wine usually shows fruit and avoids heaviness with no loss of Gigondas typicity, including a hint of "forme oxidative" in the nose. Recently, however, the wood flavors seem less well married with the other taste components, perhaps, as sometimes is paradoxically the case, because of the shorter time in wood.**

Until his retirement in 1983, M. Francois Ay, president of the Gigondas growers, was proprietor of this 18–ha single estate (slope). It is one of four parts into which the property assembled at Gigondas by 19th-century journalist, politician, and savant Eugène Raspail was eventually divided by inheritance through his wife's family. The Ays no longer own Raspail's château, for which this wine was named until 1978. 70–75% GR, 15% SY, 10% diverse *cépages,* including MV, CS, CT. ❧ M. Ay's son continues to employ CL, 10 to 21 days; hydraulic press. ❧ The wine once spent as much as 3 to 4 years in oak, beginning in foudres and racked progressively into smaller barrels. The latter practice continues, but heavy demand has pressed the wood age down to an average of 2 years, while an American importer who demanded 1983 early cut 6 months off that.

Domaine de Saint-Cosme, Henri Barruol

A cooler micro-climate in a little wooded valley that descends the north slope of the Dentelles from Les Florets gives the wine a floral fruit and concentration. Nevertheless the tannins can be hefty, as in the 1984 tasted not long after its bottling by Mousset.

15.5 ha was planted until 1985 rule change to 70% GR, 10% SY, and the rest CS and a little CT. M. Barruol is convinced that the ancient vats carved in the bedrock of his cave date to Gallo-Roman times and a major winemaking complex that must have occupied this site. ❧ ST, 10 days average. ❧ The wine is estate-bottled and commercialized by the *négociant* firm Louis Mousset of Châteauneuf-du-Pape.

H **Domaine du Terme,** Roland Gaudin

CDR; Gigondas red and rosé. **I consistently prefer M. Gaudin's Mouvèdre *cuvée* (plus old-vine Grenache and Cinsault) to that with Syrah. Fortunately, so does his U.S. importer. A clean, floral, plummy wine with a whiff of stone and truffles, it is at once solid and fine. The 1981 shows the best balance yet between fruit and wood, with the still developing 1978 not far behind. The 1979 is just rounding out (1986), and one can anticipate a similar wait for the 1983 red. The 1983 rosé is quite simply the best Gigondas rosé I have ever tasted.**

12 ha of Gigondas (plateau). 65% GR, of which some was planted in 1929, 15% SY, 10% MV, plus CT and CS. 10 ha of CDR at Sablet is 65% GR, 10% SY, 10% MV, plus CS and CT. M. Gaudin is also part owner, with M. Pierre Lambert, of Gigondas (slope) **Domaine de la Mavette, a very floral but up to now much heavier wine than Terme.** M. Gaudin, president of the official tasting commission for AOC at Gigondas, is

decreasing SY and augmenting MV in his plantation. 🍇 OT2, 12 to 15 days; rosé "par saignée." 🍇 1 year in oak casks.

H Château du Trignon, Charles Roux et Fils

CDR red and white; CDR-Rasteau; CDR-Sablet; Gigondas. **The characteristically dark-colored Gigondas smells of stones, truffles, even tar (1978), and is generally a bit fatter than other Trignons. Anyone who thinks CM method only good for early maturing wines should taste an old Rasteau from Trignon's library (back to 1964) or in nearby Séguret's restaurant, Table du Comtat. It is as true to its Mourvèdre component, beginning with flowers, red plum skins and vanilla, as Roux's Sablet is to its Syrah. Among wines that stand out are 1981 for both, with 1974 as great Sablet.**

8 ha of Gigondas (slope). 5 ha of CDR-Villages at Rasteau (GR and MV); 31 ha of CDR and CDR-Villages at Sablet (GR, SY, CS); 16 ha of CDR at Violès. All properties: 60% GR, 10% CS, 5% SY, 5% MV, 1% CR, plus GR blanc, CT, MR, and VN. 🍇 Severe selection of incoming grapes followed by CM, 18 days. Integral CM has been practiced here since 1962. 🍇 No wood.

Cave des Vignerons de Gigondas

CDR white; Gigondas red and rosé. **Through vintage 1981 the cave made a *cuvée* "Beaumanière" for the famous restaurant, in which no press wine was incorporated. This *cuvée* is now known as "Les Hauts de Gigondas." "Cuvée du Président" (exported to the U.S.) is from a special selection of grapes and was in part made by CM through 1984. My personal favorite tends to be the plain Gigondas "Cave des Vignerons," which while never thick, retains full, spicy, stony Gigondas character.**

Founded 1956. 84.73% AOC. Small cooperative of 125 members, all of whom are from Gigondas, is one of the best for regional character in the whole Côtes du Rhône. 🍇 CL, in part OT (bottom of each vat), 8 to 12 days. 🍇 The cooperative has invested in 117 oak casks, stored underground, in which the Gigondas spends 2 years before bottling.

ROBUST STYLE

Domaine du Cayron, Georges Faraud et Fils

This is a big, often late-harvest, even port-like Gigondas, jam-packed with tannin and extract, that I would love to like better than I do. Regrettably, some cellar aromas extraneous to its "forme oxidative" appear in the bottled wine.

13.6 ha, dispersed in 18 parcels. 65% GR, 30% CS and SY, with 5% white *cépages* that enter into the red wine. 🍇 Formerly ST, now OT2, 15 days; hydraulic press. 🍇 After a year or more in vat, the 2 years minimum wood age begins in cask; then the wine is gradually assembled during the course of racking into successively smaller barrels. It is finally bottled, without fining or filtering, by gravity from *pièces*.

H Domaine Les Gouberts, Jean-Pierre Cartier

CDR red; CDR-Beaumes-de-Venise red; CDR-Sablet red and white; Gigondas red and rosé. **Like a Burgundian *vigneron* with parcels in a number of named *crus*, M. Cartier consistently realizes the type of each of his AOCs. The Gigondas is rich, supple, and solid, with hints of cut hay and cedar, and deep black raspberry fruit** that develops spiciness and tar, as exhibited in 1981. His strong, floral, resinous Beaumes-de-Venise is almost bigger than his Gigondas. His red Sablet, characteristically scented of truffles, was especially tender and fragrant in 1984. The Sablet blanc, which has been made only since 1983, bids fair, as the vines mature, to be one of the greatest of all southern Rhône whites. 1983, with malolactic, was rich, Chardonnay-like; 1984, without malolactic, was more like a Loire, then developed a smell of apple-blossom honey also found in the just-finished 1985.

7.2 ha of Gigondas of which about 5 in qrt les Blaches, an area of sandy soil (plateau), and about 2 ha just bought in qrt Montmirail (mountain). 2.8 ha CDR-Villages in AOC Beaumes-de-Venise (GR, SY, CS); 1.1 ha of CDR-Villages red at Sablet (GR, SY); .6 ha CDR-Villages white at Sablet (BR, RS, CT); 3.1 ha CDR at Sablet and Beaumes-de-Venise. All properties: 72–75% GR, 20% SY, 8% CS, a little MV. ❧ ST, 15 days. ❧ No wood age for the reds since M. Cartier used to make a wooded "Réserve" Gigondas, until the 1985 "Cuvée Florence," an experiment in aging Gigondas from the Montmirail parcel in new oak *pièces*. Otherwise 23 months in vat.

H **Domaine du Grand Montmirail,** SC du Grand Montmirail (Denis Cheron)

Mountain herbs and flowers dominate in a deeply berry-fruited wine that combines freshness, sturdy structure, roundness and length—all superbly demonstrated after 24 hours aeration in monumental 1983 (tasted 1986). 1982 is lighter bodied than 1981, 1983, and 1984.

26-ha single estate on the south side of the Dentelles de Montmirail mountains lies between the Beaumes-de-Venise of Domaine Les Gouberts in Lafare and Domaine de Coyeux in Beaumes-de-Venise. It is well ventilated but not directly in the path of the mistral. 95% GR, average age of vines 35 years. Will eventually have 10–15 % SY not yet in production. ❧ Before he was this estate's proprietor, its grapes were taken for 20 years to M. Cheron's *négociant* house, Pascal, to be vinified as part of that *marque*'s Gigondas. There they were destemmed. Since 1981 the estate-bottled version has been vinified OT2, 10 days average; Vaslin press. ❧ Aged in underground cement vats, because owner Cheron believes that the climate makes it "a heresy to age wines in wood." Second labels for this wine reflect the names of portions of the property and include **Domaine de St.-Gens, Domaine de Pradas, Domaine de Roucas de St.-Pierre.**

Domaine du Grapillon d'Or, Bernard Chauvet

A big and burly wine that nevertheless seems well proportioned for its weight, and neither thick nor dry. Color and fruit are dark, in the plum to prune range, with a Gigondas cut-hay nose that was excessive only in the somewhat cooked and port-like 1982. 1981 and 1983 were well balanced and 1984 (barrel-tasted in 1985) promisingly buttery and fresh.

14 ha of Gigondas are divided between slope (qrt Les Bosquets) and plateau (qrt Le Péage). 80% GR, 15% SY, and 5% CS. The product of 7 ha of CDR at Vacqueyras is sold in bulk. ❧ ST, 12 to 15 days; hydraulic press. ❧ 12 to 18 months in oak casks. The wine is bottled unfined and unfiltered.

Domaine de la Jaufrette, André Chastan et Fils, Orange

Gigondas; CDR-Vacqueyras; CDR red and rosé; Châteauneuf-du-Pape. **Best wine seems to be the warm, black cherry and plum fruit Gigondas—chewy, particularly well balanced in 1980 by contrast to somewhat overwooded 1976.**

6 ha of Gigondas (slopes). 80% GR, 20% SY and MV. 4¹/₂ ha of Vacqueyras, 80% GR, 15% SY, plus a little MV and CS. Exploits 8 ha of CDR at Orange, 90% GR plus CS, CR, and a little SY. Sharecrops 2 ha of Châteauneuf-du-Pape at Orange (N), almost pure GR. ❧ OT2, 20 days. Press juice not incorporated. ❧ 1 year in oak casks. 6 months bottle-age before sale.

Domaine de la Mavette, Pierre Lambert and Roland Gaudin

See **Domaine du Terme.**

H **Château de Montmirail**

See Vacqueyras.

H **Domaine Les Pallières,** SCEA Les Fils de Hilarion Roux

The first domaine at Gigondas to bottle its own wine still produces one of the most typical in the "forme oxidative," i.e., with a deliberately achieved mature bouquet from wood age before bottling. Solid structure, concentrated fruit, though tending to dried rather than fresh.

Single estate with 25 ha in vine (slope), near the border of Sablet, uphill from Trignon and St.-Gayan. 54% GR, 20% SY, 18% MV, 5% CS, and a little CT. ❧ ST, 12 to 15 days. ❧ 3 to 4 years in oak casks.

H **Domaine du Pesquier,** GAEC Raymond Boutière et Fils

CDR-Villages; Gigondas. **Once perhaps the most robust Gigondas of all. 1980 seemed to strike a new balance continuing in 1981, the best balanced I've had from this estate. Deep fruit, pleasantly oaked.**

15 ha of Gigondas (mainly plateau). 65–70% GR; 25% SY(most), MV, and CS. 10 ha CDR-Villages at Sablet and Vacqueyras. ❧ OT2, 12 to 14 days; Vaslin press. ❧ 1 to 2 years in wood.

Domaine du Pourra

See Sablet.

Pradets

See Châteauneuf-du-Pape, Château Maucoil.

H **Domaine Saint-Gayan,** GAEC du Domaine St.-Gayan (Roger and Jean-Pierre Meffre)

CDR; CDR-Villages; Gigondas. **The best Gigondas in the style for those who think a wine _must_ be rough at the start to be ageable. It is sometimes hugely tannic, runs easily to 14% alcohol, nevertheless is packed with fruit and spice. The 1980 had an unusual elegance. I have sometimes found the Villages too hard, not so in the separate presentation of CDR-Rasteau 1984.**

14 ha of Gigondas (slope). 70% GR, 20% SY, 10% CS and MV, 5% CT. 15.5 ha CDR and CDR-Villages from Sablet, Séguret, and Rasteau (where planting includes 20% MV). ❧ Formerly OT1, now OT2, 15 days; hydraulic press. ❧ 1 year in wood for Gigondas, none for Villages.

Domaine Saint-Pierre, Violès
   See "CDR of the Lower Ouvèze and Plan de Dieu."

Gigondas *Négociants:*

Etablissements Gabriel Meffre, Négociants
   Meffre commercializes a line of CDV, CDR, Lirac, Tavel, and Crozes-Hermitage wines, but most especially the proprietary wines of the "Domaines Meffre" (for details, see Gigondas, Chateau Raspail). The line also includes several domaine wines from other proprietors:

Lirac:

Château de Ségriès, Lirac
   For details see Lirac.

CDR:

Domaine Chantegut, Sarrians (Vaucluse)
   20 ha of AOC on the plateau. Majority GR, 20% SY, plus a little CS and MV. ST, some destemmed, 7 days.

Domaine Latour Paul, Violès (Vaucluse)

Les Celliers Amadieu, Pierre Amadieu, négociant-éleveur
   The firm commercializes Amadieu's proprietary Gigondas "Romane-Machotte." See Gigondas, Pierre Amadieu. Amadieu owns 60 ha of CDV in the communes of Crestet and Mazan, planted 55% GR, 25% SY, 10% CS, 10% CT, GR blanc, and diverse white *cépages.* The white Ventoux is exclusively from their property, but as Amadieu also buys red Ventoux, all the Ventoux is labeled "Pierre Amadieu, négociant-éleveur."
   As *négociant* Amadieu presents a line of CDR, CDR-Villages, and Châteauneuf-du-Pape wines that includes one estate-bottled Châteauneuf:

Domaine Père Caler, Maurice Avril, Châteauneuf-du-Pape
   5 ha (90% GR, 10% MV, CN and SY).

The firm also commercializes the only marc brandy from Gigondas, which is produced by one of M. Amadieu's sons, M. Claude Amadieu. Highly aromatic, it has the distinctive feature of being cut to potable strength with calcareous Gigondas spring water.

—— DENTELLES DE MONTMIRAIL—CDR-VILLAGES ——
(communes presented in a SW to NE order)

Beaumes-de-Venise (and **Cru** *Muscat)*

The communes of Côtes-du-Rhône-Villages Beaumes-de-Venise are Beaumes-de-Venise, Lafare, La Roque-Alric, and Suzette. With the northern part of Beaumes, the latter three contain, for the most part, steeply sloped mountain sites in the interior of the Dentelles mountain range, cooler and later to harvest than the rest. They were added to the area of

CDR in 1970, having been, like Beaumes-de-Venise itself (until 1957), part of the Côtes du Ventoux when it was VDQS. The whole area was promoted to Villages (with name of the commune) in 1979.

Since 1945, however, a delimited part of Beaumes-de-Venise has been a *cru* with its own local AOC for production of Muscat de Beaumes-de-Venise. Said to have been drunk at the papal court in Avignon, this is a sweet wine made from the "Muscat à petits grains" (Muscat de Frontignan) in the port fashion. That is, the fermentation is stopped ("muted") by the addition of alcohol while some residual sugar (110 grams per liter minimum) remains unfermented. Since the sugar is purely residual (i.e., from the grapes themselves), wines of this type in France are categorized as "natural sweet wines" (VDN). The normal maximum productivity for Muscat de Beaumes is 30 hectoliters of must per hectare. The minimum natural alcohol before "mutage" must be 15%, which requires late-harvested grapes. The addresses of producers are 84 (Vaucluse).

Domaine des Bernardins, Castaud-Maurin, Beaumes-de-Venise

CDR; CDR-Villages; Muscat de Beaumes-de-Venise. **In my experience the reds seem distinctly tannic and to be from very ripe, even raisined grapes. The Muscat, of golden hue with a very slight pink blush, is richer, less musky and acid than some. The late M. Castaud was founder of the Muscat de Beaumes-de-Venise appellation.**

15 ha in 2 hillside parcels. About 1/2 is planted to Muscat, the rest to GR, SY, and CR. ❧ ST, 7 to 10 days for red, Vaslin press. ❧ Red spends 6 to 9 months in oak casks.

Domaine de Cassan, SCIA Saint-Christophe (Paul Crozet), Lafare

CDR; CDR-Villages Beaumes-de-Venise; Gigondas. **As with the other wines of this vicinity, the aroma of flowers in the CDR and Villages is remarkable. Perhaps the Cassan finish is less satisfying, but it may improve as the vines mature. Wood almost threatens to overpower what has sometimes seemed a rather light Gigondas, but 1985 retasting of the 1979 revealed much greater harmony than at the outset.**

15.5 ha in communes of Lafare and Suzette, high in the interior of the Dentelles de Montmirail. 4 ha SY, 2 ha MV, 1 1/2 ha CS, the rest GR. 7 1/2 ha of Gigondas (plateau) is planted 1 ha to SY, 1 ha to MV, and the rest to GR. ❧ ST in part destemmed. Grapes for the Gigondas are not destemmed. 8 to 9 days, Vaslin press. ❧ 2 years in oak casks for the Gigondas, 1 1/2 for the Villages, 3 to 6 months for the CDR.

Coteaux de la Ferme Saint-Martin, Guy Julien, Suzette

CDR red, white, rosé; CDR-Villages Beaumes-de-Venise. **M. Julien's father, now retired, used to make a red which I remember as notably floral and fiercely tannic. The son became winemaker in 1979. The red wines are certainly more drinkable now, though perhaps not as aromatic. The 1981 Villages stood out from a series tasted in 1985 for combining balanced wood smoothness with the most definite fruit.**

17 ha of vine all on the spectacular slopes at Suzette and La Rocque Alric. Red *cépages*: 70% GR, 20% CS, 5% SY, 5% Aubun. Whites are GR blanc and CT. ❧ OT2, 8 to 10 days, hydraulic press. Rosé "par saignée." The white and rosé complete their malolactic. ❧ Red spends 1 year in oak casks.

H **Domaine de Coyeux,** Yves et Catherine Nativelle, Beaumes-de-Venise

CDR-Villages Beaumes-de-Venise; Muscat de Beaumes-de-Venise; Gigondas. **M. Nativelle made his first wine in 1982, and each Villages wine in the sequence 1982, 1983, 1984 has been better. The latter, reflecting presence of all the domaine's *cépages,* is dark red in color and fruit, at once fragrant, supple, liquid, and balanced. 1983 was drier, spicier, perhaps cassis tinged with cinnamon. The difference between 1983 and 1984 in the Muscat is comparable. The former is very full and floral, with the kind of sweetness that coats the mouth. The latter is leafier and fresher, very long in flavor while leaving the mouth clean.**

132-ha single estate, spectacularly located at 260m elevation, between Domaine du Grand Montmirail (Gigondas) and Domaine Durban (Beaumes-de-Venise). 71% of the surface is planted to Muscat blanc for production of Muscat de Beaumes-de-Venise; some vines are 45 years old. Red *cépages:* 50% GR, 20% CS, 20% MV, and 10% SY. Gigondas is produced from 3 ha. 🦢 CL, 10 to 12 days for red. 80% of the Muscat is free-run juice. 🦢 Red spends 12 to 18 months in vat, 8 months in bottle before sale. Some will be aged in small barrels before *assemblage*. The Muscat is given 14 months in vat, 8 to 10 months in bottle.

H **Domaine Durban,** Leydier et Fils, Beaumes-de-Venise

Muscat de Beaumes-de-Venise. **The Muscat of Durban is usually the palest in color and most delicate in flavor of Beaumes-de-Venise. Perhaps for this reason the 1983 avoided heaviness, while being definitely sugary to the nose and supple in the mouth with its hints of apricot and marzipan. For leafy freshness and remarkable acid-sugar balance, though, it is hard to beat the 1984.**

Of 40 ha of vine, 14 are Muscat blanc planted at 240m altitude in the qrt Urban. Average age of the vines is between 25 and 30 years. Only the Muscat production is bottled, with both the grapes and the wines of other AOCs sold to *négociants*. 🦢 The Muscat, produced entirely from free-run juice, is cool fermented. 🦢 It rests several months on the fine lees, is diatomaceous earth-filtered, and bottled 6 to 8 months after that. Formerly, instead of filtration and early bottling, the wine passed 2 years in cask. M. Bernard Leydier prefers to drink Muscat at about 3 years of age.

H **Domaine les Goubert,** Jean-Pierre Cartier, Gigondas
See Gigondas

Château de Redortier, Etienne De Menthon, Suzette

CDR-Villages Beaumes-de-Venise red and rosé. **M. De Menthon left the cooperative and started making wine in 1981. It develops leafy, floral aromas (seems character-istic of Suzette), good fruit, even some spice and butteriness.**

27 ha at 400m altitude, exposed to the south, in the adjacent communes of Suzette and Lafare. 60% GR, 25% SY, 10% CS, 5% diverse. 4 ha of Gigondas are 75% GR and 25% SY. 🦢 ST, 8 days; Vaslin press, of which only the first press is incorporated for Villages. 🦢 No wood. 18 months in vat.

H **Domaine de Saint-Sauveur,** Les héritiers de Marcel Rey, Aubignan
See Côtes du Ventoux.

Domaine Vaubelle, Lesbros

CDR red and rosé. **Rosé, as with the others near Gigondas, is big, flavorful, and full of minerals. Of the reds, at a somewhat lower degree is a** *cuvée* **with Mourvèdre, more "tender," which shows vanilla and flowers to the nose. Darker, bigger bodied is a** *cuvée* **of pure, old-vine Grenache.**

35 ha in 2 principal groups: 14 ha on the slopes behind Vacqueyras, 21 ha on the other side of the ridge toward Lafare. 75% GR, 10% CR, 10% CS, 5% MV. ❧ OT2, 5 to 10 days, Vaslin press. ❧ No wood. "Domaine des Bernardins" is a label used for wines from this estate bottled and distributed by the *négociant* Pierre Ferraud at Belleville-sur-Saône.

Cave des Vignerons de Beaumes-de-Venise

Working in conditions of technical proficiency and impeccable cleanliness, the Cave is the largest producer of wine for its own bottle sale of all CDR cooperatives (3.5 to 4 million bottles of AOC wine annually). Its CDR-Villages Beaumes-de-Venise comes in "Carte Noire" red, distinguished from a plain Villages by more Syrah and no Cinsault. CDR "Cuvée Spéciale" comes in red, rosé and white, with the red based on selected vats, and including Syrah and less Carignan compared to the 20% Carignan and no Syrah of CDR "Rocalinot." CDV Supérieur red is Grenache, Syrah, Mourvèdre, while plain CDV deletes Syrah and includes Cinsault and Carignan. My experience over time is that the CDVs can be impressive, having more character for their type than the Cave's Villages. The Muscat de Beaumes-de-Venise, of which the Cave produces more than 90% of the AOC's total, seems always reliable in the Cave's own bottling, if a little duller than the wine of certain private domaines.

Founded 1956. 74.88% AOC. Cooperators number 307, 90% of whom are from Beaumes-de-Venise. The CDR-Villages is from there, Lafare, Suzette, La Rocque-Alric. CDV is from Aubignan, St.-Hippolyte-de-Graveyrons, Caromb, and Le Barroux. ❧ Perhaps the most remarkable feature of the Cave's operation is that the total harvest is delivered to the Cave in hand-carried plastic cases, and is received, without pumping, on conveyor belts. Vinification for red is CL, up to 10 days, with some Villages made OT. Impulsion press for reds. White is made in the progressive fashion with settling, fining of the must, cold fermentation, and blocked malo-lactic. The Muscat is centrifuged following fermentation. ❧ All wines for bottle sale are cold stabilized. No wood aging.

Vacqueyras

The communes of Vacqueyras are Vacqueyras and Sarrians (the plateau that begins there extends north to the portions of Vacqueyras and Gigondas below the slopes). Vacqueyras has been one of the named CDR-Villages (then *communales*) since 1955. Addresses of producers are 84 (Vaucluse).

Domaine du Clos de Caveau, SCA Domaine du Clos de Caveau (Georges Bungener and family), Vacqueyras

CDR-Villages Vacqueyras red. **Conscientiously made wines from a soil and situation that make them not quite typical of Vacqueyras, they feature leafy, spicy, sometimes** smokey aromas, berry to plum-like fruit, and a hint of stemminess. The 1979 was pure Grenache. Tasted in 1985, it was remarkably well preserved.

Single estate with 9 ha in vine in the qrt Caveau, just at the border with Gigondas behind the first ridge of the Dentelles de Montmirail mountains. The situation is very windy and the soil, consequently, is calcareous sand and clay dominated by silt. 7 ha of GR, some 30 years old, 1.5 ha SY about 10 years old, .5 ha of 7– and 4–year-old CS. Though these are trained on wire, harvesting is by hand, and productivity low. ❧ The SY and CS, harvested early, are vinified ST, 4 days. The GR harvested very late is ST, 7 to 15 days; Vaslin press. ❧ Wine rests at least 2 years in vat, no wood.

H Clos des Cazeaux, Archimbaud-Vache, Vacqueyras

CDR red, white, rosé; CDR-Villages Vacqueyras; Gigondas. **Two *cuvées* of Vacqueyras are made. "St.-Roch" is 80% Grenache, 20% Syrah. "Cuvée des Templiers" at 65% to 90% Syrah has usually been my preference for its balance and fragrance. Gigondas "Cuvée La Tour Sarrazine" is buttery and long with black, cayenne, and bell peppers in the nose.**

35 ha, of which 12 are Gigondas (mountain). All properties: 60% GR, 30% SY, 5% CS, 5% whites. M. Vache and his wife are the successors at this property to the late Jean Archimbaud, who formerly commercialized wine under this label jointly with his brother Maurice. ❧ OT2, 6 to 8 days. ❧ No wood.

H Domaine le Couroulou, GAEC Pierre Ricard et Fils, Vacqueyras

CDR-Villages Vacqueyras red and rosé. **Couroulou has long been a big spicy wine, packed with sometimes jammy fruit. Because of the increasing maturity of his Syrah vines, M. Ricard began in 1982 to compose his Vacqueyras of 50% Syrah and as little as 20% Grenache. The 1984 reached 60% and 10% of the two, respectively. The wine has gained in nerve, absence of thickness, an almost Bordeaux-like concentration, and aroma of resinous herbs and noble tar. The rosé was composed of 50% Mourvèdre, 50% Cinsault in 1983, 100% Mourvèdre in 1984 (flavors of green apple, apricot, toasted almond).**

30 ha, including 1 ha of CDR at Jonquières (Vaucluse). 1½ ha CS, 8 ha SY, ½ ha CR, 2 ha MV, the rest GR. ❧ Wine assembled from 70% CM, 17 to 19 days, and 30% ST, 4 to 5 days. Rosé "par saignée." ❧ 6 to 12 months in oak casks.

H Domaine de la Fourmone, Roger Combe et Fils, GAEC Vignerons, Vacqueyras

CDR red, white, rosé; CDR-Villages Vacqueyras red; Gigondas. **After development in bottle, which they very much require, the wines of Fourmone define the herbal/spicy end of the Vacqueyras taste spectrum. When young, and sometimes when first opened, they often smell vegetal, though they are neither thick nor astringent. Several *cuvées* of Vacqueyras are regularly distinguished by the weight of the wine and, consequently, the amount of wood age they are given. "Réserve du Paradis" spends the least time in wood, tends to be light, raspberryish, and peppery. The raspberries are blacker, the body more concentrated in "Trésor du Poète," kept longer in wood. "Selection du Maître de Chai" represents a late harvest from the oldest vines, including a hectare of centenarians, hence a higher alcohol degree and the longest time in wood; it can have, as in 1981, an astounding balance and**

DOMAINE DE COYEUX

CÔTES DU RHÔNE-VILLAGES
BEAUMES DE VENISE
APPELLATION CÔTES DU RHÔNE-VILLAGES CONTRÔLÉE

MIS EN BOUTEILLE AU DOMAINE
YVES & CATHERINE NATIVELLE
PROPRIÉTAIRES-RÉCOLTANTS À BEAUMES DE VENISE (VAUCLUSE)
PRODUCE OF FRANCE

750ml

DOMAINE LES GOUBERT

Beaumes de Venise

CÔTES DU RHÔNE   75 cl

APPELLATION CÔTES-DU-RHÔNE BEAUMES-DE-VENISE CONTRÔLÉE

JEAN PIERRE CARTIER PROPRIÉTAIRE RÉCOLTANT A GIGONDAS (Vse) FRANCE
MIS EN BOUTEILLE AU DOMAINE

PRODUIT DE FRANCE

MUSCAT DE BEAUMES-DE-VENISE

APPELLATION D'ORIGINE CONTRÔLÉE
vin doux naturel
DOMAINE ST-SAUVEUR

MISE EN BOUTEILLES AU DOMAINE par
MARCEL REY, PROPRIÉTAIRE RÉCOLTANT A AUBIGNAN (VAUCLUSE)

Muscat
de
Beaumes de Venise

APPELLATION MUSCAT DE BEAUMES DE VENISE CONTRÔLÉE
DOMAINE DE DURBAN

75 cl

LEYDIER et FILS PROPRIÉTAIRES, 84190 BEAUMES de VENISE (Vse) FRANCE

DOMAINE LE COUROULU

73 CL

Vacqueyras
CÔTES-DU-RHÔNE

APPELLATION CÔTES-DU-RHÔNE CONTRÔLÉE

Dépôt léger, Estomac rassuré
Elevé et mis en bouteille par :
Pierre RICARD et Fils - Propriétaires Récoltants - 84190 VACQUEYRAS

RAÇO-   RACÉJO

domaine "La fourmone"
VACQUEYRAS
APPELLATION CÔTES DU RHÔNE CONTRÔLÉE
Mis en bouteilles au Domaine
ROGER COMBE & FILS
G.A.E.C. VIGNERONS A VACQUEYRAS - VAUCLUSE - FRANCE

75 cl

Domaine de Cabasse
Séguret
Côtes-du-Rhône
Appellation Côtes-du-Rhône Contrôlée

73 cl

Elevé et mis en bouteille par :
Nadine LATOUR propriétaire - Séguret 84110 Vaison-la-Romaine France

CHATEAU DU TRIGNON

MISE EN BOUTEILLE AU Sablet

CÔTES-DU-RHÔNE
Appellation Côtes-du-Rhône-Villages Contrôlée
CHARLES ROUX ET FILS PROPRIÉTAIRES A GIGONDAS
84190 - BEAUMES DE VENISE
PRODUCE OF FRANCE   75cl e

complexity of richness with aromatic intensity. The elegant Gigondas often adds a floral nose and an extra "coteaux" distinction to the Combe spiciness.

18 ha of Vacqueyras: 65% GR, 15% SY, 10% MV, and .5 ha CS. 9 ha of Gigondas in the qrt "Petit Montmirail" (mountain) bear the name **L'Oustau Fauquet:** 65% GR plus 1.39 ha SY and 1 ha MV. An additional 3 ha of CDR include 1.3 ha in the commune of Beaumes-de-Venise. ❧ ST, 4 to 6 days, longer for Gigondas; hydraulic press. ❧ According to the *cuvée* the wines spend 6 to 12 months in oak casks, longer for Gigondas. They are neither fined nor filtered before bottling.

Domaine La Garrigue, GAEC A. Bernard et Fils, Vacqueyras

CDR red; CDR-Villages Vacqueyras red, white, rosé; Gigondas. **Bernards produce a robust red Vacqueyras, a full-flavored rosé that contains Mourvèdre, and a pure Clairette white whose fresh, round, full, lemon and nut-oil character in the 1983 was a pleasant surprise. All these are easy to sample at family-owned, spectacularly located hotel Les Florets in Gigondas where the carafe wine is Garrigue's VDT.**

30 ha of AOC in Vacqueyras, Sarrians, and Gigondas (1½ ha). All properties, red *cépages:* 65% GR, 10% each SY and MV, 15% CS. ❧ ST, 7 to 10 days. ❧ Reds age 2 to 3 years in cask.

H **Domaine des Lambertins,** Lambert Frères, Vacqueyras

CDR red, white, rosé; CDR-Villages Vacqueyras red. **If the wines of Vacqueyras form a spectrum from the herbal/spicy to the fungal/truffled, Lambertins defines the truffle type, with plums, cedar and vanilla besides. It is consistently the most elegant Vacqueyras.**

25 ha dispersed, with the Vacqueyras from the slopes portion. 80% GR, plus SY, CS, CR. Oldest vines 50 years of age. ❧ ST, 4 days, Vaslin and hydraulic presses. ❧ 6 months in wood.

H **Le Domaine du Château de Montmirail,** SCE Maurice Archimbaud and Monique Bouteiller, Vacqueyras

CDR red, rosé, white; CDR-Villages Vacqueyras red; Gigondas red. **Definitely marked by Syrah, Vacqueyras "l'Ermite" displays good acid balance and pronounced blackberry fruit. More typically Vacqueyras, including a smell of provençal herbs and tar, is the "Deux Frères," especially concentrated in 1983. The wooded character of Vacqueyras "Saint-Papes" is pleasantly in balance. Gigondas "Beauchamp" is a big, frankly tannic wine, sometimes a little "dusty," that gains a truffly, tarry Gigondas typicity with age. Especially notable for cleanliness and balance were 1983 and 1980.**

20 ha of CDR and CDR-Villages Vacqueyras, dispersed at Vacqueyras (most) and Sarrians, plateau. 60% GR, 15% SY, 10% CS, 10% CR, 5% diverse, including MV, BR, CT. M. Archimbaud inherited the Vacqueyras part of the estate from his father, Gabriel, who was the first estate-bottler of Vacqueyras. The family Archimbaud have been *vignerons* at Vacqueyras since the 16th century. Now mayor of Vacqueyras, M. Archimbaud has been joined in the estate by his daughter Monique and her husband, Jacques Bouteiller. The current name of the estate derives from the Gigondas part of the property, a vineyard entirely the creation of M. Maurice Archimbaud. This represents a

single estate with 30 ha in vine, surrounding the Château de Montmirail (mountain): 65% GR, 15% SY, 10% MV, 10% CS and CT. ❧ Following a "severe" triage of the harvest, ST with a "light" crushing and some destemming, 8 to 12 days; Vaslin press, only the first press is sometimes incorporated. ❧ The policy here is to rack as little as possible. The wood-aged wine passes 6 to 12 months maximum in oak casks. This includes the Vacqueyras "Cuvée des Saints-Papes" and Gigondas "Cuvée de Beauchamp." Vacqueyras "Cuvée des Deux Frères" (70% GR) and "Cuvée de l'Ermite" (50% SY) are not wooded.

H Domaine de Montvac, Jean Duserre-Audibert, Vacqueyras

CDR; CDR-Villages Vacqueyras; Gigondas. **M. Duserre lists himself as an oenologist on his label, and certainly is a producer to watch. Vacqueyras wines are clean, well balanced and complexly fragrant, tending toward flowers, "sous-bois," and truffles, with a very deep berry fruit, especially well exhibited in the 1981 after some development in bottle. Very aromatic 25% Mourvèdre _cuvée_ of 1984. Gigondas was commercialized in bottle for the first time in the 1982 vintage.**

18 ha dispersed in Vacqueyras and Sarrians (slopes and plateau). 3 ha of Gigondas (mountain). All properties: 62% GR, 8% CR, 14% SY, 12% MV, 4% CS. Some 70-year-old vines. ❧ CL, 8 to 12 days. ❧ Wood age is dependent on the character of the wine, the time in wood tending to be less the more MV is in the _cuvée_.

Château des Roques, Dusser-Beraud, Sarrians

CDR; CDR-Villages Vacqueyras red and rosé. **M. Edouard Dusser, president of the Vacqueyras growers, makes a robust, strong-flavored red Vacqueyras and regularly wins prizes for a delicious Vacqueyras rosé ("par saignée").**

30 ha of AOC in Vacqueyras and Sarrians. GR, SY, CS. ❧ ST, 8 to 10 days, Vaslin press. ❧ 12 to 18 months in vat. "A little" wood age.

Domaine Le Sang des Cailloux, SCEA Domaine Le Sang des Cailloux (Jean Ricard et Serge Férigoule), Sarrians

CDR-Villages Vacqueyras red and rosé. **Somewhat "violent" Syrah aroma used to make M. Ricard wish he had more old-vine Carignan. Nevertheless, it is an attractive wine, warm, tending to black cherries, spice, vanilla, and a touch of licorice.**

17 ha all plateau, 60% GR (some 100-year-old vines), 30% SY, 5% CS (40 years), 5% CR (40 years). The name of the domaine ("blood of the cobblestones") refers apparently to the red clay under the stones of the Sarrians plateau. ❧ OT (about ⅓ used to be made CM), 4 to 5 days; Vaslin press. ❧ At least 6 months in wood.

Cave des Vignerons de Vacqueyras, "Les Vins du Troubadour," Vacqueyras

The Vacqueyras wines tend to be "high-pitched," light bodied, with good berry fruit and definitely at the fungal end of the Vacqueyras taste spectrum. My preference is currently the CDR-Villages Vacqueyras "2 Bunches" (30% CM). The Vacqueyras rosé, as with others from the area, should not be overlooked. It is fresh, full of raspberries, and while dry, pleasantly round. The Gigondas, pleasant enough, seems lighter-colored than most.

Founded 1957. 77.14% AOC. 134 members, all of whom have land either at Vacqueyras or at Sarrians. Some members also have parcels in Gigondas and Beaumes-de-Venise. The cooperative of Vacqueyras produces more than half of the CDR-Villages Vacqueyras wine, plus Gigondas, and Muscat de Beaumes-de-Venise (first time in 1985). ❧ About half the Vacqueyras is produced by CM, then assembled with ST ($^2/_3$ destemmed), with more of the latter in *cuvées* for aging. Rosé "par saignée." The Cave made a white for the first time in 1985, also "par saignée," that is, by drawing off after skin contact. ❧ The wines are filtered through diatomaceous earth before being lodged in vat or barrel for aging. Vacqueyras "1 Bunch" and "2 Bunches" are not wood aged, whereas that labeled "Vieilli en Foudre" is aged in oak casks. Gigondas is produced in both unwooded and "Vieilli en Foudre" versions. The Cave joined the trend among cooperatives to produce "Domaine" wines from the properties of individual members in 1985. CDR **De la Mourelle, Du Grand Prieur,** and **De la Curnière** will not be wooded. Vacqueyras **Château des Hauts Garrigues** will be. Wines are millipore-filtered before bottling. Some labels identify the Cave des Vignerons as **Les Vignerons Réunis** or as **Les Producteurs Associés.**

Vacqueyras *Négociants:*

Pascal S.A., Négociant-vinificateur, Vacqueyras

I view Vacqueyras "Cuvée Spéciale" as Pascal's best wine, usually dark, rich, and long-lived, developing a bouquet of truffles and even tar—a wine usually at or near the top of all Vacqueyras. Outstanding years include 1972, 1978, 1981.

As a *vinificateur,* the house of Pascal buys grapes and makes them into wine. The vinification is ST, with some destemming, 6 to 8 days. The wines are aged in vat, not wood, "because of the tendency of Grenache to maderize." Owner Denis Cheron says he "got rid of barrels 20 years ago" in response to the exigencies of southern Rhône climate and *cépages*. The wines of Pascal's making are:

Gigondas
    Until 1981 made from grapes produced at what is now Cheron's own Domaine du Grand Montmirail vineyard. For details on that wine, now estate bottled, see Gigondas.
CDR-Villages Vacqueyras
H CDR-Villages Vacqueyras "Cuvée Spéciale"
CDR "Vinification Personelle"
    Regarded by Cheron as his top of the line, it is made from old-vine GR and SY, mostly from Vacqueyras. The wine is given an especially long aging in underground vats, a process that Cheron calls the "opposite" of wood aging.
CDR
CDV
VDP de Vaucluse

Also in the Pascal line are wines that are bought from their producers, including Châteauneuf-du-Pape, Tavel, Crozes-Hermitage, Saint-Joseph, CDL, and three wines from particular domaines:

CDR Domaine de la Brune
　　Vineyards at Vacqueyras.
CDR Domaine de Roquevignan
　　For details see Rochegude.
CDT Terroir Saint-Rémy
　　For details see Coteaux du Tricastin.

Vieux Clocher, Arnoux et Fils, négociant-vinificateur-éleveur, Vacqueyras

　　As a *vinificateur* M. Arnoux buys grapes for his Vacqueyras "Vieux Clocher" from his own property's production, which several years back was 18 ha at Vacqueyras and Sarrians: 80% GR, 10% CS, 5% SY, plus CR and MV. 🐝 At that time vinification was ST, 6 to 8 days for the Vacqueyras, 8 to 10 days for Arnoux's Gigondas. 🐝 The wines were aged up to 2 years in oak casks.

Sablet

The sole commune is Sablet. Addresses are 84110 Sablet unless otherwise noted.

H Domaine Les Goubert, Jean-Pierre Cartier, Gigondas
　　See Gigondas.

Domaine du Pourra, Jean-Claude Chassagne

CDR; CDR-Villages Sablet; CDR-Villages Séguret; Gigondas; Rasteau VDN. **There is considerable variation in quality from barrel to barrel, and some of the bottled wine I have tasted might have benefited from additional racking. The best wine from here may be the Séguret "La Combe."**
　　16 ha of Gigondas in the qrt Pourra (slope) is 75% GR, 15% MV, 5% SY, 5% CS. M. Chassagne makes Villages from 8 ha at Sablet (slopes and plateau) and 6½ ha at Séguret (slope). The Sablet **"Les Abeilles"** is planted 75% to GR, plus CS, CR, and CT. Séguret **"La Combe"** is 75% GR, 10% MV, 10% CS, and 5% whites. 4 ha of CDR at Violès is 90% GR plus CS. 1½ ha of VDN Rasteau vines. 🐝 OT1, at least 10 days, Vaslin press. 🐝 1½ years in oak casks for reds. VDN Rasteau is cold-stabilized and then also wood-aged.

H Château de Trignon, Charles Roux, Gigondas
　　See Gigondas.

Domaine de Piaugier, Marc Autran et Fils

CDR red; CDR-Villages Sablet; Gigondas. **Formerly sold in bulk to the *négociants*, wine from this estate was sold by the proprietors in bottle for the first time in 1982. The beginnings have been auspicious, especially the berry-smokey 1984 CDR and the 15% Mourvèdre Sablet 1984 (tasted from vat). Even this little Mourvèdre, from 50-year-old vines, was enough to mark the wine intensely with its solidity, finesse, and florality. Gigondas was made for the first time in 1985.**
　　23 ha at Sablet (slope and plateau) are planted 60% to GR, 20% MV, 15% SY, 5% CS. Half the vines are more than 50 years old, some 80. Also 2 ha of Gigondas (slope):

80% GR, 20% SY. 🍇 OT2, 9 to 10 days for Sablet, 12 for Gigondas; hydraulic press. The press juice is incorporated immediately in the Sablet, later in the Gigondas. 🍇 The CDR is not wood-aged, the Sablet is given about 6 months in oak casks, and the Gigondas will be given 1 year followed by 8 months in bottle before sale.

H Domaine de Verquière, GAEC Chamfort Frères

CDR red and rosé; CDR-Villages Sablet; Rasteau VDN. **The big, dark wines of Verquière have usually been strong enough to benefit nobly from their prolonged pre-bottle aging, developing in a truffle, tar, licorice direction. Nevertheless, the truffles plus cedar were already present in the livelier, leafier, unwooded 1979. The rosé, usually not vintage dated, is strong and minerally in the Gigondas fashion. The Rasteau VDN, produced only in certain years, is one of the best.**

30 ha dispersed in Sablet (15 ha), Vacqueyras, and Violès: 65–70% GR, plus MV, CS, SY, CR. Former proprietor M. Louis Chamfort is now retired; it was he who presented the dossier that earned for Sablet its Villages AOC in 1974. 🍇 OT2, 8 to 10 days, hydraulic press. 🍇 Usually the Villages wine spends a considerable time in vat before aging is finished in large oak casks, the time of the whole process being regulated by the space in cask required to carry out M. Louis Chamfort's principle of selling in bottle only one mature vintage at a time. In 1983, however, while sales of the 1977 as treated in the old fashion were about to begin, a 1979 that had not been in wood was also for sale. An unwooded CDR for current drinking is available.

The cooperative is:

Cave Coopérative "Le Gravillas"

Founded 1935. 67.75% AOC. CDR from Sablet (about half), Camaret, Roaix, Séguret, Vaison-la-Romaine, Violès.

CDR red and rosé; *CDR white; CDR-Villages Sablet red; Gigondas red.

Séguret

The sole commune is Séguret. Addresses of producers are 84110 Séguret.

H Domaine de Cabasse, Nadine Latour

CDR; CDR-Villages Séguret. **Firm, leafy, sometimes floral, sometimes spicy, with good nerve and attractive raspberry fruit, that even seemed to have a touch of cream in the 1983 Villages. During the summer season one may dine or stay en pension at the attractive inn on the property.**

25 ha on the border between Séguret and Sablet. 60% GR, plus CS, SY, MV, PL, and CR. RS planted, plus GR blanc and CT. 🍇 OT1, 20 days, Vaslin press. 🍇 10 to 12 months in oak casks.

"La Fiole du Chevalier d'Elbène"; Château de la Diffre, Meffre Frères et Fils

See "CDR of the Lower Ouvèze and Plan de Dieu," Château La Couronçonne.

Domaine de l'Amandine, Jean-Pierre Verdeau

CDR red. **Big, medium-colored wine of good acidity, as the others in the vicinity**

Looking down the Ouvèze valley from Roaix toward Séguret (Vaucluse). Photo courtesy of Robert Burns.

seem to be. At one time the wine was commercialized by the *négociant* Pascal at Vacqueyras (no longer) under the name domaine de la Seraphine.

35 ha, dispersed. GR, plus SY, CS, and a little MV. 🍇 ST, around 15 days, continous press. 🍇 No wood.

The cooperative is:

Les Vignerons de Roaix-Séguret

Founded 1960. 84% AOC. CDR from the communes of Roaix and Séguret (the majority), Sablet, Vaison-la-Romaine. CDR red, rosé, and white; CDR-Villages Roaix rosé; CDR-Villages red in 4 *cuvées:* *CDR-Villages Roaix (unwooded), *CDR-Villages Séguret (unwooded), CDR-Villages Roaix "Réserve St.-Roch" (aged in oak), and CDR-Villages Séguret "Réserve Bergers" (aged in oak).

──── CDR-VILLAGES ON THE SLOPES OF VENTABREN ────

Ventabren is the name one hears at Cairanne for the "mountain," across the valley and north of the Ouvèze from the Dentelles, on the flanks of which the CDR-Villages of Roaix, Rasteau, and Cairanne are located. It is a high plateau, really, and on top, at about 400 meters, is a layer of enormous cobblestones as big as the biggest at Châteauneuf-du-Pape. It is the southwest-facing slopes that descend from there and spread onto the "garrigues" of the lower plateau (an extension of the Plan de Dieu), however, that are important to the vine. The communes are presented below from E to W.

Roaix

The sole commune is 84110 Roaix.

The cooperative of Roaix is:

Cave des Vignerons de Roaix-Séguret
    See Séguret.

Rasteau (and Cru VDN)

The commune of Rasteau has been Villages (with name of the commune) since 1966. Since 1944, Rasteau has been a *cru* with its own local AOC for red, white and rosé VDN (see Beaumes-de-Venise) produced from parcels planted at least 90% to Grenaches in Rasteau and certain parts of the adjoining communes of Sablet and Cairanne. The normal maximum productivity allowed is 30 hectoliters of must per hectare. The minimum alcohol in the finished wine must be at least 21.5%, of which 15% must be achieved before "mutage." An additional AOC Rasteau Rancio is reserved for VDN that must have been aged to the point that it has acquired the special *rancio* taste. Up to now most Rasteau VDN has been the simple white Rasteau, usually called "golden" *(doré)*. Locally, Rasteau is more often presented and identified as an *apéritif* than as a dessert wine, and I prefer it for a certain bitter sweetness to the more pronouncedly aromatic Muscat in the center of a half of Cavaillon melon.

Addresses of producers are 84110 Rasteau, unless otherwise noted.

Domaine des Coteaux des Travers, Robert Charavin

CDR red and rosé; CDR-Villages Rasteau red; VDN Rasteau. **The CDR are finer and usually peppery, where the Villages wines are frankly tannic and crammed with fruit. Their density might be excessive but for M. Charavin's liking neither oxidation nor a "goût de bois" (taste of wood) in his wines.**

25 ha, dispersed 2/3 at Rasteau, 1/3 at Cairanne. GR, CS, SY, MV, CR. 🍇 Wines are assembled from some OT2 and some CM, with very little of the latter in the Villages. 🍇 No wood.

H **Domaine des Girasols,** Paul Joyet

CDR red and rosé; CDR-Villages Rasteau red. **M. Joyet first vinified his own grapes in 1979, and began Villages in 1983. Very aromatic, they develop their own vanilla and velvety texture, with cherry and plum, when unwooded. Though they begin astringent, I prefer that to the dryness and effacement of their florality in the wooded version. Remarkable 1984 Villages with broom flowers in the finish. Unwooded CDRs of 1983, 1984, and 1985 are scarcely less fine.**

14 ha in vine on this single estate. Plateau above and descending slopes. 70% GR, plus CS, old-vine CR, MV. Average age of vines is 40 years, 70 years the oldest. 🍇 OT1,

Domaine la Soumade

Rasteau

Côtes du Rhône

APPELLATION CÔTES DU RHÔNE VILLAGES CONTROLÉE

1982   mis en bouteillé au domaine   **75 cl.**

Roméro André propriétaire récoltant à Rasteau Vaucluse

Produit de France   Nº 8927

DOMAINE DE LA GRANGE NEUVE

PRODUCE   OF FRANCE

1984

RASTEAU

CÔTES-DU-RHÔNE

APPELLATION CÔTES-DU-RHÔNE RASTEAU CONTRÔLÉE

MIS EN BOUTEILLE AU DOMAINE

BRESSY - MASSON Propriétaire-récoltant à Rasteau (Vse) FRANCE   75 cl

1983

DOMAINE DES GIRASOLS

RASTEAU

COTES DU RHONE

Appellation COTES DU RHONE VILLAGES controlée   75 cl

MIS EN BOUTEILLE AU DOMAINE

Paul Joyet Propriétaire Récoltant à RASTEAU (Vaucluse)
FRANCE

RASTEAU

APPELLATION   CONTRÔLÉE

G R E N A C H E

VIN DOUX NATUREL

Louis CHAMFORT

PROPRIÉTAIRE-VITICULTEUR A SABLET (Vaucluse)

**DOMAINE
LE CHATEAU**

CÔTES-DU-RHÔNE

APPELLATION COTES DU RHONE CONTROLEE

Mis en Bouteille au Domaine par
S.C.E.A. Domaines Rieu-Hérail - 84290 Cairanne (FRANCE)   750 ml

PRODUCE OF FRANCE

CÔTES du RHÔNE

APPELLATION CÔTES-DU-RHÔNE CONTRÔLEE

*Grand Vin de
l'Oratoire S.Martin
Cairanne*

F. ALARY & ses FILS
Propriétaires à CAIRANNE (Vaucluse)

73 cl

Domaine
Rabasse Charavin

CAIRANNE
COTES du RHONE
VILLAGES

APPELLATION COTES DU RHONE VILLAGES CONTROLEE
CORINNE COUTURIER
PROPRIÉTAIRE RÉCOLTANT A CAIRANNE VAUCLUSE
MIS EN BOUTEILLE A LA PROPRIÉTÉ

Cairanne
Côtes du Rhône Village
APPELLATION COTES DU RHONE CONTROLEE
DOMAINE BRUSSET   75cl

A. BRUSSET & FILS PROPRIÉTAIRES RÉCOLTANTS A CAIRANNE 84 290 (FRANCE)

MIS EN BOUTEILLE A LA PROPRIÉTÉ

8 to 10 days, Vaslin press. ❧ 1 to 2 years in vat. A part of some bottlings spends 6 months in wood.

H Domaine de la Grange Neuve (will become **Domaine Bressy-Masson**), Bressy-Masson

CDR red; CDR-Villages Rasteau red; VDN Rasteau; VDN Rasteau Rancio. **Big, flavory red wines, almost Châteauneuf in style, have achieved better balance under M. Thierry Masson. Mourvèdre usually strikes a floral note in the Villages. None was made in 1983 due to lack of Grenache, but 1984 with its dark red fruits was aromatic and finely tannic. M. Masson began to make some of the rare red Rasteau VDN in 1983.**

29 ha of Rasteau, 5 ha CDR at Sablet and Sérignan. All properties: 70% GR, 10% each SY, MV, and CR. Some 80-year-old vines. ❧ ST, 8 days, Vaslin press. ❧ Villages wine receives 6 to 18 months in oak casks. The Rasteau Rancio, a wine with its own AOC—of which the late M. Bressy and now his successor have been the only makers—is aged 5 years in oak.

Château de la Gardine, Gaston Brunel et Fils

See Châteauneuf-du-Pape.

Domaine de la Girardière, Louis Girard

CDR red and rosé (1985); CDR-Villages Rasteau red; VDN Rasteau. **First impressions are of big, chewy, high-alcohol wines with cherry-plum-prune fruit really too supple in 1982. Better balance might be achieved in 1984 with its livelier acid and fresher aromatics.**

M. Girard and his son between them have 34 ha in Rasteau (most), slope and plateau, Séguret and St.-Roman-de-Malegarde; 60% GR, 15% CS, 10% SY, 10% CR, plus Aubun. MV, and a few white *cépages* recently planted. Some 100-year-old vines. ❧ M. Girard and his son vinify their production separately. OT2, 4 to 8 days, Vaslin press. Rosé "par saignée." ❧ Wines are held in vat. M. Girard bottles, his son does not.

Domaine des Nymphes, GAEC Meyer Fils et Gendre

CDR; CDR-Villages Rasteau; VDN Rasteau. **Formerly with the cooperative, the Meyers made their first wine in 1980, first bottled in 1982. Villages is light, but well structured, raspberryish, herbal, and with a whiff of calcareous soil. Wood age does not seem to be to its advantage. The domaine makes a little of the red Rasteau Vin Doux Naturel, as well as the "doré," and is aging some of both in casks with the possibility of leaving some long enough to become "Rancio." Here my reaction to the wood is favorable, the red in particular bidding fair to be one of the very best VDN, and definitely better in the wooded than in the unwooded version.**

33 ha at Rasteau, dispersed (slopes). 80% GR; 15% SY, MV, CS together; and 5% CR. 13–ha single estate in Tulette, gravel subsoil: 85% GR, 15% CR. ❧ OT2, 7 to 12 days, Vaslin press. *Cépages* fermented separately, rosé "par saignée." VDN Doré "par saignée" also. No press juice in the VDN red. ❧ Some Villages aged in vat, some in wood.

H Domaine Rabasse-Charavin, Corinne Couturier, Cairanne

See Cairanne.

H **Château de Trignon,** Charles Roux, Gigondas
> See Gigondas.

H **Domaine de Verquière, Chamfort Frères, Sablet**
> See Sablet.

Domaine de Beaurenard, Paul Coulon et Fils, Châteauneuf-du-Pape
> See Châteauneuf-du-Pape.

H **Domaine la Soumade,** André Roméro
CDR red; CDR-Villages Rasteau red; VDN Rasteau. **M. Roméro, whose father belonged to the cooperative at Rasteau, made the property's first wine in 1979, first bottled in 1981. It is hard to make anything but a heavy wine at Rasteau, but neither CDR nor CDR-Villages Rasteau here are; the Villages especially retains a full, ripe, pleasantly stony and tannic character. Began red VDN 1985.**

22 dispersed ha in Rasteau (2/3) and Sablet (1/3). 60% GR, 20% SY, 5% CS, 5% CR, 10% MV. 🍇 OT2, 15 to 21 days, Vaslin press. 🍇 Up to 1984 1½ to 2 years in vat. Beginning with the 1985 harvest, about half the wine will be aged for not more than 1 year in oak casks.

The cooperative is:

Cave des Vignerons de Rasteau
> Founded 1925. 85.86% AOC. 204 members from Rasteau (majority) and the adjacent communes.
> CDR red, white, rosé; CDR-Villages Rasteau red; *VDN Rasteau red; VDN Rasteau doré.

Cairanne

The sole commune is Cairanne, which is one of the original CDR-Villages (then *communales*) dating from 1953. Addresses of producers are 84290 Cairanne, unless otherwise noted.

GAEC Alary Daniel et Fils
> See **Domaine de l'Oratoire Saint-Martin.**

H **Domaine de l'Ameillaud;** H **Domaine le Château;** GAFF Le Château, proprietor; SCEA Les Domaines Rieu-Herail, producers
Members of the Albert Rieu family conduct business under two organizational hats. Previously just CDR, the first CDR-Villages Cairanne was made by l'Ameillaud in 1983; it shows a fine balance of wood and fruit. Le Château is also aimed to be of Villages quality, though it does not yet have all the required *cépages* in production. Presence of old-vine Carignan augments body in this rich wine that shows fungal and violet fragrances typical of the Cairanne "mountain" zone.

23 ha in AOC on the lower slopes with 7 additional planted (Ameillaud). Le Château is 10 ha (mountain). Château also owns and Rieu-Herail produces **Domaine la Béraude,** a 22-ha estate at Cairanne, part of which is commercialized by the Auchan

Provençal folk dancer at the village festival of Cairanne (Vaucluse). Photo courtesy of Robert Burns.

supermarket chain. All properties: 50% GR, 15–20% CR, 15% CS, 5–10% SY, 5% CN
and diverse. 🍇 Some machine-harvested grapes are automatically CL. The rest are
destemmed without being crushed in a new Vaslin *éggrappoir* (destemmer). 7 to 10 days,
Vaslin press. 🍇 Some malolactic fermentation is conducted in wood. Wine for bottle is
aged 6 to 18 months in oak casks.

Domaine du Banvin, Zanti-Cumino

CDR red, white, rosé; CDR-Villages Cairanne red. **While no disrespect is meant to
their Villages, a decent enough wine, the really exciting wine here is the CDR
labeled "Cuvée St.-Genest" for the qrt of its origin. It is a lesson in the special
aroma of old field-blended plantation in which one smells flowers, wild herbs,**

butter, vanilla—although the wine is unwooded—pepper, and in the oldest example in the series, a 1980 given 4 years of aging in vat, the cooler resins.

18 ha, almost all mountain. GR, including 7–8 ha of old vines in which other *cépages* are field-blended, 3 ha SY, plus CS, CT, and a little CR. M. Zanti works the vineyard and son-in-law M. Cumino is in charge at the *cave*. 🍇 OT1, 8 to 10 days. Rosé "par saignée." 🍇 No wood. Generally about 2 years in vat.

H **Domaine Brusset**, André Brusset et Fils

CDR red and white; CDR-Villages Cairanne red, white, rosé; CDR-Villages red. **Very soft, gold-green CDR-Villages Cairanne white. CDR-Villages Cairanne rosé is big and flavory, includes about 15% Mourvèdre. Regular Cairanne red is Grenache with about 20% Syrah, 10% Mourvèdre, plus some Cinsault. Cairanne "Réserve des Templiers" is around 75% Grenache and 25% Mourvèdre. While the two latter are robust, warm, wooded wines, perhaps it is the new press that makes the tannin of recent years less rough than formerly.**

30 ha dispersed, some *garrigues,* some mountain. Red *cépages:* 60% GR, 5% CS, 20% SY, 15% MV. Whites: 65% CT, 25% BR, 10% UN. 15 ha CDR "Coteaux des Bruyères" from Mondragon. Red *cépages:* 25–30% GR, 25% CS, 25% SY, 10–15% MV, 10% CR. Whites: 40% CT, 40% BR, 20% UN. CDR-Villages without commune name was made from this property in 1984. 17 ha Gigondos added 1986. 🍇 OT2 7-8 days, impulsion press. Rosé part direct pressing, part "saignée." 🍇 1 to 2 years in oak casks for Cairanne. "Serre-Blanc" is a second Cairanne label for reds. "Coteaux des Travers" (on the neck label) is the traditional name for the Brusset Cairannes.

Le Château, Domaines Rieu-Herail

See Domaine de l'Ameillaud.

Cave des Coteaux de Cairanne

The cooperative puts almost half its production into an extensive line of bottled wines. Of these, "Saignée de Queyran" is a Cairanne rosé, distinguished by more Grenache, less Cinsault and less Carignan from the plain CDR rosé. CDR Domaine des Combes (no wood) comes from the property of the cooperative's president, M. Michel Lacrotte, and is composed of Grenache, a little Carignan, and 20% Syrah. The Villages red comes in 4 grades. CDR-Cairanne "Cave des Coteaux" with about 15% Cinsault is for drinking young. The next 3, now each at about 80% Grenache, show increasing amounts of Syrah, with "Grande Réserve" at about 10%, "Réserve des Voconces" at 15%, and "Cuvée Antique" at 20%. Formerly the Voconces was at about 95% Grenache. The change reflects increasing maturity of the Syrah vines. Future will see addition of Mourvèdre when they attain similar maturity. My preference has always been for the "Grande Réserve" and for the unwooded version of "Cuvée Antique."

Founded 1929. 84.18% AOC. 260 members from Cairanne and adjacent communes of St.-Roman-de-Malegarde and Travaillan. 🍇 Grapes from the 3 zones of Cairanne, *garrigues,* mountain, and bank of the river (Aygues) are received separately. OT2, in part CL. CM for some wines beginning with 1985. 🍇 Cairannes "Grande Réserve" and "Réserve des Voconces" are aged in oak casks, the Voconces somewhat longer. Cairanne "Cuvée Antique" is aged two ways. Part is aged in new oak small barrels. Some bottled earlier is not aged in wood, but is aged in bottle before sale.

H Domaines de l'Oratoire Saint-Martin, Frédéric Alary et ses Fils

CDR red, white, rosé; CDR-Villages Cairanne red. **The Alary family have been vignerons at Cairanne since 1692, and were among the first on the eastern bank of the Rhône to refer to their wines in the 19th century as Côtes du Rhône (in the plural form). They were first at Cairanne to bottle. The two Alary sons, Bernard and Daniel, conducted their properties together and assembled wines from their two productions until 1983. A small part of the production was a Villages Cairanne, which happened to have the most finesse of all. 1981 "Réserve des Seigneurs de Saint-Martin" (the stock of which was still for sale in 1985 by both brothers) is representative of its class, with concentrated fruit, fine, full, buttery, and at the same time lively. Now the brothers have separated their properties and winemaking facilities into 2 domaines reported on separately below.**

GAEC Alary Daniel et Denis

19 ha, of which 1/3 are AOC on slopes and garrigues. Red *cépages* for 90% of the property: 40% GR, 15% CR, 20% SY, 20% MV, 5% CS. Whites for 10% of the property: 50% CT, 30% BR, 20% RS. 🍇 Reds 20% vinified CM, 8 to 10 days; will be sold separately as CDR "Cuvée Spéciale" (20% MV in 1984). 80% OT in stainless steel vats, 6 to 7 days. Vaslin press. 🍇 Reds given 6 months (CDR) to 2 years (Villages) in oak casks. AOC wines of their separate vinification for sale in 1985 were CDR rosé 1983, CDR white 1984, CDR red 1983, and CDR red "Cuvée Spéciale" 1984.

GAEC Saint-Martin (Alary Bernard et Fils)

17 ha, of which 12 are on the slopes near the new cave in qrt St.-Martin, which first operated in 1985. 55% GR, 20% SY, 7– 8% CR, a little CS, CL, MR. 🍇 OT2 with optional destemming in stainless steel vats, 7 to 8 days. A few batches CM are assembled with the rest. Vaslin press. 🍇 12 to 18 months in oak casks for red. M. Alary had not yet marketed red wines of his separate vinification by fall 1985.

Domaine le Plaisir, Gérard Pierrefeu

At its best, this full, rich, fairly compact, dark-fruited Cairanne tends to ripeness and an intriguing suggestion of smoke. Spicy and with good nerve in 1981, not as full in 1982, drier in 1983. M. Pierrefeu is president of the Interprofessional Committee of the Côtes du Rhône.

10 ha of Cairanne, mostly on the lower slopes out onto the *garrigues*. 10 ha of CDR on the Plan de Dieu at Travaillan. 60% GR, 15% SY, 15% CS, some CR and 2 ha of 5– year-old GR blanc, CT, BR. 🍇 OT2 with fewer crushed for lighter wines, more for *vins de garde*. 3 to 4 days for *primeur*, 6 to 7 days for others. Vaslin press. 🍇 Aging is conducted for about 18 months in stainless steel.

Domaine de la Présidente, SCEA Max Aubert, Sainte-Cécile-les-Vignes

CDR red, white, rosé; CDR-Villages Cairanne red. **Sound Cairanne, leaning to prune and licorice, that misses being of the first quality. CDR "Cuvée Simon Alexandre" 1982 showed a balanced handling of the wood, for those who want to taste the effect of oak. My preference from the domaine, however, remains the fresh, fruity,** peppery CDR. M. Aubert, who is president of the wine fraternity La Commanderie des Costes du Rhône as well as of the Université du Vin, is one of the very few producers of Marc des Côtes du Rhône brandy.

A single estate with 30 ha of Cairanne on the flat between the villages of Cairanne and Ste.-Cécile-les-Vignes. 60% GR, 15–20% SY, 10% each CS and CR. Wine from an additional 50 ha of CDR **Domaine de la Beaume** at Suze-la-Rousse (Drôme) is commercialized with the name of the estate by *négociant* firm Louis Mousset of Châteauneuf-du-Pape. 1985 was Aubert's first wine from 30-ha **Château de Gallifet** at Cairanne. ➋ CL, 4 to 5 days, with the Cairanne including 10% to 15% SY by CM, 15 days. ➋ CDR "Cuvée Simon Alexandre" receives 6 to 8 months in small oak barrels, 1/3 new by rotation.

H **Domaine Rabasse-Charavin,** Corinne Couturier

CDR red, white, rosé; CDR-Villages Cairanne red; CDR-Villages Rasteau red (first 1985); CDR-Villages red; VDN Rasteau. **Mme. Couturier made her first wine here in 1984, and this traditionally rich, compact, well-balanced Cairanne as made by her father, M. Abel Charavin, was if anything intensified in its fragrance of violet, black pepper, even mint, and cassis-to-black-raspberry lozenge fruit. In July 1985, a 20% Syrah batch with a dustier tannin was resting in vat before lodgement in cask. Already bottled was a minuscule quantity of an unwooded version with a little less Syrah, more Mourvèdre, which if it can be found will be a stunning revelation of the pure originality of this wine. The wooded lot was released in 1986 as "Cuvée d'Estevenas."**

7.5 ha of Cairanne, mostly on slopes. 7.5 ha at Rasteau. 5 ha CDR at Mondragon (which can also be declared Villages without the commune name). All properties: 62% GR, 13% SY, 5.3% CS, 5% MV, 9.7% CR, 3% CT, 2% BR. Some 100–year-old vines. CDR tends to be produced from younger vines, Villages from older ones. ➋ OT2, 5 to 8 days, horizontal and hydraulic presses. ➋ Normally Cairanne gets about 1 year, CDR about 6 months in oak casks. It was the late M. Charavin's idea to "soften" not "oxidize" the wine.

GAEC Saint-Martin (Alary Barnard et Fils)

See **Domaines de l'Oratoire Saint-Martin.**

10

North of the Aygues

I N GENERAL this is an area that begins to harvest ten days to two weeks later than the southern Vaucluse, often making it later to harvest than the northern Rhône. An exception to the pattern of movement northeast toward cooler climates is in the Aygues valley itself, where at Vinsobres, the mistral overhead clears the air, while the slopes are at the same time sheltered from the wind and exceptionally sunny and warm.

MASSIF D'UCHAUX

CDR-Villages Rochegude

The sole commune is Rochegude (Drôme). Addresses of producers are 26130 Rochegude.

Domaine de Roquevignan, Pierre Bourret

CDR red, white, rosé; CDR-Villages Rochegude. **M. Bourret bottles his own Villages, the production of which he is increasing. The wine is composed of Grenache and 20–25% Syrah. The CDR white, distributed by Pascal, is nearly 100% Ugni blanc: characteristically floral, rich and Burgundy-like in 1982, distinctly tart in 1984, suppler and a little woody in 1985. The Pascal-bottled CDR red can also taste wooded (isn't).**

55 ha in vine, dispersed in Rochegude and Mondragon (slope and lower plateau). All properties: 75% GR, 10% CR, 5% SY, 5% MV, 5% UN, plus CT, GR blanc. Part of the property is within sight of Château de la Fonsalette at neighboring Lagarde-Paréol. OT2, 8 days, Vaslin press. CDR rosé "par saignée." Likes to avoid malolactic for white. 90% of the production is *élevé* and put in the bottle with the Domaine name by the *négociant* firm Pascal of Vacqueyras. 3 months in casks for estate bottled Villages.

Domaine du Gourget, Louis Tourtin

CDR red and rosé. **Berry-lozenge fruit and resinous herbs, including lavender, show well in the wines from vat (e.g., 1984) and from a short time in cask (e.g., 1983). M. Tourtin believes his clients, however, want the bottled wine to have a taste of wood, which it does, sometimes to excess. Nevertheless, a superb balance was achieved in the 1980.**

A 65-ha single estate, all in the commune of Rochegude, on slopes, lower plateau and plain (siliceous soil) just below Domaine de la Guicharde in Mondragon. 70% GR, 20% SY, 5% MV and CS together, 5% CR, and a little CT. Some 60-year-old vines. ST, in part destemmed, 3–4 days; pneumatic press. Rosé "par saignée." Red is aged first in vat, then filtered through diatomaceous earth before being lodged in oak casks, sometimes for several years according to the pace of bottle sales. At present only about 10% of the production is estate-bottled.

The cooperative is:

Société Coopérative Agricole de Vinification, "Cave des Vignerons de Rochegude"

Founded 1959. 71.6% AOC. CDR from the communes of Rochegude (Drôme), Bollène, Cairanne, Lagarde-Paréol, Mondragon, Orange, Piolenc, Ste.-Cécile-les-Vignes, Travaillan, Uchaux (Vaucluse), Suze-la-Rousse (Drôme). CDT from Baume-de-Transit, Chamaret, Colonzelle, and Valaurie.

CDR white; CDR-Villages Rochegude in 4 *cuvées:* *"Cuvée du Président," "Cuvée le Boulidou" (the lightest), *"Cuvée la Cassuise" (more *corsé),* and "Vieilli en Futs de Chêne" (oak-aged); CDT.

CDR of the Massif d'Uchaux

(The producers are listed around the *massif,* beginning by moving south from Rochegude.)
Addresses of producers are 84 (Vaucluse).

H Château de la Fonsalette, Lagarde-Paréol

See Châteauneuf-du-Pape, Château Rayas.

Domaine de la Renjardière, SC de la Renjardière (Family Dupond), Sérignan-du-Comtat

CDR red and rosé. **The present *encépagement* represents recent increase in the proportion of Syrah, which now allows a better balance of both Grenache and Syrah to Carignan than formerly. The result is more roundness and length in these characteristically light bodied and spicy wines.**

110 ha in vine, single estate. 11% SY, 4% CT (employed in the rosé), 51% GR, 10% CS, and 24% CR. Renjardière is one of 4 adjacent large estates that surround the same lower plateau south of the hill of Uchaux, the others being Renjarde, St. Esteve, and Aigueville. The Dupond family, four generations at Sérignan, are also *négociants* and proprietors at Villefranche-sur-Saône in the Beaujolais country. 🍇 CL, 3 to 4 days, impulsion press. Rosé "par saignée" (same day). 🍇 Red ages 1 year in oak casks.

Domaine de la Renjarde, Sérignan-du-Comtat

CDR red. **The youth of the vines (most less than 15 years) makes real assessment of the wine's type here premature, as does its earlier history of shipment from the estate in bulk for bottling and mass distribution by the Damoy Society in Paris. Now it is in the hands of the large *négociant* firm David et Foillard, while still directed by the capable M. Alain Dugas. Of the 2 wines tastable at the estate in 1985, the 1984 with its buttery berry-fruit nose seemed livelier and more liquid than the drier, warmer, already more evolved 1983.**

55 ha in 3 large parcels, 2 of which are south-facing rectangular terraces on the slope behind the winery. Dynamite was needed to clear these sites, which are clearly visible to the east out the train window north of Orange. 60% GR, 20% SY, 10% CS, 5% MV,

plus CR and PL. 🙠 Production has been machine-harvested since 1981. CL without crushing, 5 to 6 days, Vaslin press. 🙠 Aging in enamel-lined and stainless steel vats, no wood. By 1985 all the wine will have been bottled at this estate. **Domaine de Coste Clavelle** is a label reserved for restaurants.

H **Château Saint Esteve d'Uchaux,** G. Français-Monier de Saint Esteve et Fils, Uchaux

CDR red, white, rosé; CDR-Villages red. **The wines here are clean and well made in the progressive fashion, and seem to have eliminated an earlier stemminess. CDR Blanc de Blancs, based on Grenache, Clairette, Bourboulenc, Roussane, gains a very particular aroma from a touch of Viognier, and was especially classy in 1984. Less distinctive was the 1984 CDR rosé at 30% Cinsault, 30% Clairette, 20% Grenache, 10% each Syrah and Mourvèdre. The red "Tradition" (60% Grenache, 35% Cinsault, 5% Syrah) is at present a fuller bodied wine than the Villages (30% Grenache, 30% Cinsault, 30% Syrah, 10% diverse), first made in 1983. Best (1985 tasting) was the very full, spicy, buttery red "Grande Réserve" 1980 which may have contained some of the last St. Esteve to be aged in wood.**

55 ha in vine in the communes of Uchaux and Sérignan (all the Villages from the former). Red *cépages:* 45% GR, 25% CS, 20% SY, 5% CR, MV, CT rose. Estate has been in the hands of the same family since 1809. 🙠 50% of the production has been machine-harvested since 1983. ST with up to 50% destemmed, depending on the year (a lot in 1984). Cuvaison has been lengthened to 10 to 15 days. Continuous press. Rosé "par saignée." The white is cold-settled, fermented cool, undergoes no malolactic. 🙠 Aging of the "Grande Réserve," formerly conducted for up to 2 years in cask, is now done in stainless steel.

Château d'Aigueville, GAEC Château d'Aigueville, Uchaux

CDR red. **1983, 1984 and especially 1985, show by their increased fruit and finesse that improvements have been made at this estate. Until now, sturdy, somewhat hard structure and cherry fruit made it a good illustration in tastings of high percentage of Carignan. The estate has been in the Arène family for more than 100 years.**

Single estate of 75 ha on same lower plateau as Renjardière. 50% GR, 21% CR, 8% CS, 8% SY, plus CT and PL. 🙠 CL, 8 days, 1/3 machine harvested since 1983. Vaslin press. 🙠 Earlier, had already decreased aging time in cask from 3 years to 1. The wine is bottled by *négociants* and commercialized with the name of the estate.

H **Château du Grand Moulas,** M. Rykwaert, Mornas

CDR; CDR-Villages. **Clean, fluid reds show the Syrah to start, with cassis fruit, black and bell pepper, and leafy, even floral fragrances that move toward butter and cedar with bottle age. A CDR-Villages, quite a bit weightier, was produced for the first time in 1984.**

The property is named for the château at Mornas where it is made, but the 30 ha in vine are in the commune of Uchaux. The land is new to vine and had to have its scrub growth and green oak removed; unlike other proprietors in the region, the Rykwaerts did not rework the contours of their land in clearing it. The clay-lime soil, covered with enormous flat limestone rocks, is planted 2/3 to GR, and 1/3 to SY. 2 ha of MV and 2–3 ha of white *cépages* will be added in 1985. 🙠 OT2, 5 to 12 days, depending on the *cépages* and the temperature. Vaslin press. The Rykwaerts aim to have finished wine by Christmas. 🙦 No wood. The wine rests in stainless steel vats before bottling within its first year.

Domaine de la Guicharde, François Biscarrat, Mondragon

CDR red, white, rosé. **In my limited experience here, I have found the most interesting wine to be the CDR white, 100% GR blanc, with good acidity even in 1982 and almost a Sauvignon nose.**

35 ha in vine, almost a single estate, all in Mondragon, mostly on sandy slopes. 80% GR, plus SY, CS, and diverse *cépages.* 🙦 OT2, 4 to 5 days, Vaslin press. 🙦 Reds age in vat.

Château de Gourdon, Sanchez et Gauchet, Bollène

CDR red and rosé. **Light, flowing-style reds. 1982 was almost too pale for a red, 1981 had more substance and length.**

45 ha in vine on south-facing sandy slopes around the 18th-century château. 60% GR, 20% CS, 15% SY, 5% MV and CR. 🙦 Production is machine-harvested. CL, 4–5 days average; hydraulic press, none incorporated for CDR. 🙦 Aged in vat and 3 months by rotation through 3 oak casks.

The cooperatives of this zone:

Cave Coopérative de Mondragon
Founded 1951. 31% AOC.

Cave Coopérative "Les Coteaux du Rhône," Sérignan-du-Comtat
Founded 1926. 50.9% AOC. CDR from Sérignan, Camaret, Orange, Piolenc, Travaillan, Uchaux.

─────── CDR OF THE LOWER AYGUES AND GARRIGUES ───────

In effect a continuation northward of the Plan de Dieu all the way to Richerenches, this area of ancient riverbed and low plateaus formerly covered by green oak scrub has seen extensive new plantation to reach its present virtual monoculture of vine since World War II.

At Suze-la-Rousse, in the magnificently restored 12th-century château, the Université du Vin is housed. Founded in 1978, largely under the impetus of the local growers from this zone, it is now sponsored by numerous producer, professional, and governmental bodies. The wine university provides the wine profession with laboratory and official tasting facilities, libraries of both wines and books, and information-retrieval services based on an international data base. The academic program offers courses and sequences for both professionals and amateurs, including tourists. (The director is M. Patrick Galant, 26790 Suze-la-Rousse.)

The producers are presented below in roughly SW to NE order. Addresses are 84 (Vaucluse) or 26 (Drôme) as indicated.

Domaine de la Presidente, SCEA Max Aubert, Ste.-Cécile-les-Vignes (Vaucluse)
See Cairanne

Domaine de la Grand' Ribe, Abel Sahuc, Ste.-Cécile-les-Vignes (Vaucluse)
Working in conditions of strictest cleanliness, M. Sahuc normally has 2 years of reds for sale. One, sold early for drinking young, comes—with the rosé—from the Ste.-Cécile-Rochegude part of the property (down the road from Roquevignan). Supple, spicy, and light-colored almost to a fault, it makes pleasant summer drinking. From the Suze part comes an older wine that, while still light-bodied, has more substance and savor (not made in 1982).

30 ha dispersed. One principal part straddles the boundary between Rochegude and Ste.-Cécile, whose gravel subsoil sometimes requires irrigation of the vines. The other principal part is on *garrigues* with stones and red soil at Suze. GR, CR, MV, SY. 🍇 CL, Vaslin press; rosé "par saignée." 🍇 Red is stocked in below-ground vats.

Chateau de Ruth; Vignoble de la Florette, Ste.-Cécile-les-Vignes (Vaucluse)
See Gigondas, Château Raspail

H **Château La Borie,** SCA Château La Borie (Emile Bories), Suze-la-Rousse (Drôme)
Excellent berry fruit and a leafy freshness that leaps from the vat characterize the wine when sampled at the estate. The best representation of its quality in bottle is from the *négociant* house Chauvenet of Nuits-St.-Georges, with the name Château La Borie as well as that of the proprietor on the label.

This single 70-ha estate lies north of Suze-la-Rousse, on the border with the Coteaux du Tricastin, and is adjacent to the Château de l'Estagnol. Here the country is rolling, and the soil is sometimes stoney, sometimes sandy on either gravel or clay. 50% GR, 40% SY, 10% CS, and a very little CR. 🍇 ST with some destemming, 7 days, vertical press. 🍇 No wood age. None of the wine is estate-bottled.

Château de l'Estagnol, Chambovet, Suze-la-Rousse (Drôme)
CDR red, white, rosé. **Wines are produced here under several labels named for different parts of the property, and reflecting different compositions, methods, and *élevage*. Red fruity CDR Domaine Ste.-Marie was composed (1984) of Grenache, Carignan, Mourvèdre, and Syrah. Sturdier 1984 CDR Château de l'Estagnol added 20% Syrah to the *cépage* mix. 1984 CDR La Serre du Prieur was 80% Syrah, 20% Grenache (its typical composition), and is vinified with the highest proportion of whole berries. Unusally tender for its high percentage of Syrah, it combines blacker fruit with decent fat and liveliness. CDR Château de l'Estagnol blanc de blancs has the characteristic green apple scent of its 100% Bourboulenc origin, and some refinement.**

85 ha in vine, all in the commune of Suze-la-Rousse, north of the village in an area of mostly sandy soil. The property touches that of Château La Borie. 50% GR, 20% SY, plus CR, CS, MV, and BR. 🍇 About 80% of l'Estagnol is machine-harvested now. The arrangement of the *cave* allows the grapes to be loaded directly into the vats by gravity. About 80% of the wine is produced CL; the other 20%, though destemmed, is not crushed. The *cépages* are vinified separately. Rosé "par saignée" and undergoes a malolactic. The white is also "par saignée," which is to say, after skin contact; the must is

fined, the fermentation cool, and the malolactic is blocked. ❧ The reds are given aging in oak casks according to *cuvée*. In 1984, **Ste.-Marie** was not in wood, **L'Estagnol** received 8 months wood age. As a rule **Serre du Prieur** gets 1 to 2 years.

Domaine Chante-Bise, Rieu Frères, Suze-la-Rousse (Drôme)

CDR red, white, rosé; CDR-Villages red; CDT red. **While the white and rosé show promise, the reds are excitingly concentrated, round, and aromatic, especially the CDR "Cuvée Spéciale" and the Villages (75% Mourvèdre in 1984).**

20 ha of CDR and CDR-Villages generally on plateau is dispersed in the communes of Suze, Rochegude, and Bollène. Taken together: 50% GR, 20% SY, plus CS, MV, CR, GR blanc, UN, BR, and Chardonnay. Also 4 ha of CDT in the commune of Montségur has 60% GR, 30% SY, and 10% CR. ❧ OT2, with the option of some destemming; 10 days; Vaslin press. Rosé "par saignée." ❧ A "Cuvée Vieillie en Foudres" is aged in oak casks, otherwise the aging takes place in vat.

Domaine du Petit Barbaras, SCEA R. Feschet et Fils, Bouchet (Drôme)

CDR red, white, rosé; CDR-Villages red. **The very particular white, with a slight blush to the color and an aroma of fruit salad, is made from Grenache gris, Bourboulenc, Ugni blanc, Maccabéo, and Marsanne. The reds have the fruit to sustain their passage in wood, but in my view the aroma suffers a bit from wood dryness.**

30 ha in vine almost all plateau, about half in Bouchet and half in Suze. About 70% GR, 15% old-vine CR, with the rest SY, CS, and a few whites. Among the diverse *cépages* are some rarities that result from the elder M. Feschet's interest as a former commercial grower of vine plants. ❧ OT2, 5 to 8 days, Vaslin press. Rosé "par saignée." ❧ 6 months to 1 year in oak casks and used small barrels for reds.

Domaine Mazurd et Fils, Tulette (Drôme)

CDR red, white, rosé; CDR-Village [sic] red. **These big, full-bodied, high-alcohol wines are presented in a somewhat confusing multitude of versions that have won medals and are bottled separately. Most are actually from particular parcels, while not always indicated as such. Thus CDR "Carte Marron" 1984, 1983, and 1982 are unwooded "St. Quénize." Unwooded CDR "Carte Blanche" is, like wooded CDR Village 1981, from Valréas. "Cuvée Exceptionelle" 1982 (wooded) and "Cuvée Mazurka" 1979 (wooded) are from Tulette.**

75 ha dispersed in Suze, Tulette, and Bouchet (Drôme), and Visan and Valréas (Vaucluse). The parcels at Bouchet ("St. Quénize" and "Coteaux de Claras"), Tulette ("La Cruzère"), and Valréas ("Grande Belanne") are on slopes. All properties: 70% GR, 15% CR, 10% SY, 5% CS and MV. Vines average 65 to 68 years old. White *cépages:* GR blanc and BR. ❧ OT2, 8 to 12 days. Continuous press, from which only the free-run juice is used for AOC wine, will be replaced by an impulsion press. ❧ Some wines receive wood age, either 7 to 8 months in oak casks, or 5 to 6 months in small barrels. All the wood-aged wine is estate-bottled.

H **Domaine de la Berardière,** Pierre Bérard, Tulette (Drôme)

CDR red; CDR-Villages red. **I have really enjoyed the CDR with old-vine Carignan, purple, fruity, salty, "high-pitched." The Villages, from Valréas, was pure Grenache**

Espalier-pruned old vines on the Feschet estate at Bouchet (Drôme). Elsewhere (Châteauneuf-du-Pape and Plan de Dieu), the reader will have noticed the system of bush pruning *(en gobelet)* more prevalent in the southern Rhône valley. Photo courtesy of Rosalind Srb.

in 1979 and 1980, 90% Grenache in 1981, very well balanced and fragrant, at 13.5% alcohol. 1984 had a finer tannin even with 25% Carignan than the rougher 1983, both at 14.4% alcohol.

40 ha in AOC is divided between 25 at Tulette and 15 at Valréas "la Petite Belanne." Most of this is on slopes, and some of the vines are more than 80 years old. 80% GR, 10% SY, and 10% CR from old vines for red *cépages*. White: UN and BR. 🍇 OT2, 7 to 10 days, Vaslin press. 🍇 1 year in vat, with some wines, particularly those that have won medals, receiving 6 months in reused small barrels. M. Bérard began to bottle his own wine in 1979.

Cellier des Dauphins, Union des Vignerons des Côtes du Rhône, Tulette (Drôme)

The Cellier is owned by a union of 10 cooperatives from the northern Vaucluse and southern Drôme departments. This is the area of the southern Côtes du Rhône with the highest local proportion of cooperative growers (90%) and the largest cooperatives (average capacity, in round numbers, of 79,000 hl; average annual production of 49,000 hl; average membership, 335).

The member *caves* are those of (roughly from east to west) St.-Pantaléon-les-Vignes (Drôme), Nyons (Drôme), Vaison-la-Romaine (Vaucluse), Vinsobres (Drôme), St.-Maurice-sur-Eygues (Drôme), Tulette "Costebelle" (Drôme), Tulette "Costes-Rousses"

(Drôme), Suze-la-Rousse (Drôme)—largest in the whole CDR, Ste.-Cécile-les-Vignes (Vaucluse), and Rochegude (Drôme). Together the member *caves* produce approximately 700,000 hl of wine per year, of which about 400,000 hl is CDR. Each contributes from 1/3 to 1/2 of its production for conditioning and sale by the Cellier. This is enough to make the Cellier the largest single supplier of CDR wines in bottle. The Cellier also bottles the wines for the member *caves* that they commercialize under their own labels. Export of members' wines, however, is supposed to be handled by the Cellier, which exports 30% of its annual production of 30 million bottles. When the union's bottle sales are taken together with those of the member *caves*, the effect of the union has been to allow the members to sell about 50% of their production directly in bottle, thus liberating these cooperatives, as they would see it, from depending on low-price sale of wine in tankcars to *négociants* (shippers) who specialize in sale *en gros* (bulk).

The sales policy of the Cellier is to guarantee to its clients a large stock of bottled wines whose quality can be "followed," that is, bought in quantity again and again without radical variation in quality level or style. The following (with sources) are the most particular wines available from the Cellier:

CDR red with name of Domaine
    Cave "La Vinsobraise" of Vinsobres.
CDR-Villages Saint Maurice
    Cave of St. Maurice-sur-Eygues.
CDR-Villages Vinsobres
    Cave "La Vinsobraise" of Vinsobres.
CDV
    Cave of Vaison.

Wines commercialized by Cellier des Dauphins affiliate **Cellier de l'Abbaye,** housed in the former Cistercian Abbey of Bouchet (Drôme), are bottled by the Cellier des Dauphins, which is the source of the Abbaye's CDR wines. For appellations that are not produced by the union's members, Cellier de l'Abbaye acts as a *négociant*. Cellier de l'Abbaye specializes in direct sale to individual clients. Cellier des Dauphins now also owns the formerly independent *négociant* firm **Boissey et Delaygue** of Cornas (Ardèche). Boissey et Delaygue act as *négociants* for CDR *septentrionales* wines, and specialize in sale to fine restaurants and wine stores. The Cellier des Dauphins has recently joined in an additional union (SICA) with the Cave du Prieuré at Vinsobres (see Vinsobres). On some labels, especially of non-CDR wines, the Union des Vignerons des Côtes du Rhône is identified as **"Vignerons Réunis à Tulette"** or as **"Chai des Vignerons."**

The cooperatives of this zone follow (C = member of the Cellier des Dauphins; E = member of the Cellier de l'Enclave):

C **Cave Coopérative Vinicole "Cécilia,"** Ste.-Cécile-les-Vignes (Vaucluse)
    Founded 1927. 73.09% AOC. CDR mostly from Ste.-Cécile.

Cave des Vignerons Réunis, Ste.-Cécile-les-Vignes (Vaucluse)
    Founded 1936. 77.5% AOC. CDR from Ste.-Cécile (about 50%), Bollène (Vaucluse), Bouchet (Drôme), Buisson, Cairanne, Camaret, Lagarde-Paréol (all Vaucluse),

CHATEAU DE FONSALETTE
1er GRAND CRU
APPELLATION CÔTES-DU-RHÔNE CONTRÔLÉE

PROPRIÉTÉ DE   LA GARDE PAREOL
Mᵉ L.REYNAUD   VAUCLUSE

1983
CHATEAU
SAINT ESTÈVE
d'UCHAUX

TRADITION

Produce of France
ALC. 13 % VOL.

Mis en bouteille au Château
CÔTES DU RHONE
APPELLATION CÔTES-DU-RHÔNE CONTRÔLÉE

75 cl

G. FRANÇAIS-MONIER DE SAINT-ESTEVE ET FILS PROPRIETAIRES RECOLTANTS UCHAUX 84100 ORANGE

CHÂTEAU DU GRAND MOULAS
1984

CÔTES-DU-RHÔNE
Appellation Côtes-du-Rhône Controlée

Produce
of France

e 750ml

M.RYCKWAERT CHATEAU DU GRAND MOULAS MORNAS VAUCLUSE FRANCE

MIS EN BOUTEILLE AU CHÂTEAU

1979

CUVÉE-DE   LA VIERGE
VISAN
APPELLATION COTES DU RHONE VISAN CONTROLÉE
DOMAINE DE LA CANTHARIDE

MIS EN BOUTEILLE A LA PROPRIETE

J. Roux

Propriétaire récoltant à Visan (Vaucluse)
Produce of France

75 cl

Domaine "Les Aussellons"

Vinsobres
CÔTES-DU-RHÔNE

e 75cl

APPELLATION CÔTES-DU-RHÔNE VINSOBRES CONTROLEE

BENOIT-EZINGEARD PROPRIÉTAIRES-RÉCOLTANTS 84 VILLEDIEU
Mis en bouteille au Domaine
PRODUIT DE FRANCE

Domaine du Coriançon

COTES-DU-RHONE
Vinsobres
1982
APPELLATION CÔTES-DU-RHÔNE CONTRÔLÉE

Mis en bouteille par :
François VALLOT Viticulteur à Vinsobres 26110 - France

75 cl

Imp. Couston Vaison

DOMAINE DE LA FUZIÈRE
VALREAS
CÔTES du RHÔNE
APPELLATION COTES DU RHONE CONTROLEE

VINIFIÉ ELEVÉ ET MIS EN BOUTEILLE A LA PROPRIETE PAR
LÉO ROUSSIN, VITICULTEUR à VALREAS (84)
TELEPHONE: 35.05.15

Un léger dépôt est dû au vieillissement naturel de ce vin.

DOMAINE DES GRANDS DEVERS
Côtes-du-Rhône
APPELLATION CÔTES-DU-RHÔNE CONTRÔLÉE

SINARD Père et Fils
PROPRIÉTAIRES RÉCOLTANTS 84600 à VALRÉAS (FRANCE)

73 CL

Rochegude (Drôme), St.-Roman-de-Malegarde and Sérignan-du-Comtat (Vaucluse), Suze-la-Rousse (Drôme), Travaillan (Vaucluse), Tulette (Drôme), Valréas and Visan (Vaucluse).

C **Cave Coopérative Vinicole "La Suzienne,"** Suze-la-Rousse (Drôme)
Founded 1926. 71.9% AOC. Largest cooperative in the CDR region, CDR wines principally from Suze, Bouchet, Rochegude (Drôme). CDT, of which the Cave is the largest single producer, made in separate facility from Baume-de-Transit, St.-Paul-Trois-Châteaux.

C **Cave Coopérative "Costebelle,"** Tulette (Drôme)
Founded 1925. 73.7% AOC. CDR from Tulette (80%), Bouchet and St.-Maurice (Drôme), St.-Roman-de-Malegarde (Vaucluse).

C **Cave Coopérative "Costes Rousses,"** Tulette (Drôme)
Founded 1939 (hence used to be known as the Cave Nouvelle of Tulette). 73.7% AOC. CDR from Tulette (2/3), Bouchet (Drôme), Cairanne, Ste.-Cécile-les-Vignes, St.-Roman-de-Malegarde, Valréas, Visan (all in Vaucluse). CDT from Baume-de-Transit, Chamaret, Montségur.

E **Coopérative Vinicole "Le Cellier des Templiers,"** Richerenches, (Vaucluse)
Founded 1966. 76.91% AOC. CDR principally from Richerenches and Grillon (Vaucluse). CDT from Baume-de-Transit, Donzère, Grignan, Montségur, La-Roche-St.-Secret.

– CDR-VILLAGES AROUND THE PLATEAU OF VINSOBRES –
(Communes are roughly from SW to NE)

Visan

The sole commune is Visan (Vaucluse). Addresses are 84820 Visan.

H **Domaine de la Cantharide,** J. Laget-Roux

CDR red and rosé; CDR-Villages Visan. **Mme. Laget and her husband have both studied oenology and are responsible for the best Visan. Two cuvées were once distinguished: "Cuvée l'Hermite" (Grenache and about 20% Syrah), darkly fruity and distinctly tannic, evolves into peaches and truffles; "Cuvée de la Vierge" (Grenache and about 30% Mouvèdre), more discrete, classically structured, with flowers, red plum skins, and vanilla. No Villages was produced in 1981, and only l'Hermite in 1982 and 1983. In 1984 the Mourvèdre and Syrah were placed in a single *cuvée* (with Grenache, of course).**
16 ha, dispersed but nearby on SW-facing slopes. 70% GR, 5% CS, 15% SY, 5% MV, plus a little CR and some recently planted whites (1982). 🍇 OT2, 4 to 12 days, according to the *cépages,* which are vinified separately. 🍇 Aged normally in vat, except for some experiments in wood.

Cave Coopérative "Les Coteaux"

Cave produces a very consistent line of CDR-Villages Visan reds: all about 70% Grenache, sturdy, round, tending to plums, spice and pepper. "Grande Réserve" has

more Syrah, and less Cinsault, than plain Visan. Mourvèdre, even less Cinsault, and a proportion of CM distinguish the richer, suppler "Notre Dame des Vignes." "Confrérie Saint-Vincent" to my mind is less aromatic and drier than the others. The distinctive quality of the citrussy, minerally Visan white is said to result from the presence of old-vine Clairette and the location of Grenache blanc in Visan's best exposures. Visan rosé is perhaps less interesting.

Founded 1937. 76.11% AOC. 95% of the 370 members come from Visan. ✦ The Villages wine is vinified in a separate facility. Part of the wine destined for the Cave's own bottling is produced CM, 12 to 15 days. The rest is CL, 6 to 8 days. ✦ About 30% of the Visan "Notre Dame des Vignes" spends a year in oak casks. All the "Confrérie St.-Vincent" is wood-aged.

Clos du Père Clément, Depeyre Père et Fils

CDR red and rosé; CDR-Villages Visan. **Fairly light, with good nerve and red or plum fruit, the wines seem best when not overbalanced by wood.**

20 ha Visan: 75% GR, 10% SY, plus CS, CR. Some CDR is from the adjacent commune of Tulette. ✦ CL, 5 to 10 days in water-cooled stainless steel vats; Vaslin press. Rosé "par saignée." ✦ Reds are aged for the most part in vat. Several wines are labeled separately. CDR **"Domaine du Vieux Caveau"** is assembled from the whole property (including Tulette) and sees no wood. CDR **"Clos du Père Clément"** is only from the Visan part, receives oak age in Burgundian *pièces*. The Villages is labeled **"Cuvée Notre Dame"** for the qrt of that name, and is also unwooded.

Saint-Maurice-sur-Eygues

The sole commune is 26650 St.-Maurice-sur-Eygues.

Cave Coopérative des Coteaux de Saint-Maurice

CDR red, white, rosé; CDR-Villages St.-Maurice red and rosé. **Smooth, clean, even delicate, the wooded reds here add a pleasant vanilla to their basic raspbery fruit, while successfully avoiding an overt taste of wood. Nevertheless, I prefer the greater intensity of the unwooded versions. In my view the outstanding wine is the St.-Maurice rosé.**

Founded 1939. 57.4% AOC. 160 members from St.-Maurice, where there are no private proprietors outside the cooperative; Buisson, Valréas, Villedieu, Visan (Vaucluse) and Mirabel-aux-Baronnies, Piégon, Tulette, Vinsobres (Drôme). ✦ CL in self-emptying vats. Some of the 1985 harvest was to be experimentally vinified with the stems. ✦ Some CDR-St.-Maurice is aged in oak casks. CDR-St.-Maurice "Grande Réserve" is aged in *pièces*. Bottling is conducted for the cooperative by the proprietors' union Cellier des Dauphins at Tulette.

Vinsobres

The sole commune is Vinsobres (Drôme). It has been one of the CDR-Villages (then *communales*) since 1957. Addresses are 26490 Vinsobres, unless otherwise noted.

H **Domaine Les Aussellons,** SCEA Benoit-Ezingeard, Villedieu (Vaucluse)

CDR red and rosé; CDR-Villages Vinsobres. **As growers of Vinsobres who reside outside the village, since 1978 this Domaine has been a source of top-quality estate-bottled Vinsobres wine that has passed neither through the Cave du Prieuré nor the Cellier des Dauphins. The wines combine chewiness with finesse, deep berry fruit with resins, truffles, and even licorice. The discrete handling of wood allows these nuances to show outstandingly well in the somewhat light-colored 1983.**

17 ha at Vinsobres; 13 ha of CDR at Villedieu. All properties: 50-60% GR, 15% SY, 10% CR, 6-8% CS and diverse. Excellent 1980 CDR, a year with no Villages declared, contained their Vinsobres production as well. 1982 CDR was pure GR from Vinsobres. ❧ OT2, about 7 days for Villages; Vaslin press. ❧ 1 year in vat, up to 1 year in oak casks depending on the character of the wine (delicate 1981 Vinsobres was not wooded). The wine is withdrawn from wood by taste and placed in enamelled vat to await bottling.

H **Domaine du Coriançon,** François Vallot

CDR red, white, rosé; CDR-Villages Vinsobres. **M. Vallot now sends almost no wine to the Cave du Prieuré proprietors' union, having begun his own bottling and commercialization in 1982. The production of the field-blended parcel, in particular, is reserved for his bottled Vinsobres, a particularly fragrant and solid wine with good acidity.**

60 ha in production, all in Vinsobres. 65% GR, 10% SY, 10% CS, 5% MV, 10% whites including GR gris, UN, CT. One parcel planted in 1978 returns to the principle of field-blending the other *cépages* right in the plantation with GR. ❧ OT2, 8 to 10 days for Vinsobres, Vaslin press. Rosé "par saignée." ❧ At least 1 year in oak casks for Vinsobres. All wines are cold-stabilized before bottling.

Château de Deurre, Le Comte de Saint Priest d'Urgel

CDR red and rosé; CDR-Villages Vinsobres. **Good raw material should show better in bottle when aging facilities are improved. Interesting 1983 CDR contains no Grenache.**

Recently expanded to 20 ha in vine (slopes), of which 14 are planted to relatively young vines. 40% GR, 30% SY, 20% CS, 5% each MV and CR. ❧ OT2, 4 to 6 days. ❧ Until recently had to stock wine in metal vats. Will age longer when cement or wood storage is installed.

Claude et Nicole Jaume, GAEC Cave C. N. Jaume

CDR red and rosé. **The Jaumes formerly produced and estate-bottled the most robust Vinsobres Villages wines, but switched exclusively to CDR following the institution of the very strict 1974 regulations on productivity, which limited excess production to VDT. In recent years the wines have gained considerable finesse as a result of modern equipment in the new cave the Jaumes have used since 1981.**

27 ha in AOC, 80% on slopes. 6–10 ha between Vinsobres and St.-Maurice will soon be added. 72% GR, 15% SY, plus CS, MV, CT. ❧ CL with very gentle crush, 5 to 10 days (in stainless steel vats since 1981); Vaslin press. Rosé "par saignée." ❧ Red is aged first in cement vats, then receives 6 to 12 months in oak casks.

Domaine du Moulin, Denis Vinson

CDR red, white, rosé. **Like his father Jean, M. Denis Vinson sends the estate's Villages production to the Cave du Prieuré. Only CDR is sold under their own label. The white and rosé, usually having not undergone malolactic fermentation, retain considerable nerve. The reds have been made in a "junior" Châteauneuf style and pick up lots of wood tannin. This may change under M. Denis Vinson's direction, with more Syrah in the composition.**

20 ha of CDR, 19 of which are in Vinsobres, 1 at Nyons. Red *cépages:* 70% GR, 15% SY, 15% each CS and MV. The white, planted in lower, less sunny slopes for acidity, are CT, UN, and GR blanc. ❧ ST, 8 days, hydraulic press. Rosé "saignée." ❧ Reds get 6 to 12 months in oak casks.

Domaine de Saint-Vincent, Fernand Durma

CDR red and rosé; CDR-Villages Vinsobres. **M. Durma used to send his Villages wine to the Cave du Prieuré, but the Cave informs me that he has withdrawn. My earlier notes, limited to CDR under his own label, show big, ripe, burly wines, sturdy if none too subtle. More recently tasted 1983 Villages was clearly a *vin de garde,* with noble tar reduction and a little dustiness.**

30 ha dispersed in Vinsobres, most on slopes. 60–70% GR, plus CS, SY, MV, Oldest vines 60 years. ❧ ST, 5 to 10 days, hydraulic press. ❧ A part is aged 6 to 12 months in wood.

Cave "la Vinsobraise" des Vignerons de Vinsobres

Some of the best raw material in CDR-Villages Vinsobres is produced by the cooperative, not always as good from the bottle as when tasted from the vat. The 1981, which had 6–8 months in cask, is nevertheless a reasonable representation. CDR white is Clairette and Ugni blanc. CDR rosé is Grenache, Cinsault, and Syrah. A considerable line of Domaine wines from the properties of particular members is now produced for sale by the Cellier des Dauphins.

Founded 1949. 68.9% AOC. 320 members from Vinsobres, St.-Maurice, Mirabel-aux-Baronnies, Nyons, Piégon, La-Roche-St.-Secret, St.-Paul-Trois-Châteaux, Venterol (Drôme), and Valréas (Vaucluse). ❧ CL, 7 to 8 days for Villages; impulsion press. Rosé "par saignée." ❧ Wine to be sold by the coop under its own label is *élevé* and given wood age at the Cave, then bottled for it by the Cellier des Dauphins at Tulette.

Cave du Prieuré, Propriétaires-Réunis

Founded in 1959, the Cave du Prieuré is a joint-share company owned by about 120 proprietors of Vinsobres, including the Cave Coopérative "La Vinsobraise," which makes the wine for its members who also belong to the Prieuré. The original purpose of the union was to age, bottle, and commercialize the Villages-quality wine produced by its members. Finished wines were submitted some months after harvest and had to pass muster with a tasting panel before being aged separately and often extensively in oak casks before *assemblage*. Existence of the Cave is one reason that a number of producers of CDR-Villages Vinsobres wine, who otherwise bottle their own wines, sell no Vinsobres under their labels.

Recently the Cave joined in a further union with the Cellier des Dauphins (Tulette) as majority partner. This new "SICA" Cave du Prieuré will assume essentially all the functions of the old, except, of course, production of the members' wines and ownership of the facilities. All this will presumably be little noticed by consumers, except that quality may improve from the more rapid movement of the wine stock out of wood, in which it has been more nearly stored than brought up *(élevé)*.

The most particular wines available from Prieuré are:

CDR red with name of domaine

The domaines tend to change according to availabilities, but often include *Domaine de Coriançon (see).

*CDR-Villages Vinsobres "Prieuré" red, white, rosé

CDR-Villages Vinsobres "Prestige" red

Valréas

The sole commune is Valréas (Vaucluse). Addresses are 84600 Valréas, unless otherwise noted.

Domaine de la Deydière, Maurice Laurent et Fils, Grillon

CDR red, rosé, white. **A new estate to me (1985) produced a notable CDR 1982 "Vieilli en Foudres" of 80% Grenache, 15% Carignan, and 5% Syrah, lively enough to sustain the wood of a "junior Châteauneuf" style over its plum and dark cherry fruit.**

15 ha in vine in Valréas and Grillon, half on plateau, half on sandy slopes. 70% GR, plus SY, CS, CR. ॐ OT2, 10 to 15 days, hydraulic press. M. Laurent also makes the wine for Domaine Gramenon from Montbrison-sur-Lez (see "CDR of the Pre-Alps"). ॐ Wine that spends a year in oak cask is separately labeled "Vieilli en Foudres."

H Domaine de la Fuzière, Léo Roussin

CDR red; CDR-Villages Valréas red. **Seems to be less in the "forme oxidative" than formerly, perhaps from the advent of destemming. Now one can see the depth of fruit in a wine with notable acidity—herbal, berryish, sometimes plummy—which develops apricot and pepper with age.**

Around 21 ha, plateau. About 70% GR, 15% CR, 10% CS, plus SY and MV. ॐ OT/CL, i.e., up to 80% destemmed but not all crushed. 8 to 12 days, Vaslin press, no press wine incorporated. ॐ 2 to 6 months in oak casks.

H Domaine de Grand Devers, Sinard Père et Fils

CDR red and rosé; CDR-Villages Valréas red. **The Villages, almost pure Grenache, is remarkable for its intense berry lozenge fruit and buttery, vanilla nose with no excess of thick or astringent tannin.**

25 ha of vine dispersed but nearby. 1.35 ha of the CDR is at Ste.-Cécile-les-Vignes. 5½ ha of SY, 4 ha CR. 1.3 ha MV, the rest GR. ॐ OT1, 10 to 12 days. Rosé "par saignée." ॐ No wood.

Domaine de Notre-Dame-des-Veilles, Albert et Annie Bonnefoy

CDR red. **Leafy, raspberry, candyish, sometimes spicy wine when young. We will know more when more is bottled, but a 1985 tasting showed the 1979 had evolved in a tar, truffle, Burgundy direction—intense, stylish, and surprising.**

45 ha in vine, single estate, plateau on the border of Valréas and Grillon. 60% GR, 15% SY, 8% CR, plus CS, CT, UN. ☙ OT2, 7 to 8 days, Vaslin press. ☙ 2 to 3 months in oak casks for bottled wine. Bottled a small fraction of the 1979 and 1982 vintages.

Domaine de la Prévosse, GAEC Henri Davin et Fils

CDR red, white, rosé; CDR-Villages Valréas red. **M. Davin, now president of the Valréas growers, would sometimes like less wood for a wine that his clients prefer in a distinctly wooded style. A little white is made from Bourboulenc and Clairette rose.**

20 ha on slopes across the lower plateau from those on the north slope of the plateau of Vinsobres. South exposure. 70% GR, 20% SY, 10% CS and CR. Also, **Château de Montplaisir,** 5 ha at Valréas, on slopes between routes to Orange and to Vinsobres. Only GR for the moment. Will plant SY, CS, MV to produce Villages from this property. ☙ ST, some destemming. 5 to 8 days. Rosé "par saignée." ☙ Reds spend 8 months in *foudres,* 6 months in *demi-muids.*

Domaine de Saint-Chétin, SCP André F.C. Gras et Fils (Robert and Isabelle Schuimer)

CDR red and white; CDR-Villages Valréas (last made 1978). **The white, known as "Gloire de St. André," is especially and genuinely distinguished, at once stony, round, fresh, floral, and honeyed. The quality of the reds, big-scaled and dense with ripe fruit whether wooded or not, is also high.**

25-ha single estate, just west of Domaine du Séminaire. GR plus 4 ha of SY, 2 ha MV, 2 ha CS, 4 ha together of CT, GR blanc, UN, BR, and RS. ☙ 8 ha of the estate are machine-harvested, therefore automatically CL. The rest is ST, 3 to 4 days, Vaslin press. ☙ Wine under the principal label **"Trésor de St.-Chétin"** is aged 2 to 3 years in oak casks. **"Hauts de St.-Pierre"** is a label for an early bottled red without wood age.

Domaine du Séminaire, Denis Pouizin

CDR red. **A dark wine usually crammed with fruit and "goût de terroir" that could do with less of the sort of tannin that finishes dry. Particularly harmonious 1980.**

30 ha in vine on south-facing slopes at 300m altitude. 60% GR, 10% CS, 10% SY, 5% CR, plus a few MV and whites. Vines average 50 years old. ☙ OT2, 8 to 10 days, hydraulic press. ☙ Wine for estate bottling—up to now a very minor part of the production—is given about 1 year in oak casks.

H **Domaine du Val des Rois,** Romain Bouchard

CDR red and rosé; CDR-Villages Valréas. **A scion of the famous Burgundian wine merchant family, M. Bouchard since 1978 has usually composed the red Villages Valréas of 75% Grenache and 25% Syrah. 5% Gamay was added in 1980 and 1983. Full of resinous smells and deep blackberry to cassis fruit, the wines have real "nerve" from the cooler Valréas climate, and are excellent examples of light wines with the structure to age. The pre-1978s, almost pure Grenache, develop a more peachlike and almost Burgundian fungal nose in aging, with wines tasted back to the 1964 in excellent condition. M. Bouchard also used to make a Villages rosé with extraordinary keeping qualities.**

14.36 ha in vine, slope, dispersed but grouped nearby. One parcel is exposed SE at 400m altitude. 6.78 ha GR, 3.44 ha SY, 1.87 ha CS, .48 ha MV, .55 ha CR, and 1.19 ha

Gamay. ✌ CL, 5 to 6 days. Rosé "par saignée." ✌ No wood beginning 1978. Before that reds received a few months in oak casks.

Ferme La Verrière, Pierre Rosati

CDR red, rosé, and "blanc de blancs;" CDR-Villages Valréas red. **A young producer to be watched with interest for what could become a distinguished white, already promising in fine, nervy, citrus-to-apple, honeyed 1984. His reds see too much wood for my taste, with the possible exception of the old-vine Villages 1981.**

22 ha in vine, of which 2 are in St.-Pantaléon-les-Vignes and the rest in Valréas, plateau and slope (in this case, sandy). 60% GR, 10% CR, 10% CS, 5% SY, and the rest in CT, UN, and BR. ✌ ST, 6 to 15 days, (the latter for Villages); hydraulic press. Both white and rosé "par saignée." No malolactic for the white. ✌ All reds 12 to 18 months in oak casks.

Cellier de l'Enclave des Papes, Union des Vignerons de l'Enclave des Papes

The Cellier is owned by a union of cooperatives, including a "cooperative" of proprietors from within the Enclave des Papes. This is a portion of the Vaucluse department, historically of the Comtat Venaissin, north of the rest and entirely surrounded by the Drôme, as it was by the old Dauphiné. It is made up of Valréas, Visan, Richerenches, and Grillon. Valréas and Visan are home to the private proprietors in this union. The cooperative caves are those of Valréas and Richerenches. Members contribute a portion of their production, aged according to the union's instructions, for bottling and commercialization by the union. In turn, they may use the facilities of the union to bottle wine that they will commercialize under their own labels.

The Cellier's wines by AOC, with sources, are:

CDR red
> The whole of the Enclave.

CDR **"Marquis de Simiane"**
> Red: whole of the Enclave.
> Rosé: usually the Cave Coopérative of Valréas.
> White: the cooperatives of Valréas and Richerenches.

CDR **"Enclave des Papes"** red (margue exclusive to Union until 1987)
> Whole of the Enclave, especially private proprietors.

CDR-Villages red (including the **"Cuvée de Petit St.-Jean"** sold in Québec)
> Private proprietors and cooperative of Valréas.

CDT red and rosé
> Cooperative of Richerenches.

A recent change in French law will allow the Cellier to sell as *négociant* a limited quantity of wines that are not of the members' production. For the moment these are, with sources:

Châteauneuf-du-Pape
> Domaine du Caillou, Courthézon (see "CDR in the Environs of Châteauneuf-du-Pape").

CDV
> Union des Vignerons des Côtes du Ventoux, Carpentras.

Crozes-Hermitage
> Cave Coopérative de Vins Fins, Tain l'Hermitage.

Gigondas
> Cave Coopérative de Gigondas.

Tavel
> Les Vignerons de Tavel.

The cooperative is:

E Cave Coopérative "La Gaillarde"

Founded 1928. 73.43% AOC. Members from Valréas, Grillon, Richerenches (Vaucluse); Le Pègue, Rousset-les-Vignes, St.-Pantaléon-les-Vignes, and Taulignan (Drôme).

CDR red, white, and rosé; CDR-Villages Valréas red; *CDR-Villages Valréas rosé.

11

Near the Pre-Alps

ITH THE EXCEPTIONS of Rousset, St.-Pantaléon, and Taulignan (Drôme) and Vaison and Villedieu (Vaucluse), a considerable portion of this zone was added to the Côtes du Rhône in 1970, having until then been part of the old VDQS Haut-Comtat or of the Côtes du Ventoux when it was VDQS. Due to the mountain influence, the climate already counts as "Rhodanian" (northern Rhône valley) rather than Mediterranean.

In this chapter, C = member of the Cellier des Dauphins (Tulette). For other abbreviations see the master list at the beginning of this book.

CDR-Villages Rousset-Les-Vignes and Saint-Pantaléon-Les-Vignes

The sole producer-bottler of wine from the two named communes is the cooperative at 26230 St.-Pantaléon.

C Cave Coopérative Vinicole de Saint-Pantaléon-les-Vignes, Union des Producteurs de St.-Pantaléon-les-Vignes; Union des Producteurs de Rousset-les-Vignes

Founded 1960. 72.7% AOC. 217 members producing CDR from Rousset-les-Vignes, St.-Pantaléon-les-Vignes, Montbrison-sur-Lez, Le Pègue, Taulignan (Drôme) and Valréas (Vaucluse). CDT from La-Roche-Saint-Secret (Drôme).

CDR red, rosé, and white (the last three years); CDR-Villages Rousset red; CDR-Villages Saint-Pantaléon red; CDR-Villages red; *CDR-Villages rosé; CDT.

CDR of the Pre-Alps (producers arranged N to S)

The following addresses are 26 (Drôme).

Domaine Gramenon, Philippe Laurent, Montbrison-sur-Lez

CDR red. **In my limited experience of this estate, I have tasted one extraordinary wine—CDR "Vieux Ceps" 1982, from 80-year-old Grenache, Carignan, and diverse field-blended *cépages*. Black, rich, chewy without being thick, the fruit was of sour cherries, with a little licorice in the finish.**

20 ha in Montbrison across the road from Domaine des Treilles. 80% GR, 1.5 ha CT, plus CS, SY, CR. 🍇 OT2, 10 to 15 days; hydraulic press, not incorporated. 🍇 No wood.

H Domaine des Treilles, Patrice Méry, Montbrison-sur-Lez

CDR red and rosé. **Cool, well-ventilated microclimate makes for remarkably aromatic Grenache. For their intense fruit I have preferred the unwooded versions of some wines, including 1982—99% Grenache—and equally fragrant, tighter-structured 1984.**

23 ha in vine, almost a single estate that straddles the boundary between Montbrison and Valréas. Many old vines. 80% GR, 15% SY, plus CS and CR. ❧ ST, 4 to 5 days, Vaslin press. A *primeur* was produced for the first time in 1983. Rosé is directly pressed (vinified *en blanc*). ❧ Some wines receive 9 to 12 months in oak casks.

H **Domaine de la Taurelle,** GAEC Domaine de la Taurelle (Mme. Roux et Fils), Mirabel-aux-Baronnies

CDR red, white, rosé. **These sturdy hillside wines seem to have gained considerable fruit and balance in recent years, particularly if one follows the history of the very good "Cuvée Spéciale" (Grenache, Syrah, and sometimes Cinsault).**

15 ha of CDR. Red *cépages:* 50% GR (some planted in 1928), 20% CR, 20% SY, 10% CS. Whites: ⅓ BR, ⅓ GR, ⅓ CT, plus a little UN. Also 2.5 ha of VDP du Comté de Grignan in Mirabel. In addition, this domaine produces black olives and extra-virgin "Nyons" olive oil. ❧ ST, 5 to 6 days, hydraulic press. Rosé "par saignée." ❧ Since 1979, no wood. 2 to 3 years in vat.

Domaine du Grand Relais, Daniel Pélissier, Mirabel-aux-Baronnies

CDR red, white, rosé. **For the moment the crisp Clairette/Grenache white, fined before cool fermentation, and the fresh, full-flavored rosé seem more distinguished in bottle than the slightly too woody smelling reds of 1983. The promise is there, however, in the fruit of the new wines and the seriousness of the winemaker.**

Since 1982, M. Pélissier has owned the Mirabel part of the former "Vieux Relais" vineyards that belonged to M. A.R. Mangin, who was also a *négociant-éleveur.* 17 ha of CDR in Mirabel. 50% GR, 10% SY, 8% CS, 8% MV, 5% CT and GR blanc, plus old-vine CR. Also 3.5 ha of VDP du Comté de Grignan in Mirabel. ❧ OT2, 5 to 7 days for most *cépages.* About half the CR is vinified *en blanc* for light red *cuvées* in the "café" style. Vaslin press; rosé "par saignée," no malolactic. ❧ Red wine is filtered before being lodged 8 to 10 months in oak casks.

The following addresses are 84 (Vaucluse).

H **Domaine Les Aussellons,** Villedieu
See Vinsobres.

H **Domaine Saint-Claude,** GAEC Claude Charasse et Associés, Le Palis, Vaison-la-Romaine

CDR red, rosé, white. **Supple, lively, floral white supports the view that the Vaison-Villedieu-Puyméras vicinity is one of the best in the southern Rhône for white. The rosé has flavors of peach and apricot, the red is fruity, sometimes resinous (1982, 1984), tender and long.**

32 ha in AOC CDR dispersed in Vaison, Villedieu, Roaix, and Buisson, mostly on sandy slopes. 60% GR, 25% CS, 10% SY, plus CN, UN, CT. ❧ CL because of machine harvesting, but no crushing, 3 to 5 days; Vaslin press. Rosé "par saignée." ❧ Reds spend 1 year in vat on the fine lees. No wood.

Domaine de la Cambuse, Pierre Brun, Vaison-la-Romaine

CDR red and rosé. **M. Brun carries his earlier interest in painting into the art of winemaking, for which, he says, one must have a love. Still a member of the cooperative at Vaison, he began to make some wine on his own in 1979 and to**

A classic of provençal romanesque architecture, the present parish church, Nôtre Dame de Nazareth (principally 12th century), was originally the cathedral of Vaison-la-Romaine (Vaucluse). At this end of the church, below the view of the camera, the foundation has been excavated to show that it rests on fragments of Roman buildings of the 1st and 2nd centuries. Photo courtesy of Rosalind Srb.

bottle in 1981. **Greatest success so far may be the rosé, as in the pale pink, peach-colored-and-tasting 1984, at once lively and round. He deliberately aims for his red to resemble a Gigondas, which the 1982 did, perhaps to a fault with its very ripe prune and dusty hay nose.**

15 ha in vine, dispersed in Vaison. About 35% is on clay-lime slopes, the rest on sandier flat land. 80% GR, 15% SY, 5% CS (which will be augmented). ✿ OT2, 10 to 15 days. Rosé is part "saignée," part directly pressed, and undergoes a malolactic. Vaslin press. ✿ The red is aged about 7 months in vat and then rests in bottle before sale.

Domaine Saint-Apollinaire, SCA Daumas, Puyméras

CDR red and white. **M. Daumas, who is oenologist and technical director for the Interprofessional Committee of the Côtes du Rhône, conducts the family vineyard** at Puyméras, where there is some downhill airflow from the nearby Mont Ventoux. His wines include a floral, slightly spritzy, apricot-flavored Viognier, a Blanc de blancs (45% Grenache blanc, 45% Clairette, 10% Ugni blanc), red "Cuvée d'Apolline" (1/3 each Grenache, Cinsault, Syrah), red "Réserve du Domaine" (Grenache, Cinsault, Mourvèdre), and a *cuvée* of pure Syrah. The latter, perhaps from the locally sandy soil and cool microclimate, I find nearer to the northern type than most southern versions. Tasted at the *cave* (1985), the 1982 seemed outstanding, full of such characteristic overtones as smoke, tobacco, sorrel, and cinnamon or nutmeg, over a black raspberry fruit. Older versions show tar, leather, and truffles.

15-ha dispersed estate in Puyméras is conducted according to organic farming principles. 60% GR, 25% SY, 10% CS, 15% MV and diverse whites. ❧ The grapes are harvested in hand-carried cases. OT1, 1 to 3 weeks, Vaslin press. In principle no SO_2 is employed except to clean barrels. The whites are allowed to undergo malolactic and are bottled *sur lies*. ❧ The reds spend 1 to 2 years in oak casks, the SY being given the longest time.

The following are cooperatives of this zone:

C Coopérative Agricole du Nyonsais, Nyons (Drôme)

Founded 1923. 47% AOC. CDR communes include Mirabel-aux-Baronnies, Nyons, Piégon, Rousset-les-Vignes, St.-Pantaléon-les-Vignes, Venterol. VDP Coteaux des Baronnies is produced at a special annex in Les Pilles (Drôme). Cooperative also produces appellation d'origine Olives Noires de Nyons and Huile d'Olive Vierge de Nyons.

Cave Coopérative Vinicole "Comtadine-Dauphinoise," Puyméras (Vaucluse)

Founded 1939. 53.16% AOC. CDR from Puyméras, Faucon, St.-Marcellin-les-Vaison, St.-Romain-en-Viennois, Vaison-la-Romaine (Vaucluse); Mérindol-les-Oliviers, Mirabel-les-Baronnies, Mollans-sur-Ouvèze, Piégon (Drôme). CDV from Crestet, Entrechaux, Veaux (Malaucène).

CDR red and rosé; CDR red "Natur et Progrès" ("organically" produced from the properties of 4 members); *CDR white; CDV; VDP des Coteaux des Baronnies.

C Cave Coopérative des Vignerons de Vaison et du Haut Comtat, Vaison-la-Romaine (Vaucluse)

Founded 1925. 66.25% AOC. CDR principally from Vaison-la-Romaine, Faucon, St.-Marcellin-les-Vaison, St.-Romain-en-Viennois (Vaucluse), Mérindol-les-Oliviers, Mollans-sur-Ouvèze (Drôme). CDV from Crestet, Entrechaux, Malaucène.

CDR red and rosé; CDV red and rosé.

Cave Coopérative "La Vigneronne," Villedieu (Vaucluse)

Founded 1939. 67.09% AOC. CDR from Villedieu and Buisson (most), St.-Roman-de-Malegarde, Vaison-la-Romaine (Vaucluse); Mirabel-aux-Baronnies (Drôme). Certain whites tasted from vat can be better than the Cave's own bottling. Wood age seems to add licorice, remove cedar in the reds.

CDR white "Cuvée des Templiers;" CDR rosé "Cuvée des Templiers;" *CDR red; CDR-Villages red; CDR red "Cuvée St.-Laurent" (aged in oak casks).

Domaine des Treilles
1982
Côtes du Rhône
75cl. APPELLATION CÔTES DU RHÔNE CONTROLÉE
MISE EN BOUTEILLE AU DOMAINE
PRODUCE OF FRANCE
PATRICE MÉRY, RÉCOLTANT - 26230 MONTBRISON S/LEZ - (75) 52.51.69

Domaine de la Taurelle
G.A.E.C.
côtes du rhône
APPELLATION CÔTES DU RHÔNE CONTROLÉE
CUVÉE SPÉCIALE
Mis en bouteille au Domaine
Mme Roux & Fils · Propriétaire-Récoltant · Mirabel aux Baronnies - Drôme
PRODUIT DE FRANCE
75cl

Domaine "Les Aussellons"
Côtes du Rhône
APPELLATION CÔTES·DU·RHÔNE CONTROLÉE e 75cl
BENOIT-EZINGEARD PROPRIÉTAIRES-RÉCOLTANTS 84 VILLEDIEU
Mis en bouteille au Domaine
PRODUIT DE FRANCE

DOMAINE St CLAUDE
CÔTES DU RHÔNE
APPELLATION CÔTES DU RHÔNE CONTRÔLÉE
Claude CHARASSE et Associés, Propriétaires-Récoltants
LE PALIS — 84110 VAISON-LA-ROMAINE
75 cl

PRODUCE 1981 OF FRANCE
MIS EN BOUTEILLE A LA PROPRIÉTÉ

Domaine St Sauveur
CÔTES DU VENTOUX
APPELLATION CÔTES DU VENTOUX ÇONTROLÉE
élevé et mis en bouteilles au domaine
par les héritiers de MARCEL REY propriétaire récoltant
DOMAINE ST SAUVEUR à 84 AUBIGNAN (FRANCE)
vol. net 0,74 L

DOMAINE TROUSSEL
CÔTES du VENTOUX
APPELLATION CÔTES du VENTOUX CONTRÔLÉE 75cl
DOMAINE TROUSSEL PROPRIETAIRE RECOLTANT/route de Serres
84200 CARPENTRAS/VAUCLUSE/FRANCE/Tél. 90/63.16.56-67.28.35
MIS EN BOUTEILLE AU DOMAINE

1978
Net contents 750ml
(25.4 FL.)
Alcohol by vol. 12.5 %
PRODUCE OF FRANCE
Domaine des Lônes
COTEAUX DU TRICASTIN
Appellation Côteaux du Tricastin Contrôlée
O.& H. BOUR
VIGNERONS A ROUSSAS · DROME · FRANCE
750 ml
RED TABLE WINE
Imported by AWARD WINES L.T.D. · NEW YORK · NEW YORK 10017
N.Y. State permit WW 584

DOMAINE DU VIEUX MICOCOULIER
Coteaux du Tricastin
appellation d'origine contrôlée

SO.C.G.E.A. - CAVE VERGOBBI
viticulteur-récoltant
LES GRANGES-GONTARDES
(Drôme)

12
Satellite Appellations

VDQS FROM 1951, the Côtes du Ventoux was promoted to AOC standing in 1973. The center of gravity of the region is around Carpentras, which was capital of the old papal state, the Comtat Venaissin. For this reason some of these wines had a fame at the papal court as early as Châteauneuf's.

The region is on the whole sheltered from the mistral by the Mont-Ventoux to its north, at 1900 meters the highest mountain in France outside the Alps or Pyrenees. This means the CDV runs more risk than the CDR of spring frosts. Because of altitude, the climate is cooler the farther east one goes, with the coolest of all the farthest south, the valley of the Calavon. There an additional particularity is that CDV is found on the south and south-facing slopes of the Plateau of Vaucluse, north of the river, while south of the river are Côtes du Lubéron on the north slopes of the Montagne de Lubéron. The eastward portion of the CDV is one of the latest to harvest in all France.

The region is generally and irregularly hilly ("accidenté")—the plateau of Mazan is one exception—so that almost all the vineyards are on *coteaux*. In many cases the vineyards have replaced plantations of table (eating) grapes that were occupying the best sites, with care being taken during the process to augment the proportion of Grenache and Syrah and to cut back on that of Carignan in the CDV's *encépagement*. The soils are meager, arid, and on the whole calcareous.

For a long time the wine economy of the region, dominated by cooperatives, was dependent on the bulk sale of the style of wine called "café," intermediate between red and rosé because the product of a very short *cuvaison*. (The name derived from the market, which was principally over-the-counter sale in the cafés of industrial areas farther north.) In the last decade, there has been a major effort, by private growers and cooperatives alike, to sell more wine in bottle and hence to make more of it true red wine.

The AOC is accorded to red, white, and rosé wines produced at a normal maximum productivity of 50 hectoliters per hectare and with a minimum natural alcohol of 11%. Principal *cépages* for the reds and rosés are Grenache, Cinsault, Syrah, Mourvèdre and Carignan; for white, Clairette and Bourboulenc.

In this chapter, U = member of the Union des Vignerons des Côtes du Ventoux. For other abbreviations see the master list at the beginning of this book. Addresses of Ventoux producers are 84 (Vaucluse).

North of the Mont-Ventoux

Pierre Amadieu, Gigondas

See Gigondas, Les Celliers Amadieu.

Domaine Champ-Long, GAEC M. Gély et Fils, Entrechaux

CDV red and rosé. **Substantial reds, leafy and cherry-flavored when tasted from vat, with a decent level of acidity. My impression is that the bottled wine (except for the "Cuvée Spéciale") is actually hardened by wood.**

20 ha dispersed in Entrechaux (sandy soil) and Malaucène (clay-lime soil). 80% GR, plus SY, CR. 🦗 ST, 4 to 5 days, hydraulic press. 🦗 Wine spends 3 to 6 months in oak casks for the regular bottling, 12 to 18 months for "Cuvée Spéciale."

The following are cooperatives of this zone:

U Coopérative Vinicole de Beaumont-du-Ventoux

CDV from Beaumont, Le Barroux, Crestet, Entrechaux, and Malaucène (most)—in general one of the most elevated regions of France for vinegrowing. CDR from Mollans-sur-Ouvèze (Drôme), the eastern limit of AOC CDR.

Cave Coopérative Vinicole "Comtadine-Daphinoise," Puyméras

CDV from Crestet, Entrechaux, Veaux (Malaucène). Long time among principal sources of CDV "La Vieille Ferme" (See "CDR in the Environs of Châteauneuf-du-Pape"). See "CDR of the Pre-Alps" for CDR.

Cave Coopérative des Vignerons de Vaison et du Haut Comtat, Vaison-la-Romaine

CDV from Crestet, Entrechaux, Malaucène. Source of CDV for Cellier des Dauphins (see "CDR of the Lower Aygues and Garrigues").

South of the Mont-Ventoux

H Domaine du Saint-Sauveur, GAEC Les Héritiers de Marcel Rey (Guy Rey), Aubignan

CDR; Muscat de Beaumes-de-Venise; CDV. **M. Rey's wines all come from the same terroir, a cobble-covered plateau south of Beaumes-de-Venise that is crossed by rows of cypresses marking the boundaries between the appellations. He distinguishes the CDV as a lighter, suppler wine than the CDR by including Cinsault in the *encépagement*. The CDV is usually one of the best. The rose-gold, almost smokey Muscat may be the most fragrant of all Beaumes-de-Venise.**

28 ha of CDV at Aubignan, 50% GR, 25% CS, 14% SY, 8% CR, 2% MV, 1% CN. 2.10 ha CDR at Beaumes-de-Venise, 80% GR, 20% SY. 5.50 ha of Muscat de Beaumes-de-Venise, with both Muscat blanc and noir. 🦗 CM, 3 to 5 days (CDV), 7 to 8 days (CDR), hydraulic press. 🦗 No wood.

Domaine de Champaga, M.M. d'Ollone (Philippe et Olivier d'Ollone), Le Barroux

CDV red and rosé. **A Ventoux from the border with CDR, which was lively, leafy, berryish in 1984, more in the café style and not quite as much of a red wine as M. d'Ollone likes to make. 1983 was in fact a bigger wine, with the tannin a little on the dusty side. Pleasant rosé.**

20 ha from slopes at 300m altitude in Le Barroux. 65% GR, 15% SY, 15% CS, 5% CR. 🦗 Machine-harvesting began in 1984, to reach 70% of the production by 1985.

ST, 50% destemmed, 8 to 10 days; Vaslin press. Rosé "par saignée." 🍃 By rotation between vat and cask, the red spends 3 to 4 months in wood before bottling.

Domaine du Vieux Lazaret, Caromb

See Châteauneuf-du-Pape, Domaine du Vieux Lazaret

H **Domaine des Anges,** Malcolm Swan, Mormoiron

CDV red. **Mr. Swan is an Englishman who left advertising to become a *vigneron*. He makes medium-dark, quite substantial Ventoux—definitely a red rather than a café wine. Behind an intense, sun-warmed blackberry to black raspberry fruit lurks a tannin that sometimes smells a little dusty, for which reason I preferred a green-capsuled bottling of 1982, which had been double-filtered.**

19 ha total, most on east-facing slopes high above the village of Mortmoiron. 11.8 ha ore red GR, SY, CS, CR and 7.5 ha are white, MR, RS, BR, GR, UN and Chardonnay (VDP). 🍃 OT2, 8 days, Vaslin press. 🍃 Wine is aged in vat.

H **Domaine Troussel,** GAEC Domaine Troussel, Serres-Carpentras

CDV red and rosé. **A true *vigneron* spirit is evident here when father, son, and son-in-law present unassembled wines for a tasting that is a virtual lesson in the diversity of Ventoux *terroirs,* the greater acidity of wines from high altitude being much in evidence. The bottled wine shows more than the usual capacity for development in a "Junior Châteauneuf" or even Burgundy direction, already apparent in a 1983, stronger in a 1981, strongest in the still lively (in 1985) 1978.**

39 ha of CDV, 8 in the hamlet of Serres, 12 elsewhere in Carpentras, 12 at Flassan, 5 at Mormoiron. 60% GR, 20% CR, plus CS, SY, CT, RS. The grapes of Flassan can ripen as much as 3 weeks later than those from Carpentras. 🍃 OT2, 6 days, Vaslin press. Rosé "par saignée." 🍃 Most red wines are aged in vat, but some of the SY (from Carpentras) is being tried in oak cask, which seems to remove a vegetal character.

Union des Vignerons des Côtes du Ventoux, Carpentras

Headquartered on the Route de Pernes just south of the old capital of the Comtat Venaissin, this is a union of cooperatives from within the area of AOC CDV. The members are the *caves* of Beaumont-du-Ventoux, Bédoin, Goult-Lumières, Maubec-Gare, Maubec-Lubéron, Mazan, Mormoiron, St.-Didier, and Villes-sur-Auzon, plus the SICA Viticole du Comtat (a cooperative of private growers). As with similar unions, it functions to condition, bottle and commercialize under the union's label an important supply of CDV of "followed" quality—together the members produce more than half of all CDV—as well as to bottle for them the wines the members will sell under their own labels.

The following wines are offered under the Union's label:

CDV white
CDV rosé
CDV red "Tradition" (Burgundy bottle)
*CDV red "Prestige" (Bordeaux bottle)
CDL (from cooperatives with members in the Lubéron)

The cooperatives of this zone (roughly from N to E, then S, then W) are:

Cave des Vignerons de Beaumes-de-Venise
*CDV, from Aubignan, Le Barroux, Caromb, St.-Hippolyte-de-Graveyrons. (See Beaumes-de-Venise for CDR-Villages and Muscat.)

Cave "Saint-Marc," Caromb
CDV from Caromb, Le Barroux, Modène, St.-Hippolyte-de-Graveyrons, St.-Pierre-de-Vassols. Having specialized in café style, Cave returned to long *cuvaison* red in 1980.
     *CDV St.-Marc "Cuvée Spéciale."

U Les Vignerons du Mont Ventoux, Bédoin
CDV from Bédoin, Crillon-le-Brave, Flassan, St.-Pierre-de-Vassols.
     *CDV Château Crillon; *CDV "Cuvée des 3 Messes Basses."

U Coopérative Vinicole "La Montagne Rouge," Villes-sur-Auzon
*CDV from Villes-sur-Auzon, Bédoin, Blauvac, Flassan, Méthamis, Mormoiron. Cave has always specialized in red wine.

U Cave Coopérative "Les Roches Blanches," Mormoiron
CDV from Mormoiron, Bédoin, Blauvac, Caromb, Carpentras, Flassan, Mazan, Villes-sur-Auzon.
     *CDV Syrah.

U Cave Coopérative de "Canteperdrix," Mazan
CDV from Mazan (most), Caromb, Modène, St.-Pierre-de-Vassols.
     *CDV "Seigneur du Carri."

U Coopérative Intercommunale "La Courtoise," St.-Didier
CDV principally from St.-Didier, Malemort-du-Comtat, Venasque. Vinify with the stems, interesting experiments in CM, especially Carignan.
     *CDV rosé; *CDV "Carte d'Or."

Société Coopérative Vinicole "La Pernoise," Pernes-les-Fontaines
CDV from Pernes, Aubignan, Carpentras, Loriol-du-Comtat, Saumane.

The Valley of the Calavon

Domaine de la Coquillade, Cyprien Percie du Sert, Gargas
CDV red. **M. Percie du Sert made his first wine here in 1976. Very deep black raspberry fruit is sometimes masked by a surprising amount of rough tannin (for a Ventoux), which made a 1979 once shipped to the U.S. unexpectedly take a while to come around.**
     Single estate of 15 ha in vine, all on slopes, about half on soil with iron oxide. The winery is at 300m altitude. 40% GR, 40% SY, 10% CR, 10% CS. 16-year average age of vines. 🍇 Through 1982 about half the wine, including all the Syrah, was made CM, the other half OT1, 8 to 10 days. 🍇 Aged about 1 year in vat.

Domaine de la Verrière, Bernard et Françoise Maubert, Goult

CDV red. **Fruity, supple, tender wine when tasted from vat that is darkened and soured a bit in flavor by oak age before bottling. Magnums of unwooded Verrière were once taken by U.S. importer.**

20 ha of vines on clay-lime slopes with some iron oxide. 50% GR, 20% CR, 10–15% CS, 10% SY, 5% MV. 🐚 ST with partial destemming according to the year, 3 days average; Vaslin press, none incorporated into CDV. 🐚 Wine for bottling (about 60% of the production) is given 6 to 12 months in oak casks.

The cooperatives in this area (listed W to E):

U **Cave Coopérative Vinicole de Maubec-Lubéron,** Coustellet (Maubec)
CDV from Cabrières-d'Avignon, Gordes, Goult, Lagnes, Robion.

U **Cave Coopérative Vinicole de Maubec-Gare,** Coustellet (Maubec)
CDV from Cabrières-d'Avignon, Gordes, Rousillon, St.-Pantaléon.

Coopérative Agricole de Vinification de Goult-Lumières
CDV from Goult, Gordes, Joucas, Murs, Rousillon, St.-Pantaléon.

Coopérative Vinicole de Bonnieux
CDV from Apt, Bonnieux, Gargas, Gordes, Goult, Joucas, Murs, Rousillon. Founded in 1920, Bonnieux was the first *cave coopérative* in the Vaucluse.

Cave Coopérative Vinicole "Le Vin de Sylla," Apt
CDV from Gargas, Gordes, Lioux, Murs, Rousillon, Rustel, St.-Saturnin d'Apt.

COTEAUX DU TRICASTIN

Once having been VDQS and also promoted to AOC in 1973, the Tricastin has some areas with as much historical claim to usage of Côtes du Rhône in the plural as those that eventually gained that AOC. Nevertheless, the terrain has a distinct look that seems to declare a different *pays* north of Suze-la-Rousse, an aspect dominated by cracked, green-oak-covered limestone plateaus with almost no soil that really look like buttes pointed at the Rhône. On top of one of these sits La Garde Adhémar, the first Provençal "perched village" with octagonal-towered Romanesque church one sees to the east of the train south of Donzère.

Below this village, stretching northwest toward Donzère, is one of the two principal zones of production for CDT, a Châteauneuf-type plateau covered with enormous cobblestones, which happens to be one of the areas of the southern Rhône receiving the strongest mistral. This, plus the limestone slopes to the north, is the area with the highest concentration of private growers and the most substantial wines. Even so, they are less full-bodied than the high plateau wines of the CDR farther south, partly because the area is farther north and partly because the *encépagement* is more varied and the vines younger. The plateau was replanted after phylloxera only recently, for the most part by repatriated Algerian French families.

The other important zone, including the commune that is the biggest producer of

CDT, La Baume-de-Transit, is part of the northward continuation of plain and *garrigues* that begins with the Plan de Dieu. Production is dominated by cooperatives in the neighboring CDR. At La Baume-de-Transit there is also a cooperative (SICA) for the production, off calcareous, oak-covered soils, of *appellation d'origine Truffes noirs du Tricastin* from the Tricastin and neighboring Enclave des Papes.

The AOC is awarded to red, white, and rosé wines whose productivity is limited to a normal maximum of 50 hectoliters per hectare. Minimum natural alcohol is 11%. Principal *cépages* for red and rosé are Grenache, Cinsault, Mourvèdre, Syrah, Picpoul, and Carignan, with up to 20% white *cépages* admitted. White are Grenache blanc, Clairette, Picpoul blanc, Bourboulenc and Ugni blanc.

The following producers are listed alphabetically. Their addresses are 26 (Drôme), unless otherwise indicated.

Domaine du Devoy, Yves Aubert, Tulette

See **Domaine de la Tour d'Elyssas.**

H **Domaine de la Grangeneuve,** O. and H. Bour, Roussas

CDT red and rosé. **The wines of Grangeneuve exhibit an interesting transitional character between northern and southern Rhône, with lighter body than the north, but less cooked or jammy than some in the south. The result is a certain flavor nuance of the north with southern roundness. Very concentrated and powerfully aromatic "Cuvée Spéciale" 1983. An almost always convincing pure Syrah, in the 1982 hints at meat fat and vanilla, though unwooded.**

100 ha divided between 70 at Roussas (more stony) and 30 at St.-Paul-Trois-Châteaux (more sandy). 50% GR, 30% SY, 20% CS, a little MV. 🍇 Production has been machine-harvested since 1983. Up until then "some" whole berries were used in CL, 6 to 15 days, "never" above 28° C. Now straight CL. 🍇 No wood. **Domaine des Lones** is an additional label.

Domaine Saint-Rémy, SCI Le Terroir St.-Rémy (Famille Reynaud), La-Baume-de-Transit

CDT red and rosé; CDR red and white. **Light, pleasant berry-filled fruit CDT reds of which my notes indicate that the "Réserve" (Grenache/Syrah) has more concentration than the "Cuvée Tradition" (essentially with Grenache, Syrah, Cinsault, Mourvèdre, Carignan). CDRs are "Sélection" (old-vine Grenache) and "Prestige" ("mainly" Grenache).**

120 ha in vine dispersed in Baume-de-Transit (CDT), Ste.-Cécile-les-Vignes, Roche-gude, Suze-la-Rousse, Visan, Richerenches (CDR). Having been cooperators at 4 different *caves*, the Reynauds began making their own wine in 1976. 🍇 CL, 4 to 6 days, Vaslin press. 🍇 Wine is aged in below-ground vats. Some is commercialized with the name "Terroir St.-Rémy" by the *négociant* firm Pascal (Vacqueyras).

Domaine de la Tour d'Elyssas, formerly Pierre Labeye, Les Granges-Gontardes

CDT red and rosé. **Under M. Labeye's proprietorship, 3 selections were produced. "Cru du Devoy" in red and rosé was Grenache, Cinsault, and Carignan. "Cru du Meynas" added 10–15% Syrah to these. Then came "Vin de Syrah" pure.**

At one time a property of 135 ha, divided between Granges-Gontardes (Meynas)

and Donzère (Devoy). M. Yves Aubert of Tulette is now owner of the latter part, known as Domaine de Devoy. At last report the rest of the property, including the striking open-air vat-house tower, was in the hands of la SAFER, a non-profit government-supervised corporation that buys and resells agricultural land to prevent speculative pricing and to promote economically viable holdings among neighboring proprietors.

H **Domaine du Vieux Micocoulier,** SCGEA Cave Vergobbi, Logis de Berre, Les Granges Gontardes

CDT red. **Until 1982 a lighter and a richer** *cuvée* **were distinguished. All vats in the** *cave,* **however, contain 20% or more Syrah. The 1983 and 1984** *cuvées* **were all of the rich style, which develops leafy, floral, lemon-orange peel fragrances, often of violet and truffles, in a wine that though fairly high in alcohol, is never heavy.**

The Vergobbi family were *vignerons* in Algeria for 4 generations before repatriation and a fresh beginning in the Tricastin. They have cleared 125 ha on the plateau of Donzère, covered with Châteauneuf-sized cobblestones and hard limestone rocks. 60% GR, 30% SY, 7% CS, 3% MV. Average age of vines is 12 years. 🐌 Machine-harvesting began in 1981. Even before, vinification was CL, 5 to 6 days, Vaslin press. 🐌 No wood. 1 to 2 years in vat. Vergobbis do not bottle their own wine, but sell a large part direct to individual clients who drive to the *cave* for it. In the recent past, however, some was bottled and sold with the name Cave Vergobbi by *négociant* Romaine Bouchard of Valréas (Vaucluse). Now *négociant* firm De Launay of l'Etang Vergy (Côte-d'Or) commercializes it with the name of the domaine, and an important part is sold to the state monopoly of Sweden.

A peculiarity of CDT has been that none of the cooperatives producing it is located within the AOC; instead they are found in surrounding parts of the CDR. Among them are the following, listed in alphabetical order by commune.

Société Coopérative Vinicole de Bourg-St.-Andéol (Ardèche)
CDT from Donzère, La-Garde-Adhémar, Pierrelatte. Source of CDT for the Union des Coopératives Vinicoles d'Ardèche "Vignerons Ardèchois," Ruoms (Ardèche). (For CDR see "CDR of the Northern Gard and Southern Ardèche.")

Coopérative Vinicole "Le Cellier des Templiers," Richerenches (Vaucluse)
*CDT from Baume-de-Transit, Donzère, Grignan, Montségur, La-Roche-St.-Secret. Source of CDT for Le Cellier de l'Enclave des Papes (see Valréas). (For CDR see "CDR of the Lower Aygues and Garrigues.")

Société Coopérative Agricole de Vinification, Rochegude
CDT from Baume-de-Transit, Chamaret, Colonzelle, Valaurie. (For CDR see Rochegude.)

Cave Coopérative Vinicole de Saint-Pantaléon-les-Vignes
CDT from La-Roche-St.-Secret. (For CDR see Saint-Pantaléon-les-Vignes.)

Cave Coopérative Vinicole "La Suzienne," Suze-la-Rousse
CDT from Baume-de-Transit, St.-Paul-Trois-Châteaux. The Cave is the largest single producer of CDT and principal supplier of CDT to the Cellier des Dauphins. (For the Cellier and CDR from the Cave, see "CDR of the Lower Aygues and Garrigues.")

Cave Coopérative "Costes Rousses," Tulette

CDT from Baume-de-Transit, Chamaret, Montségur. (For CDR see "CDR of the Lower Aygues and Garrigues.")

Cave "la Vinsobraise" des Vignerons de Vinsobres

CDT from La-Roche-St.-Secret, St.-Paul-Trois-Châteaux. (For CDR see Vinsobres).

THE NORTHERN RHÔNE VALLEY

Church of St. Croix (12th century), La-Baume-de-Transit (Drôme). Photo courtesy of Rosalind Srb.

GRANDE CUVÉE

Chante-Alouette

APPELLATION HERMITAGE CONTRÔLÉE

M. CHAPOUTIER S.A.

NÉGOCIANTS-ÉLEVEURS A TAIN L'HERMITAGE (DROME) FRANCE

le Chevalier de Sterimberg

MARQUE   DÉPOSÉE

HERMITAGE

APPELLATION HERMITAGE CONTRÔLÉE

PAUL JABOULET AÎNÉ

TAIN (DRÔME) FRANCE

C.M. 11.115

LES VOUSSÈRES

PRODUIT DE FRANCE

Crozes-Hermitage

Appellation Crozes-Hermitage Contrôlée

MIS EN BOUTEILLE A LA PROPRIÉTÉ   75 cl

G.A.E.C. LES GAMETS FAYOLLE FILS

PROPRIÉTAIRES - VITICULTEURS A GERVANS (DROME) FRANCE

TRADE   MARK

CROZES HERMITAGE

APPELLATION CROZES HERMITAGE CONTRÔLÉE

Domaine de Thalabert

MARQUE DÉPOSÉE

75 cl   ## PAUL JABOULET AÎNÉ

Mis en bouteilles par

PAUL JABOULET AÎNÉ, NÉGOCIANT ÉLEVEUR A TAIN L'HERMITAGE DRÔME FRANCE

PRODUIT   DE FRANCE

Cornas

APPELLATION CORNAS CONTRÔLÉE

MIS EN BOUTEILLE A LA PROPRIÉTÉ

Auguste CLAPE, Propriétaire-Viticulteur à CORNAS (Ardèche)

75 cl

PRODUCE   MÉTHODE
OF FRANCE   CHAMPENOISE

Saint-Péray

APPELLATION CONTROLÉE

J.-F. CHABOUD Propriétaire-Viticulteur   78 cl.

07130 SAINT-PÉRAY - FRANCE   BRUT

IMP. PLANCHER ST-PÉRAY

GRAND VIN DES COTES-DU-RHONE

CUVÉE C

Cornas

APPELLATION D'ORIGINE CONTROLÉE

PRODUIT FRANÇAIS   75 cl

MIS EN BOUTEILLE A LA PROPRIÉTÉ

MARCEL JUGE - PROPRIÉTAIRE-VITICULTEUR A CORNAS (ARDÈCHE)

IMP. REYNAUD, VALENCE

Saint-Joseph

APPELLATION D'ORIGINE CONTROLÉE

MIS EN BOUTEILLE A LA PROPRIÉTÉ

BERNARD GRIPA   37,5 cl

PROPRIÉTAIRE-VITICULTEUR A MAUVES (07) FRANCE

PRODUCE OF FRANCE

13
Generalities

— LOCATION OF *LES CÔTES DU RHÔNE SEPTENTRIONALES* —

THOUGH THEY SHARE one name and geographical situation, the Côtes du Rhône as they gradually came to be known in the 19th century are by climate and geology two distinct winegrowing regions. By far the smaller is the northern region, *les Côtes du Rhône septentrionales*. While it contains some vineyard sites at least 2000 years old, for reasons that will become clear, it represents at present only about 3% of the area and production of the Côtes du Rhône. In other respects as well, the distinction between the southern and northern regions is as pronounced as their difference in size.

Compared to the vast extent of southern vineyards, located principally along the Rhône's tributaries and often on flat ground, the vineyards of the northern Rhône are confined, except at Crozes-Hermitage and Saint-Péray, to the steep, granitic banks of the Rhône River itself. They extend from just south of the old Roman city of Vienne to just south of Valence. As a general rule the pitch of the slopes is so severe that the vines have to be planted on terraces, called "chaillées," "chayées," or "chalets." The terrace walls, called "cheys" or "murgeys," are dry-constructed of the local stone. Their maintenance is a regular vineyard chore to prevent escape of soil that, when it washes down the slopes, must be carried back up, as does the grape harvest down, they say in the north, "on a man's back."

But not only the difficulty of labor in these arduous circumstances limits the production of northern Rhônes, although in fact it does threaten some of them with disappearance. Some flat ground to plant is found on the plateau at the top of some *coteaux,* and at the bottom of others. With very few exceptions the wine from such sites is the source of what little regional CDR is still produced in the north. Thus the specific *terroirs* of these *coteaux* is responsible for the originality of the northern *crus,* and hence their inherent rarity. Almost all the northern Rhônes are *crus* and have been accorded their own local AOCs. Even so they represent but 21% of the area and 24.1% of the production of all Rhône *crus* (Le Plâtre et Sarfati 1983).

──────── CLIMATE, SOIL, SUBREGIONS ────────

These *terroirs* are conditioned by the general climate. Compared to the mistral-dominated, Mediterranean climate of the south, the northern Rhône region is a southerly outpost of temperate continental climate. Summers are warmer, but winters are also colder than parts of France farther north that are under greater maritime influence. As to humidity, Lyon is famous for its mists, so that the climate of the northern valley may also

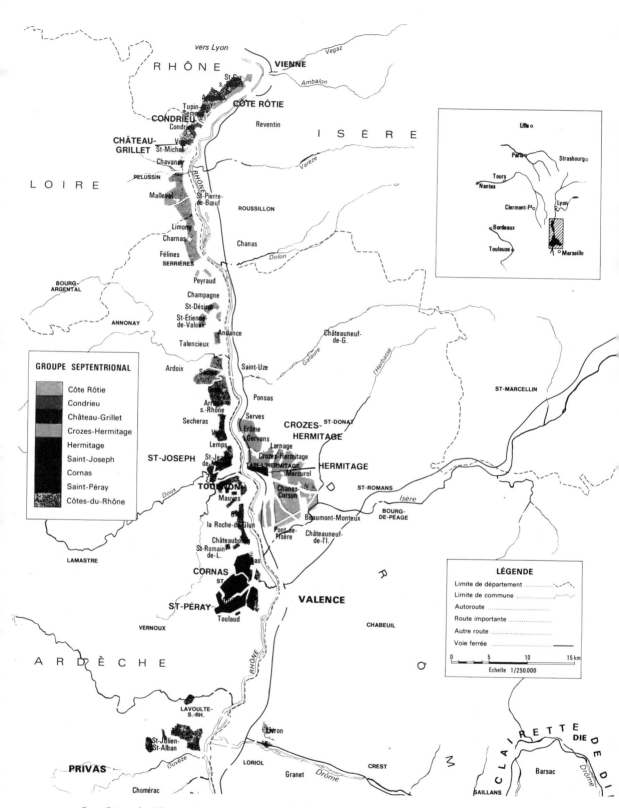

Les Côtes-du-Rhône, Group Septentrional. Reprinted with permission from *Atlas de la France Vinicole L. Larmat.* Copyright 1976, *Revue du vin de France.*

be described as transitional between the more regularly occurring humidity of the Lyonnais and the torrential rains and summer drought of the lower Rhône.

In general the red wines themselves seem to share this character of "triple transition" (Bordas 1946). From a situation far enough north that they can be balanced when produced from a single *cépage*, they are nevertheless simultaneously more alcoholic (like southern Rhônes) and more tannic (like Bordeaux) than Burgundies, while more acid (like Burgundies) than southern Rhônes.

But specific *terroirs* are also the result of microclimates. The Rhône valley south and north is windy, and being in effect a corridor between mountain ranges to either side, there is a fairly clear-cut alternation between north and south winds. Again, the northern sector as a whole has a difference that comes from the confinement of the vineyard to the river banks. The whole corridor is protected from winds in the northwest quadrant by a series of ridges just west of the river. Microclimates are created by the orientation and contours of the river banks. They are in effect bluffs that, as they jut out toward the river from the already protected west side, often turn their backs to the north wind, simultaneously sheltering their south sides and creating exposures that face south and southeast. To locate vineyards on these sunny, protected slopes is the classic solution to the problem of achieving sufficient ripeness in a northerly winegrowing region. For this reason part of the unity of the northern Rhône is the tendency of the *crus* to be clustered on the right bank in situations that create microclimates.

In the southern Rhône the extent of the region as a whole produces important modifications into subregions along east-west lines. In the northern Rhône the narrowness of the valley and the climate transition make the modifications happen north to south. The north wind increases in strength and frequency the farther south one moves in the valley. It begins to be called *mistral* (which means master), and to be regarded as a factor for sanitizing the vineyards by evaporating excess moisture, not far north of Tain-l'Hermitage. From this hotter, periodically drier middle part of the valley, come wines that are higher in alcohol and somewhat more grossly tannic. (An exception is St.-Joseph, whose slopes are not exposed as much to the south.)

When one is driving north along the Rhône from Tain, the climate seems to change in the vicinity of Serrière. Suddenly the trees seem taller and all vegetation lusher and more verdant than in areas under the mistral's influence. In any case, by the time one reaches Ampuis, the north wind is called a "bise." Here the vineyard's health is said to depend more on good ventilation than on the influence of one wind. And protecting the vines from the strength of the south wind is apparently what required the old, purely local system of training the vine on three stakes (called "echalas," of which two are still employed). From this more regularly humid, far northern valley come more delicate, lower alcohol, somewhat more finely tannic and acid wines.

A series of additional exceptions to unity coincide to mark the same distinction between middle valley and northern valley subregions of *les Côtes du Rhône septentrionales*. Some of these are technical. In the middle valley they tend to use *pigeage* (punching down) to keep the floating cap of grape skins and stems below the surface of the fermenting wine; in the northern valley the cap is more often held down and submerged by a grid of planks. *Elevage* (literally "raising," in the sense of upbringing of the wine) follows the lines laid down by climate. By contrast to the southern Rhône where reused large casks *(foudres)* are the norm, a mixture of medium-sized casks *(demi-*

muids) and small barrels *(pièces)* is used for the purpose in both subregions of the north. But the wood is more often reused in the middle valley, and more *pièces,* more often made of new oak, seem to be used in the far north.

There are white *cépages* unique to each subregion. In the middle valley (around Hermitage), the white varieties are Marsanne and Roussanne. The northern valley (Côte-Rôtie and Condrieu) has as its sole white *cépage* the Viognier.

Great wines are grown on the left bank only in the middle valley, at Hermitage, where the ancient Rhône cut the famous south-west facing hill off from the granite *coteaux* of the right bank, and a further line of south-angled slopes falls back a little distance from the river. As the gentler slopes extend south and east and the growing area eventually spreads onto plateaus, the vineyards of the middle valley are no longer confined to the Rhône corridor and to granitic soil. First there are calcareous soils on the slopes; then the plateaus are covered by "rolled" cobblestones of alpine origin, such as one sees in the southern Rhône, and by gravel. These are the detritus of glacial times deposited by the Rhône and its tributary the Isère. (The well-drained lower plateaus in the Crozes-Hermitage AOC provide another exception to the robust character of middle valley reds.)

In the middle valley some cobblestones also appear on the right bank at St.-Péray, where the vineyards up behind the town occupy a side valley, one side of which is based on granite, and the other (beneath the crumbling château of Crussol, now virtually indistinguishable from the bedrock) is based on limestone.

The northern valley has its exceptions to granite too, and the principal one is at the same time distinctive, being the micaschist of Côte-Rôtie. Further variations are

Remains of the Château de Crussol, above St.-Péray (Ardèche). Photo courtesy of Rosalind Srb.

localized within the areas of the *crus* themselves. These include, almost everywhere, the possibility of sand, clay, or a little calcareous soil. With *encépagement* of the reds not really a variable, and with the scale of the region as a whole being intimate, these minor differences show up with a force and interest somewhat comparable to those among *climats* in Burgundy. As a result interest has increased in the northern Rhône for putting the name of the "lieu-dit" of origin on the label.

CÉPAGES

Red

SYRAH

Syrah is the sole red *cépage* of all the northern *crus*. In certain AOCs, because the northern Rhône is a southerly outpost of temperate climate, it may be blended with a small portion of white grapes to take off the very roughest edges. One hears additional details in the northern Rhône about the distinction between Petite and Grosse Syrah. The Grosse Syrah is said to be the "Syrah de Gervans"; the Petite, "Syrah de Mauves." At Côte-Rôtie the real native or "old" Syrah is called "La Sérine pointu," for its ovoid berries.

On their home ground, Syrah wines are definitely more dominated by their tannins than in the south. The vegetal side of Syrah is almost always in evidence in the younger wines. The scent of violets among their leaves is part of it. The leaves seem to be sorrel in the Hermitage area. To pepper and cinnamon can be added a fresh, resinous aspect that may be especially intense at Côte-Rôtie. The Latin naturalist Pliny noticed this quality millennia ago in what were then the wines of Roman Vienne; it may have been behind the too-much-of-a-good-thing custom that grew up of artificially resinating ancient Côte-Rôtie ("vinum picatum"). In maturing, the resinous aspect often seems to mingle a pitchy-tarry character with truffles.

On the right bank of the Rhône more than on the left, the Syrah can have an aroma of meat fat, almost surely a smoked pork product, which some say makes St.-Joseph especially harmonious with *charcuterie*. The animal side can extend to leather and general barnyard. All this is over a deep, basic, fruit in the blackberry (a little cooked and spiced) to black raspberry (with vanilla) to cassis range, which some would localize as cassis at Hermitage, and raspberry at Côte-Rôtie.

Try:
Any northern Rhône red wine.

White

MARSANNE

Marsanne is thought to have originated in the town of the same name near Montélimar (Drôme). Its presence (with Roussanne) is distinctive of the middle Rhône valley, perhaps because it is a "3rd epoch" ripener. There it is the *cépage de base* for the great white wines of Hermitage, St.-Joseph and St.-Péray, as well as being allowed in small quantities (with Roussanne) for the refinement of red Hermitage, Crozes-Hermitage and, since 1980, St.-Joseph. It is also admitted to regional CDR in the south and is making some inroads there in the search for more aromatic whites.

This seems somewhat paradoxical since it is one of those *cépages* whose wine from the very start gives an impression, which is actually varietal, of being oxidized. This is on account of its green apple fruit combined with a grassiness that can easily pass into hay. In the grass there are also clover, clover blossoms, and honey, with richer (Hermitage) or steelier (St.-Péray) variations. Marsanne also seems, like Chardonnay, to develope a lemon flavor in contact with oak.

As a result, two schools of thought have grown up on how to treat Marsanne. One says to keep it very fresh and protected from oxidation through all the steps until early bottling, preferring the bottle to the barrel as a medium for its development. The other, believing that the varietal aroma destines Marsanne wines to be "aged" in any case, advocates fermenting and maturing at least in part in wood. There is no doubt that Marsanne is the basis at Hermitage of one of the longest-lived white wines of France.

Try:

The white St.-Joseph of **Jean-Louis Grippat** (see St.-Joseph). 100% Marsanne.

White Hermitage **"Chante-Alouette"** (see Hermitage), of which Max **Chapoutier** says the same.

J.F. Chaboud still St.-Péray (see). Conveniently now presented in pure Marsanne and Roussanne labelings.

ROUSSANNE

Probably a native of the middle Rhône and Isère valleys, Roussanne at present is much less a factor in northern Rhône whites than Marsanne, or (according to what one reads) than it was historically. Affected by infectious degeneration (fan-leaf virus), its lower productivity than Marsanne's made it less attractive to the growers, as did its susceptibility to oidium (a fungus infection). It is somewhat ironic that recovery of virus-free strains has made pure Roussanne easier to encounter in the south, where it is one of the 13 cépages of Châteauneuf-du-Pape and where it (but not Marsanne) is admitted to CDR-Villages. Thus my sense of its varietal character comes from southern examples, in which it seems notably floral, and while rich and even honeyed, at the same time is perhaps leaner, more structured, and less metallic than (southern) Marsanne.

Try:

Châteauneuf-du-Pape **Château de Beaucastel** white (see Châteauneuf-du-Pape). Has reached 90% Roussanne in composition in recent years.

CDR-Villages white from **Domaine Ste.-Anne** (see St.-Gervais). 100% Roussanne in the 1983.

Both Crozes-Hermitage blanc **"Mule Blanche"** and Hermitage blanc **"Le Chevalier de Stérimberg"** (see **Paul Jaboulet Aîné**). 55% and 45% Roussanne, respectively.

VIOGNIER

Although legends relate that it was brought to Condrieu by Greeks, or from Dalmatia by the Romans, Viognier's origin is uncertain. By a number of ampelographic criteria, it seems to belong with the other northern Rhône *cépages* to a group that may well be indigenous (Allobrogian) (Charnay 1985). Its presence as the sole white *cépage* in Condrieu and Côte-Rôtie (for refinement again) defines the far northern valley subregion as surely as Marsanne and Roussanne define the middle valley.

Viognier's rarity is enhanced by being an ungenerous producer, but it is well adapted to dry, steep, granitic *terroir*. There it produces a rich juice, once difficult to ferment to completion. This gave rise to a semi-sweet, *pétillant* style of Condrieu that earned the wine the reputation, now undeserved, of not traveling well. Yet even the dry Viognier of the present era smells as if it were going to be a sweet wine, probably German, though even more floral than a Riesling. Thereafter richness follows rather than sweetness, played off against acidity, in a wine tasting anywhere from pear (with bananas) through peach and, in the most intense examples, a truly startling apricot.

Its noble reputation has induced some southern growers to plant Viognier, as they have the other northern white *cépages,* in their quest for aromatic wines. (Viognier is admitted as a "principal" *cépage* in regional CDR.) There, the pure examples certainly do not have the fullness of Condrieu's, but those I have tasted, especially M. Steinmaier's at St.-Gervais, are interestingly leaner and in a way less exaggerated than the northern original. I am more dubious of Viognier as a component in assembled white wines, where even the tiniest percentage seems to mark the wine with an almost unassimilable varietal presence.

Try:

Any Condrieu.

Côte-Rôtie **La Mouline** (see **E. Guigal**). Shows the use of Viognier, a factor principally in the Côte Blonde vineyards, in the refinement of red Côte-Rôtie.

14

Crus and Producers
of the Middle Valley

LEFT BANK—*CRU*: HERMITAGE

THE VINEYARD OF TAIN (Latin Tegna) dates from Roman times and the wines were among those known as wines of Vienne. Later in the Middle Ages they were known as wines of Tournon, when they belonged to the *seigneurs* of that city just across the river. The present name, which began to be used at the end of the 16th century, came from the cultivation of vineyards on the site by hermits, the first of whom is reputed to have been the 13th-century knight Henri-Gaspard de Stérimberg. He became a hermit here after the Crusade against the Albigensians, and planted and tended vines near the chapel of St.-Christophe, still to be seen at the top of the hill.

Besides being sought out for its own sake—and it was prized in various European courts, including the 17th-century Russian, as being one of the greatest French wines—Hermitage, like Châteauneuf, was bought by *négociants* to use as a corrective in other wines. In this case it was Bordeaux that received its benefits, where the wines of certain châteaus were quite openly and proudly declared in the 18th and 19th centuries to be "hermitagé."

The famous hill, exposed south-west, is traditionally divided into three chief sectors, named for their principal *quartiers*. Their soils gradually become less granitic as the granite bedrock descends deeper beneath the surface, moving from west to east. The steepest sector, with a soil largely of decomposed granite, is Bessards. Second comes Méal, above, sandier and with some *calcaire,* and Greffieux below, with a soil that is richer by receipt of materials washed down from above. From Bessards come the biggest reds, those from Méal are more complex and fine, and those from Greffieux more supple. Third and farthest east is Murets, particularly important for white *cépages,* a gentler slope with clay. Within each sector there are particular *quartiers* whose characters, well recognized by the *vignerons,* elude these generalizations.

The Hermitage AOC is for red (Syrah and no more than 15% white *cépages*) and white (Marsanne and Roussanne). Productivity must not exceed a norm of 40 hectoliters per hectare (almost never achieved, incidentally), with a minimum alcohol of 10.5% for red, 11% for white. Chaptalization can be authorized.

The AOC also extends to *vins de paille* (straw wines), sweet wines made from white grapes that have been raisined by drying on straw mats. A tradition once almost abandoned, it has recently been revived by several important growers. Some say the lingering influence of the old tradition created the local taste for white wines in the "forme oxidative."

The communes of AOC Hermitage are just those parts of Tain-l'Hermitage,

The hill of Hermitage looms above downtown Tain-l'Hermitage (Drôme). Photo courtesy of Rosalind Srb.

Larnage, and Crozes-Hermitage, as determined by judicial delimitation, that occupy the hill. Addresses of producers are 26 (Drôme) or 07(Ardèche) as indicated.

M Chapoutier SA, Négociants-Éleveurs à Tain-l'Hermitage (Drôme)
Steady and deliberately untrendy quality in their chosen style is the mark of Chapoutier. The pillars on which the style of the red wine rests, according to M. Max Chapoutier, are destemming and aging in small, used barrels—he thinks stems and new wood both produce gross tannin. Among wines from Chapoutier's properties, the successes usually include a floral, tobacco and truffle-tinged Côte-Rôtie, with a fat in 1984 that others lack. The Chapoutier treatment of Saint-Joseph "Deschants" red lets the attractive "primary" aromas and flavors of its youth

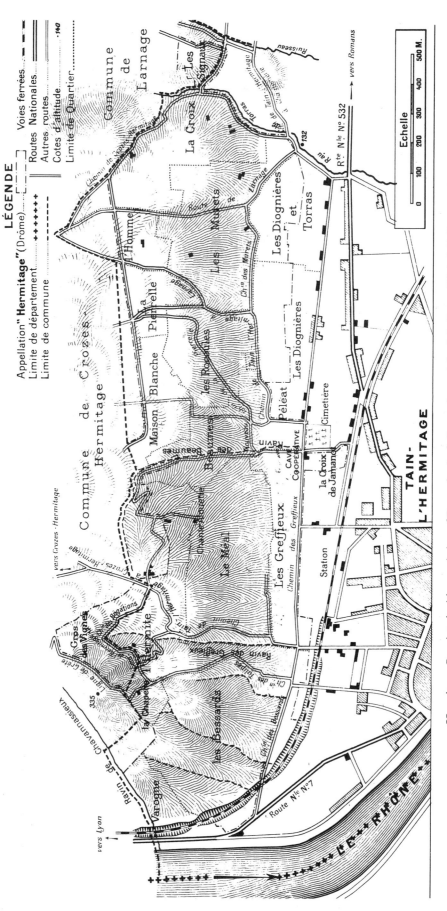

Hermitage. Reprinted with permission of *Revue du vin de France* from *Atlas de la France Vinicole L. Larmat.* Copyright 1943, Louis Larmat, Paris.

persist. Blueberry may be the note that is struck on top of raspberry and cassis in the best years of Hermitage "M. de la Sizeranne" (e.g., 1978, 1984). Among white Hermitages, H "Chante Alouette" demonstrates the potentiality for noble oxidation in a Marsanne wine that undergoes some maturation before bottling. Here again 1984 shows the youthful foundation of florality, spice, honey, lively acidity, and length that must be built into such a wine.

As proprietors, Chapoutier have about 17 ha of red Hermitage, most in Les Bessards and Les Greffieux; about 13 ha of white Hermitage, most in Les Murets, closely followed by Le Méal and l'Hermite; around 5 ha of red Crozes-Hermitage, most in qrt Les Chassis; approximately 2 ha of red Saint-Joseph, most in qrt St.-Joseph; about 3.5 ha of white Saint-Joseph, most in qrts St.-Joseph and Montagnon; approximately 2.7 ha of Côte-Rôtie, Brune et Blonde; and approximately 27 ha of Châteauneuf-du-Pape, most in qrts Le Patouillet (E) and Barbe d'Asne (S). ❧ Vinification is CL in open wooden vats, floating cap with *pigeage* by foot-treading for Côte-Rôtie, Saint-Joseph, Hermitage and Crozes-Hermitage "Les Meysonniers." Crozes-Hermitage "Les Petits Ruches" is CL in stainless steel. Châteauneuf-du-Pape "La Bernardine" is CL in closed cement vats. Whites are settled, fermented in enamelled vats. ❧ Reds are aged in used oak and young chestnut *pièces* (Chapoutier still have their own barrel-maker on the premises). White is aged 1 to 2 months "maximum" in wood and afterwards in enamelled vats. Besides presenting vintage wines, M. Chapoutier is a believer in the "grouping" into one *cuvée* of several years of the same wine. Wines of such *cuvées* are presented as "Grandes Cuvées" with additional selection occasionally producing numbered bottles of special batches such as Hermitage white "Cuvée des Boys" and Chateauneuf-du-Pape "Barbe Rac."

H Jean-Louis Chave, Mauves (Ardèche)

Hermitage red and white; Saint-Joseph red. **Barrel tasting the reds with M. Chave before *assemblage* is a lesson in the character of the "lieux-dits" at Hermitage: tannic Bessards, complex Méal, the cinnamon of Péléat, the finesse of Beaumes, the roundness of Rocoules. Together in bottle they produce a complete expression of Hermitage, perhaps weighted to the rustic side, including black raspberry but even more cassis, a little cooked, suggesting the vegetal side of Syrah—licorice and violets, but growing in a barnyard—and built to evolve slowly (wines I have tasted back to the 1952 were never tired). The almost pure Marsanne whites are also *vins de garde*—big, ripe, tending to gold, and with a complex stink of mingled oxidations and reductions that need to be cleaned out by some airing in the glass before tasting. They mix their honey—which M. Chave thinks is acacia—with some kind of bark or sap and citrus. Not to be overlooked is Chave's tiny production of an especially characteristic and intense Saint-Joseph.**

Before his recent purchase of **Domaine l'Hermite** (Gray-Dufresne), M. Chave had approximately 10 ha of Hermitage, the qrts for red given above; white from Rocoules, Péléat, and Méal; and 2 ha of St.-Joseph in Mauves and Tournon. ❧ ST in open wooden vats, floating cap wth *pigeage* beginning by foot. The qrts are vinified separately. 3 weeks *cuvaison,* Vaslin press. ❧ Reds are aged in oak *pièces* and progressively assembled in the course of racking. White is assembled from some that has been, some that has never been in wood.

Delas Frères, St.-Jean-de-Muzols (Ardèche)

The Delas *négociant* firm, founded in 1835, has been owned since 1977 by the Deutz and Geldermann Champagne house. Among several proprietary wines is an outstanding Hermitage, the red "Marquise de la Tourette," with a concentration of tannin so fine it does not mask the fruit or keep the wine from seeming cool. Smokey, truffley, even cedary, the 1983 had a hint of caramel. Cornas "Chante Perdrix" 1983 seemed more concentrated than several years back, in better balance with its wood than 1983 Côte-Rôtie "Seigneur de Maugiron," which nevertheless had violets and a "Brune" weightiness.

The Delas family own or lease properties at Hermitage (5 ha in qrt Bessards, 4 in l'Hermite), Côte-Rôtie (4 ha of Côte Brune), Condrieu (3 ha), and Cornas (1.5 ha). The following wines are exclusively from these properties:

> Condrieu **"Viognier"**
> Cornas **"Chante Perdrix"**
> Côte-Rôtie **"Seigneur de Maugiron"**
> H Hermitage **"Marquise de la Tourette"** red
> Hermitage **"Marquise de la Tourette"** white

≥ All Delas northern Rhônes are of their own vinification. For reds this is OT2, 12 days, conducted in closed, enamel-lined vats. Whites are fermented in stainless steel. The new facility Delas has occupied since 1981 has greatly enhanced capacity for temperature control and for aging. ≥ The proprietary red wines are aged 18 months in oak *pièces* and casks and in bottle before sale. White Hermitage is given 1 month in oak *pièces* Condrieu "never" touches wood.

Bernard Faurie, Tournon (Ardèche)

Hermitage red and white; Saint-Joseph red. My experience here is limited but favorable. The white Hermitage in the wood-aged style was soft, rich, fragrant, anised. Barrel-tasted red Hermitages had cinnamon, butter, and truffle overtones with the ripe skin character of their fruit, and some tendency to dryness. Excellent balance in a 1980.

1.7 ha of Hermitage on the borders of Bessards and Greffieux, a little in Méal; .5 ha of St.-Joseph in Tournon. ≥ A little crushing in the comports, OT1 in open wooden vats with floating cap and *pigeage* by foot-treading, 21 days; hand-operated press. ≥ 12 to 18 months in cask.

GAEC Les Gamets Fayolle Fils, Gervans (Drôme)

See Crozes-Hermitage.

H **Jean Louis Grippat,** Tournon (Ardèche)

See Saint-Joseph (1).

Paul Jaboulet Aîné, Négociant-éleveur à Tain-l'Hermitage (Drôme)

In my judgment Jaboulet makes three wines that are consistently at or near the top of all wines in their AOC. White Hermitage "Le Chevalier de Stérimberg" is the expression of Marsanne—and of more Roussanne than in most northern Rhônes—when it is kept from oxidation. Pale greenish-gold in color, with a good level of acidity, clean and mineral, it is more lean or fat depending on the year, and is enclosed rather than forthcoming at the start. Red Crozes-Hermitage "Thalabert" may be junior to Hermitage, but not by much. Softer, not quite as big, it is nevertheless well concentrated within its own scale, full of black raspberry, vanilla, and violets mixed with black and even bell pepper and sorrel. Great finesse. Greatest of all Jaboulets is probably red Hermitage "La Chapelle." It begins with rich black raspberry fruit, butter, sorrel, and pepper in a wine whose balanced concentration does not preclude a certain softness. With age come spices, increasing tarriness, truffles, salt, and a wet seaside-sand sort of rottenness still founded on ripe fruit that makes years like 1961 in their maturity resemble Pomerol.

The Jaboulet firm acts as sole "vendors" of wines from the Jaboulet family properties. These, all at Hermitage and Crozes-Hermitage, are:

H Hermitage **"Le Chevalier de Stérimberg"** white
    5 ha in Bessards and Méal; 1 additional ha planted.
H Hermitage **"La Chapelle"** red
    20 ha in Bessards and Méal; 2 additional ha planted.
Crozes-Hermitage **"Mule Blanche"** white
    5 ha in qrt 7 Chemins; 2 additional ha planted.
H Crozes-Hermitage **"Domaine de Thalabert"** red
    35 ha in qrt Thalabert.
    🐌 ST with optional destemming in closed cement vats, 15–18 days; Vaslin press. For whites their policy is fermentation of clear juice (previously fined, settled and racked) in glass-lined vats. No malolactic. 🐌 12 to 18 months in oak *pièces* is given to their northern Rhône reds. Their whites, "never in wood," are bottled by February or March. As *négociants* Jaboulet also buy and "bring up" a considerable line of southern Rhônes, for which their practice of discreet wood-aging and sometimes none at all assures a remarkably distinctive expression of their origin in each.

H. Sorrel, Tain-l'Hermitage (Drôme)

Son Marc Sorrel has succeeded the late Henri Sorrel at this estate. Under his father, the red Hermitage was a rich, full-bodied, earthy-truffly wine whose bouquet was dominated by spice, extending from cinnamon to cigar-box, menthol, and incense in a 6-year-old 1980 Le Méal recently retasted.

2.7 ha of Hermitage. Red is from Le Méal and Les Greffieux, with a little additional Greffieux and some Bessards recently acquired by Marc. 90% SY, 10% MR. White is from Les Rocoules, 90% MR, 10% RS. 🐌 Reds are ST in open wooden vats, with *remontage*, 14 to 21 days. Whites are fermented in *pièces* (25% new tried in 1985); malolactic is completed. 🐌 18 to 24 months oak age for reds. "Le Gréal" is now the name of a *cuvée* produced from old vines in Greffieux and Méal (85%).

Domaine Saint Jemms, Robert Michelas, Mercurol (Drôme)
    See Crozes-Hermitage.

Louis Francis de Vallouit, St.-Vallier (Drôme)
    See Côte-Rôtie.

The cooperative of this zone is:

Cave Coopérative de Vins Fins, Union des Propriétaires de Vins Fins à Tain-l'Hermitage (Drôme)

Founded 1933. About 80% AOC. In effect the cooperative of Crozes-Hermitage, since the large majority of the Cave's 550 members are small growers from that AOC, it nevertheless produces about 20% of all Hermitage as well. St.-Joseph from St.-Jean-de-Muzols, Tournon, Mauves. Newest part of the *cave* allows OT2 in closed vats for Hermitage, Cornas, St.-Joseph and part of Crozes-Hermitage.

Crozes-Hermitage red and white; Hermitage red and white; St.-Joseph red and white; Cornas; St.-Péray white and *méthode champenoise*.

———————— *CRU:* CROZES-HERMITAGE ————————

The communes, south to north, of Crozes-Hermitage are Pont-de-l'Isère, La-Roche-de-Glun, Beaumont-Monteux, Chanos-Curson, Mercurol, Tain-l'Hermitage, Crozes-Hermitage, Larnage, Gervans, Erôme, and Serves. This list represents the 1952 extension of the original AOC from the sole commune of Crozes onto land that until then had been CDR. The reasons for the extension were chiefly economic. At the time, there was insufficient demand for CDR of northern character for use in blends with the otherwise overwhelmingly southern product. Another, I have been told, was to give the northern Rhône *négociants*—who by tradition are also proprietors and vinifiers—some kind of wine to sell in relative quantity alongside the miniscule and heroically costly production of their other *crus*.

The result was in effect to create three different zones of production for AOC Crozes-Hermitage. Many vineyard sites to the north are on abrupt granite slopes similar to that of Hermitage itself, overlooking the river but somewhat less well exposed. In the middle are gentler clay-lime slopes, well back from the river, historically famous for the production of white wines (e.g., Mercurol). The transition to the third zone is made within the one commune of Mercurol, where the slopes descend first to a middle level of plateau, and then to the series of low plateaus stretching on to the south, where the soil is "ancient alluvion" made up of cobblestones on a gravel base.

The Crozes-Hermitage AOC is for red (Syrah and up to 15% white *cépages*) and white (Marsanne and Roussanne) wines, normally limited in productivity to 40 hl of wine per ha of land, and achieving a natural alcohol minimum of 10%. Chaptalization may be authorized. Addresses of producers are 26 (Drôme), unless otherwise noted.

M Chapoutier SA, Tain-l'Hermitage

See Hermitage.

Caves des Clairmonts, Société Coopérative Familiale (Borja), Beaumont-Monteux

Crozes-Hermitage red and white. **An estate whose recent wines sustain an earlier impression of good quality, especially in the pale straw-green, floral white, which tastes of peaches. Peaches, pepper, and stones seem to show up too in the light, almost southern-smelling red, especially concentrated in the 1983.**

Approximately three-quarters of a possible 100 ha suitable for vine are planted, in Beaumont-Monteux, Chanos-Curson, Pont-de-l'Isère and La-Roche-de-Glun. Much of this is cobblestone-covered. &. Was ST, then OT2 (1982), automatic *pigeane* added 1984, Vaslin press. White from pure free-run juice. &. Reds aged 1 year in vat.

H GAEC Les Gamets Fayolle Fils, Gervans

Crozes-Hermitage red and white; Hermitage red. **The wines here are all named for their qrts. The white Crozes are Les Blanc and Les Pontaix. The reds are Les Pontaix from clay soil, and Les Voussères from granite and 35-year-old vines. Both factors show in the combined finesse and compactness, liquid and firmness of the latter wine. While young it is the more enclosed, when older the more floral; very impressive in the 1980. Pontaix seems the bigger, chewier, ruder wine, showing more fruit to start but hard enough to need age. Hermitage Les Dionnières, from siliceous soil with cobblestones, seems enormously fragrant of violets and blackberry, going on to meat fat and vanilla. Tasted from the barrel, several were in an enclosed phase to the mouth, though the 1981 was notably round and full.**

8 ha total, dispersed in Crozes-Hermitage, Gervans, and Tain-l'Hermitage. &. OT2, part in open wooden vats with floating cap, *pigeage* by foot, 12 to 15 days. Part in closed cement vats, 12 to 15 days. Vaslin press. White is fermented in enameled vats. &. Reds are aged 15 months in oak casks.

H Paul Jaboulet Aîné, Tain-l'Hermitage

See Hermitage.

Jean Marsanne, Mauves (Ardèche)

See St.-Joseph (1).

Domaine la Négociale, Collonge Père et Fils, Mercurol

Crozes-Hermitage red and white. **Wine has been made at this estate since 1868, estate-bottled since 1976. Though definitely light-bodied, the 1978 here, tasted both from vat and bottle, had a tar-violet intensity less evident in reds of subsequent years, which stress leafiness and cassis. More recently the pure Marsanne white seems the more impressive wine: light yellow-green, honey-floral with a suggestion of citrus.**

15 ha at Beaumont-Monteux and the similar portion of Mercurol (cobblestones on gravel). &. OT2 in closed cement vats, 8 to 12 days; Vaslin press, press wine not incorporated. White is settled, fermented in enameled vats. &. When I first knew M. Collonge *père*, he aged both the red and white in wood (the latter "the least possible time"). Now, no wood for either.

H Domaine Pradelle, GAEC Pradelle (Jean-Louis et Jacques Pradelle), Chanos-Curson

Crozes-Hermitage red and white. **Pradelle started making Domaine wine in 1978, having sold grapes formerly to Chapoutier of Tain. A very pure blackberry to black raspberry fruit with vanilla can develop further complexity in these wines, often licorice, sometimes truffles, even a hint of sea salt. The 1979 is among the very best Crozes I have ever tasted. Whites have had apricot with a little almond, tend to be citric.**

16 ha, of which 10 are at Mercurol, 3/4 on the clay-lime slopes; 4 are cobble-covered at Beaumont-Monteux; 2 are clay-lime and gravel at Chanos-Curson. The white comes from 2 ha of pure clay at Mercurol. &. OT2 in closed cement vats, optional destemming,

10 days; Vaslin press. White is settled, fermented cool, try to avoid malolactic. ❧ Part of the red spends 12 to 18 months in oak casks.

Domaine Saint Jemms, Robert Michelas, Mercurol

Crozes-Hermitage red and white; Hermitage red and white; Cornas (beginning 1985). **The domaine has bottled since 1971. Of wines available to taste in 1985, the most impressive were a pure Marsanne 1983 white Hermitage—grassy, with round, sweet fruit, almost unctuous—and a 1983 red Crozes with a tannin one could smell over good blackberry fruit and spice in a wine, nevertheless, not heavy. 1982 red Crozes was more cassis, slightly cooked; 1981 again cassis, better structured.**

22 ha of Crozes-Hermitage dispersed in Mercurol (clay-lime soil), Pont-de-l'Isère and Beaumont-Monteux (cobblestones). 30 ares of Hermitage in qrt Les Beaumes. "2– 3" ha of Cornas, slopes, bought from Delas. The Michelas family have been *vignerons* at Mercurol since 1851, M. Michelas's parents were cooperators at Tain. ❧ OT2 in closed cement vats, 12 days, Vaslin press. White is settled, fermented cool in enameled vats, generally undergoes malo-lactic. ❧ Reds are aged a minimum of 2 years in oak casks.

GAEC de la Syrah, Charles Tardy et Bernard Ange, Chanos-Curson

Crozes-Hermitage red and white. **Brothers-in-law Mm. Tardy and Ange made their first domaine wine in 1979 (having been until then cooperators at Tain), and a good red wine that was, all from the Mercurol part of their properties. It had a smoky-truffle nose that one can recognize when barrel-tasting the wines of their separate parcels (the Monteux wines are dustier, stonier, more peppery). Bottled 1980 was very stylish, light but firm with just the right amount of tannin for its elegance. Fresh, soft white, "never" in wood.**

13 ha, mostly at Mercurol (clay-lime soil), a little at Chanos (same type), some at Beaumont-Monteux (alpine cobblestones on gravel). White (Marsanne and a little Roussanne) is exclusively from the Coteau des Pends at Mercurol. ❧ OT2 in closed cement vats, 8 to 10 days, Vaslin press. White is settled, fermented cold in enameled vats, usually does a malolactic, is bottled early. ❧ Red is aged a year in oak casks.

Louis Francis de Vallouit, St.-Vallier

See Côte-Rôtie.

The cooperative of this zone:

Cave Coopérative de Vins Fins, Tain-l'Hermitage

See Hermitage.

--- **CDR OF LIVRON** ---

The principal producer is the cooperative:

Cave Coopérative de Loriol

Since 1978 this 4–member cooperative has produced one of the rare regional CDR of the north, from 7.73 ha of vineyards in the several "lieux-dits" of Livron called Brézème. 90% SY, 10% GR.

RIGHT BANK—*CRU:* SAINT-PÉRAY

Vineyards probably grew here in Roman times, and the wines have been famous since the time of King Henri IV. It was the white that had earned the highest reputation for quality until sparkling wine began to be made by the Champagne method in the 19th century. The AOC regulations stipulate that sparkling Saint-Péray must be champagnized within the boundaries of the AOC area to earn the appellation, which extends only to still and sparkling white wines produced from Marsanne and Roussanne at a normal maximum productivity of 45 hectoliters per hectare. Minimum natural alcohol is 10% for still, 9% for sparkling. Chaptalization can be authorized. The communes of Saint-Péray are Saint-Péray and Toulaud.

Addresses of producers are 07130 St.-Péray unless otherwise indicated.

GAEC du Biguet, A. Thiers et Fils, Toulaud

St.-Péray white; St.-Péray *méthode champenoise.* **A producer I will follow, especially for the quality of the still white. For this, the grapes come from old vines on more granitic slopes, and the consequence is a higher alcohol percentage. The clean 1984 showed excellent balance of roundness and crispness, had a grassy, floral-honey nose and a pleasant, slightly metallic, reduced finish. To have more acidity and less alcohol in the sparkling wine, the grapes for it are harvested from younger vines on sandier soil at the bottom of the slopes. It is bottled without indication of the year in both *brut* and *demi-sec* (beginning 1985). Available to taste in 1985 was the "mostly 1983" *brut,* more leafy than floral, fresh, soft, slightly yeasty and with a fine *mousse* (bubbles).**

5.5 ha of St.-Péray in the qrt Biguet of Toulaud and the qrt Coupier (partly N-facing) of St.-Péray. 25 acres of Cornas 🡲 After settling and fining of the must, the wine is fermented cool in enameled tanks. Both the still and the champagne-method sparkling wine undergo malolactic. 🡲 The still wine normally spends about a year in tank before bottling (1984 was bottled early).

H J.F. Chaboud

St.-Péray white; St.-Péray *méthode champenoise.* **M. Chaboud now bottles both pure Marsanne and pure Roussanne in still St.-Péray. The former in the 1984, pale straw, had a leafy-smokey nose and plenty of nerve, with not quite the distinction I recall from earlier years. The sparkling, also pure Marsanne, has always been my preference: richer, even meaty in the 1983, around plenty of the flavor of the grape; fine *mousse.***

10 ha of St.-Péray in qrt La Hongrie (where in certain sectors there are clay-lime soil and white cobblestones). 🡲 Still wine is settled and the must is fined before a cool fermentation in enameled vats. Malolactic is finished. 🡲 The still is not aged in wood; bottled early.

H **Bernard Gripa,** Mauves (Ardèche)

See St.-Joseph (1).

CRU: CORNAS

Winegrowing here seems to have monastic origins dating to the early Middle Ages. Now, with its neighbor St.-Péray, Cornas is one of two northern Rhône *crus* whose vineyards continue to diminish. The threat to their existence from the large urban area of Valence, just across the river, is twofold: from the profitable sale of land for "suburbanization," and from the availability of work nearby that is more attractive to the young than vineyard labor.

The growers distinguish vineyards from *coteaux* and from *pied de coteaux*. (Land that is actually on the flat is CDR.) The slopes, deeply cut into by ravines, are granite of a severity that is said to resemble the qrt Bessards at Hermitage, and the wines are correspondingly robust—all the more because untempered by the addition of any white grapes. These are the biggest, if not the most nuanced, of all the northern Rhônes. The AOC is for red wines only, produced only from Syrah, at a normal maximum of 40 hectoliters per hectare, and achieving a minimum natural alcohol of 10.5%. Chaptalization can be authorized. Cornas is from the sole commune of Cornas.

Addresses of producers are 07130 Cornas unless otherwise indicated.

Guy de Barjac

There are mushrooms among the flowers in M. de Barjac's Cornas. His view is that balance more than a "great year" is the most important thing for longevity, which he illustrated in 1982 by presenting a light-colored 1970 in excellent form— pungently aromatic, combining delicacy and power (nevertheless in a lighter style than he is making now). In a more concentrated, structured 1978, tar was dominant; it finished on a note of marc brandy. A very substantial 1980. The 1983, tasted from bottle in 1986, was still severely reduced, with an impression of very ripe skins locked up in tannin and minerals.

2 ha, mid-slope. 🙠 OT1 in open wooden vats, floating cap with *pigeage* by foot; 10 to 12 days. No sulfur unless there is risk of oxidasic *casse*. "Pressoir 'd batir." Wine finishes in casks. 🙠 18 months wood age is given in *pièces;* bottled unfined and unfiltered.

H Auguste Clape

The first Cornas I ever tasted was a 1970 Clape bought in New York. Despite its enormous tannin, it was so deliciously crammed with fruit that I had drunk up my half-case practically as *primeur* before first visiting M. Clape in 1977. By then the tannin was better balanced in relation to fruit. Only by a 1981 visit had the full florality of the nose emerged. According to M. Clape, 1971 was an even better year! His blend of lower down *(bas)* and slope *(coteaux)* has the flowers, pepper and tar, and is accessible earlier. The slope wine by itself is much more concentrated and animal, shows more reduction when barrel-tasted, and can be downright hard until resolved by age. In a 1986 U.S. tasting, a 1984 was almost "pretty" with its floral, berry, and vanilla nose and fresh acidity. A bigger 1983 was already slightly orange, while its fruit was still enclosed by tannin and minerals. 1982 seemed simultaneously more evolved and less integrated.

3.5 ha of Cornas; 1.5 ha of CDR. 🙠 ST in open cement vats, floating cap with *pigeage* the first day, pumping-over thereafter; 10–15 days. ❧ 2 years aging in used *pièces*.

Delas Frères, St.-Jean-de-Muzols (Ardèche)

See Hermitage.

H Marcel Juge

Cornas; St.-Péray. **M. Juge, president of the Cornas growers, distinguishes his Cornas from "mi-coteaux" (mid-slope) and "coteaux" (slope). The latter he must label "C" for European countries because of ECC rules that retain the word "coteaux" for use only in AOCs. He also makes a "Coteaux Réserve" from late harvest grapes, labeled "SC" for Europe. "C" wines are definitely more concentrated, with an almost meaty cassis fruit. The 1984 from cask was fine, round, tender, while with good acid; 1983 from bottle, unfined and unfiltered, added even more concentration, tar, and vanilla. 1983 "SC" from cask was a dream Cornas, with its late-harvest, pitch to petrol nose, immense black pepper, and a suggestion of warm granite. All these wines seemed simultaneously tighter structured and less hard than the Juge wines of some years earlier.**

3 ha includes "a little" St.-Péray. ❧ A little crushing in the comports; OT1 in open vats, floating cap, *pigeage* by foot; 8 to 15 days. ❧ 18 months minimum age in oak casks.

Jean Lionnet

Cornas; St.-Péray. **My first acquaintance with this wine includes a 1983 that stood out for combining good liquid with the tannin of a great year, florality, and vegetal-raspberry Syrah character. Warmer, riper, drier 1982 already had chocolate in the finish (in 1985).**

9 ha of which .30 ha are old vines in the north sector of St.-Péray. Cornas in qrt Pied-la-Vigne. Oldest vines 80 years old. ❧ ST in open wooden and cement vats, floating cap with *pigeage* by foot, 10–20 days; hand-operated press. Some white is fermented in *pièces* and some in enameled tanks. High acid blocked the malolactic in 1984. ❧ Cornas receives 4 to 18 months wood age in casks and *pièces,* regulated by age of the barrel.

Robert Michel

Cornas "Pied de Coteaux" (foot of slopes) and "Coteaux" are distinguished. The **dark fruit in the latter is almost an extract, with tar to petrol resins that seem to penetrate it. Perhaps a touch of volatile with the vanilla in the 1983 caused M. Michel to say (1985) that tautly tannic 1984 was better balanced. M. Michel produced an especially pretty 1979, and a classical 1976.**

5.5 ha of Cornas, of which 5 are slope. Some 80-year-old vines. ❧ ST in open cement vats, no "foulage à pieds" (foot treading), 10 to 12 days; hydraulic press. ❧ Wine usually ages 6 to 12 months in used *pièces,* but less for "Pied de Coteaux," which is released earlier.

Domaine St. Jemms, Robert Michelas, Mercurol (Drôme)

See Crozes-Hermitage.

Noël Verset

Verset's wines seem to show a southern side to Cornas among northern Rhônes. While typically dark, tarry, floral and concentrated, they tend also to prunes, spice and licorice. Not all the wood in the *cave* tastes good, which may account for some mustiness and volatility in the nose of bottles that give a cleaner impression in the mouth.

2 ha of Cornas in qrts Les Côtes Chaillot, Renards. The 70-year-old vines are replaced, when the time comes, plant by plant. 🐌 OT1 in open cement vats (wood until 1980), floating cap, *pigeage* by foot, 15 days; vertical press. The wine finishes in barrels. 🐌 Wines age 1 year in casks and *pièces* before the first are bottled.

―――――――――――――――― *CRU:* SAINT-JOSEPH (1) ――――――――――――――――

The communes of Saint-Joseph treated here (S to N) are Guilherand, Châteaubourg, *Glun, Mauves, Tournon, St.-Jean-de-Muzols, Lemps, Vion,* Sécheras, Arras-sur-Rhone, Ozon, and Sarras. These make up the southern portion of the AOC as it has been defined since it was expanded in 1969. Those italicized above are the original recipients of the AOC created in 1956, in large measure to save vineyards famous since late medieval times from disappearing because of the unprofitability of producing their wines as simple CDR. The same logic led to the expansion. The originals include the areas traditionally known for producing the wines of Mauves, of Coteau St.-Joseph, and of Coteau Ste.-Epine. The AOC is for red (Syrah, with no more than 10% white *cépages*) and white (Marsanne and Roussanne), with a normal maximum productivity of 40 hectoliters per hectare and minimum natural alcohol of 10%. Chaptalization can be authorized.

Addresses are 07 (Ardèche) unless otherwise noted.

Maurice Courbis, Châteaubourg

St.-Joseph red and white. **M. Courbis's Marsanne vines can be seen from the door of the Hostellerie du Château restaurant when one looks across the roofs of Châteaubourg toward the** *coteau.* **They produce a white that can be fine, fresh, leafy to appley, in which I have sometimes detected sulfur in the finish. An unfiltered bottling of 1981 did not have that fault, was rounder and pleasantly yeasty. Violets, pepper, meat fat, and tar appear in the reds, but to me they feel different from other St.-Josephs, especially on the teeth, perhaps from calcareous soil.**

M. Courbis, mayor of Châteaubourg, has 7.71 ha in Châteaubourg (calcareous) and Glun (granite). 🐌 ST in closed cement vats, 12 days; Vaslin press. White ferments in enameled vats; the malolactic is blocked when it is hard to start. 🐌 Red is aged 18 to 24 months in oak casks.

Jean-Louis Chave, Mauves

See Hermitage.

Pierre Coursodon, Mauves

St.-Joseph red and white. **The Marsanne white, formerly fermented in wood and sometimes then tinged with oxidation, has gained a kind of green apple freshness from modern methods. 1984 combined roundness and acidity, tasted a bit of anise.**

Of the two 1983 reds, that labeled "Le Paradis" exceeded the simple St.-Joseph in depth of fruit, also in an almost severe tannin, and was inclined to resin more than the spiciness and classic *charcuterie* nose of the latter. Of other years available to taste in 1985, there was lots of wine left in a full, round, tender 1979 compared to a 1981 showing aldehyde. 1982, still hard, showed petrol-resin and raspberry (on another occasion, it had been red currant).

8 ha with principal parcels in qrts l'Olivet and Le Paradis (Mauves). ❧ ST in open wooden vats, floating cap, *pigeage* by foot, 1 to 3 weeks *cuvaison*. Switched from hydraulic to Vaslin press in 1985. White is settled, the must fined, fermented in enameled tanks, bottled as soon as the malolactic is finished. ❧ Red is aged 18 to 24 months in oak casks.

H **Bernard Gripa,** Mauves

St.-Joseph red and white; St.-Péray white. **Of the two whites, St.-Joseph is the bigger and rounder—floral, honeyed, with a touch of grassiness and even some Riesling-style petrol in the extraordinarily concentrated 1984 "Berceau."** The honey in the pale straw-green St.-Péray seems apple blossom, with a hint of milk in the finish. M. Gripa distinguishes his red St.-Josephs into "pieds de coteaux" (at the foot of the slopes), young-vine *coteaux,* old-vine *coteaux* (labeled "Berceau"), and an assemblage of the three. "Berceau" is much the most concentrated wine, in 1983 loaded with tannin, but so fine it did not mask the deep black raspberry, vanilla, and meat fat. The old-vine concentration shows through in the *assemblage* too, which takes the fruit in a cherry-cassis-cinnamon, slightly metallic direction; particularly intense in 1981.

4.5 ha of St.-Joseph, the "big majority" in qrt St.-Joseph—hence the label "Berceau" for the wine from the "cradle" of the appellation. 1.5 ha of St.-Péray, part near the château of Crussol (more calcareous), part on the Route de Toulaud (heavier clay). Majority of vines are 40, some 60–70 years old. ❧ OT1 in open wooden vats, floating cap, *pigeage* by foot, 10 to 15 days; pneumatic press. White is settled and the must fined before cool fermentation in enameled or fiberglass tanks. Undergoes malolactic. ❧ About 1 year in casks for reds, no wood for whites.

Jean Marsanne, Mauves

St.-Joseph red; Crozes-Hermitage red. **Despite his name, M. Marsanne produces only reds. Of the two wines, Crozes does not have meat fat and is in my experience at once sweeter seeming and more tannic (a 1982 tasted in the U.S. was marred by a smell of cigarette ash). St.-Joseph is compact, has good berry fruit, and tends to reduction, as M. Marsanne believes good fruit in a St.-Joseph "entails reduction."**

1½ ha of St.-Joseph in Mauves and Tournon, principally on slopes; .8 ha of Crozes-Hermitage in Crozes "en bas de coteaux" (at the base of the slopes). ❧ A little crushing in the comports. OT1 in open wooden vats, floating cap, *pigeage* by foot, 10 days; hand-turned vertical press. Wine finishes in oak casks. ❧ Wine ages in oak caks, is racked and sometimes withdrawn from cask to enameled vats before the next harvest because "St.-Joseph ill supports too much aging."

M Chapoutier SA, Tain-l'Hermitage (Drôme)

See Hermitage.

Bernard Faurie, Tournon

    See Hermitage.

H **Jean-Louis Grippat,** Tournon

St.-Joseph red and white; St.-Joseph "Cuvée de l'Hospice" red; Hermitage red and white. **M. Grippat's red Hermitage comes from one of the great qrts for white, which contributes to its elegant color and body—the "Burgundy" of Hermitage, he says. The best I have tasted early may have been the 1979, and berry-fruited, floral, cinnamon 1982—complex, rich, smooth, balanced and long, although it was in a more than usually reduced phase recently (1985). More Hermitage—or even Cornas—than Hermitage itself may be Grippat's tar and violet "Cuvée de l'Hospice," an especially forceful and concentrated St.-Joseph vinified separately since 1979. The regular St.-Joseph red is more elegant, with its intense aroma of cassis-cinnamon and the fat of *charcuterie,* over a wine that is clean, direct, lively, and flowing yet firm. Outstanding in 1981; 1980 was drier, 1984 had more nerve than usual. 100% Marsanne St.-Joseph white, with its dominant of clover honey, is also a fresh and refined expression, which made 1983 in bottle a puzzle with its drier, anise, orange-peel flavors. Less forthcoming at the start, white Hermitage also has honey, sometimes nuts and a hint of sourish grass, even sage (1981), truffles, much more body, nerve, minerals, and grain (it can resemble Meursault or Puligny).**

    3 ha of St.-Joseph at Tournon. Part on the original *coteau* of St.-Joseph that gave the appellation its name, just below Chapoutier's parcel. Part rented from the hospital of Tournon—source of "L'Hospice"—on the *coteau* of Tournon closest to the hill of Hermitage, which it in effect continues on the other side of the Rhône. 1½ ha of Hermitage in Les Murets. ❧ M. Grippat restored OT1 in open wooden vats in 1971. Harvests in wooden comports (some mulberry), with a little tamping down. 15 to 21 days, floating cap with *pigeage* started by foot. Switched from vertical to pneumatic press in 1985. The whites are settled and fined before fermentation—some in barrel, some in enameled vats. Undergo malolactic. ❧ Reds finish and age in oak *pièces.*

Delas Frères, St.-Jean-de-Muzols

    See Hermitage.

Raymond Trollat, St.-Jean-de-Muzols

St.-Joseph red and white. **A rustic red in which the meat fat can be smoked bacon, and there is sometimes a smell of hard wood in the nose that ranges on from floral to cinnamon to varnish. The fruit is cassis to blackberry, the finish, long. The white, pale but with a little yellow, smells classically of clover blossoms, gives an almost sweet fruit impression that verges on Riesling or Sauvignon-style reduction.**

    3 ha, all slopes, in qrt Aubert. Some 90-year-old vines. ❧ A little crushing occurs in the comports upon arrival at the *cave* (not in the field). OT1 in open wooden and cement vats, floating cap, *pigeage* started by foot. 12 to 18 days, Vaslin press. White is wood-fermented. ❧ Red ages 18 months maximum in oak and chestnut.

15

Crus and Producers
of the Northern Valley

CRU: SAINT-JOSEPH (2)

THE COMMUNES, from south to north, of the northern portion of AOC St.-Joseph are Talencieux. Andance, St.-Etienne-de-Valoux, St.-Désirat, Champagne, Peyraud, Serrières, Felines, Charnas, *Limony* (Ardèche); *St.-Pierre-de-Boeuf, Malleval, Chavanay* (Loire). Because of the extension northward of AOC St.-Joseph (explained earlier) at virtually the same time as an extension southward of AOC Condrieu, both appellations extend to the italicized communes. The AOC of a parcel included in both areas is determined by its *encépagement:* Condrieu where Viognier, St.-Joseph where Syrah, Marsanne or Roussanne.

Addresses are 07 (Ardèche) or 42 (Loire) as indicated.

Cave Coopérative de Saint-Désirat-Champagne, St.-Désirat (Ardèche)

The Cave makes St.-Joseph exclusively from an area north of the 6 original communes of the AOC that was changed from CDR to St.-Joseph in 1969. The Cave now produces about 25% of all St.-Joseph. Due to the great care taken in its operations, the wine is interesting and increasingly characteristic as the many young vines in the area mature. Berry-fruited, slightly smokey, with hints of meat fat, black, or even bell pepper, and cinnamon, good examples include 1979 (silver medal Mâcon), 1980 (silver Mâcon), and 1982 (gold Paris).

App. 23% AOC. 100 principal members of a total 300. St.-Joseph from Talencieux, St.-Etienne-de-Valoux, Andance, St.-Désirat, Champagne, Peyraud, Serrières, Félines, Charnas, Limony. In this area vineyards from the plateaus above the granitic slopes produce an interesting VDP d'Ardèche from Gamay while, according to the president of the Cave, the flat land below is for VDT. The Cave ensures undamaged fruit by supplying cases and sending its own trucks after them to bring in the St.-Joseph harvest. OT1 in closed stainless steel vats, 1 week cuvaison; Vaslin press. (VDP Gamay is CM.) The wine is fined and filtered through diatomaceous earth before being aged, first in vat, then for a year in oak casks.

CRUS: CONDRIEU AND CHÂTEAU-GRILLET

First planted under the Romans, Condrieu's recent history is perhaps even more exciting. From 8.40 hectares of vineyard in 1965 (out of approximately 400 hectares of eligible land), it had risen to 16 by 1981 (Jauré n.d.; Charnay 1985). Now it benefits from a comprehensive plan on the part of several regional agencies, including those responsible for disinfecting the soil, selecting and purifying the clones of Viognier, and training winemakers, to promote a "Renaissance of Vineyards on Terraces." Strong demand for the product is certainly behind this effort, but it represents no enlargement of the AOC area. Rather, abandoned vineyard land that had passed into production of fruits and vegetables or reverted to just plain woods is being recovered. Already 6 ha have been replanted on the Coteau de Chéry in the commune of Condrieu, and two more "slices" of 6 ha each are in the works for Chavanay.

Condrieu must not exceed a normal maximum productivity of 30 hectoliters per hectare, of course all from Viognier, and must achieve a minimum natural alcohol of 11%. Chaptalization may be authorized. The communes of Condrieu, S to N, are Limony (Ardèche); St.-Pierre-de-Boeuf, Malleval, Chavanay, *St.-Michel-sur-Rhône*, *Vérin* (Loire); and *Condrieu* (Rhône), of which those italicized were originally awarded the AOC in 1940. Addresses are 07 (Ardèche), 42 (Loire), or 69 (Rhône) as indicated.

Château-Grillet, Neyret-Gachet (André Canet)
Château-Griller près Condrieu, Vérin (Loire)

AOC Château-Grillet. **With limited experience of this wine, I cannot enter the discussion of whether or not it is what it used to be (harvesting too much and too early is alleged). Suffice it to say that I have been surprised to be able to smell the bouquet several feet from the glass, something I had encountered, before Grillet, only with La Tâche. It is a golden-greenish wine whose general ensemble of flavors is that of Condrieu with a more Burgundian texture than either Condrieu or the German wines it smells like.**

2.7-ha single estate with its own AOC. The site, in Vérin and St.-Michel-sur-Rhône, is a steep, south-facing amphitheater of broken granite, planted uniquely to VN. Normal maximum productivity is fixed at 32 hectoliters per hectare, minimum natural alcohol at 11%, after which chaptalization may be authorized. ✌ The grapes, "scarcely" crushed but not destemmed, are directly pressed in a pneumatic press. The juice is settled or not according to the year, and fermented in enameled vats. ✌ Wine is racked to barrels where it is given "2 winters," "in principle" without additional racking, before being bottled. Fined and filtered.

Pierre Dumazet, Limony (Ardèche)

A pale, peach-colored wine yielding peach and fresh apricot to the taste in an attractive 1984, which combined steeliness and a burgundy-like marriage with its wood. Resinous finish.

60 ares of Condrieu are planted, exclusively in the commune of Limony. One vineyard is predominantly granite and another, somewhat calcareous. Many old vines. ✌ After rapid pressing and settling, fermentation is conducted in oak *pièces* (some new), and the wine is left on the fine lees in wood until April. Thereafter it is withdrawn to stainless-steel tanks for *assemblage*. ✌ When it is certain the malolactic is finished, the wine is fined, optionally filtered by gravity, and bottled.

André Perret, Verlieu, Chavanay (Loire)

Condrieu; St.-Joseph red and white. **The bottled 1983 Condrieu needed some air to disperse a bit of unpleasant gas. There were also grassiness and a hint of pastry to** the nose, leading to an almost sweet taste impression as well. **Finished clean and burgundyish.**

2.5 ha of AOC Condrieu, of which .5 are 25-year-old vines in the qrt Chanson of Chavanay and 2 are on the Coteau de Chéry of Condrieu. 1.5 ha of the latter are more than 40-year-old vines. The St.-Joseph is from 2.5 ha of terraced vineyards in Chavanay, of which .5 are white *cépages*. ‍🌿 The Condrieu is fermented, after settling as necessary, partly in stainless-steel vats and partly in *pièces*. Malolactic is conducted in stainless. The St.-Joseph red is ST in stainless-steel, temperature-controlled vats. ‍🌿 The Condrieu is assembled from some that has aged in wood and some in stainless, is fined and filtered. St.-Joseph is also aged about a year in stainless, and in *pièces* and casks.

Jean Pinchon, Condrieu (Rhône)

Fresh apricot, with leaves or grass, appears in both the bottled 1983 and 1984. 1983, though soft, had a metallic edge and something not quite clean in the middle. I found 1984 higher pitched and more nuanced, with smoke, spice, and sea-salt.

1.5 ha cultivated at present will rise to 2.5 between 1988 and 1991. ‍🌿 After rapid pressing, the juice is settled in stainless-steel, and cool-fermented. "We have several *pièces*, but the tendency is to work more and more in stainless tanks." Undergoes malolactic. ‍🌿 The wine rests on the lees before fining, filtering and bottling.

H **Château du Rozay,** Paul Multier, Condrieu (Rhône)

Underneath a slightly banana, nobly reduced Rhenish aroma, is a medium yellow-gold wine that usually combines a round and golden fruit impression in the mouth with a lean streak of acidity suggestive of potential longevity. Vintages differ in which of these characteristics they bring forward. 1980 and possibly 1983 stress the former; 1984, and above all 1979, scarcely evolved in 1986, the latter. The late M. Multier once presented a 20-year-old 1961 that had been fermented in *pièces* and aged a year in wood. While it had the smell of an *apéritif,* as the French say, it was by no means harmfully oxidized.

App. 1.5 ha of Condrieu in production on the Chéry slope (next slope south of Vernon). 35- to 65-year-old vines. 70 ares of CDR (Syrah). ‍🌿 Château du Rozay is vinified in oak casks and bottled "sur lies" in April once the malolactic is completed. M. Multier described this as making wine "according to the methods of M. Vernay," who once sharecropped .80 ha of Multier's land, as well as vinifying the Rozay until 1979.

H **Georges Vernay,** Condrieu (Rhône)

Condrieu; Côte-Rôtie; St.-Joseph; CDR. **The difference between M. Vernay's two Condrieux can be dramatic. The plain Condrieu "Viognier" is no slouch, with its powerful nose often beginning with banana. With air it then develops great leafy florality, including violets, and a general cast that but for the wine being dry resembles a Rhine. Tart acidity inclines the fruit to peach. Therein lies the difference from richer, suppler, even more quintessential "Coteau de Vernon." Its fruit is unmistakably apricot—so intensely aromatic in the 1983 that it seems to be *eau de vie*—and its acid the gentler one of apricot skins.**

In 1977 M. Vernay conducted 5.20 ha of Condrieu—exactly half the surface of all Condrieu then in production—and was given credit by the late M. Paul Multier for singlehandedly creating a renaissance of the AOC. Now he owns 6.5 ha of Condrieu (whose surface had risen to 16 ha by 1981), plus 1.5 ha of Côte-Rôtie in qrt Maison Rouge, 10% VN. Also 60 ares of St.-Joseph from Chavanay, and 1.5 ha of CDR. 🐾 Condrieu is directly pressed in a pneumatic press, neither crushed nor destemmed. After settling, it is fermented 10% in new oak *pièces,* 50% in oak casks, and 40% in stainless-steel. Malo-lactic is conducted on the lees. The reds are OT1 in open wooden vats, submerged cap following initial *pigeage* by foot, 2 to 3 weeks *cuvaison,* then racked for finishing to cask. 🐾 Reds age 1 to 2 years in cask.

CRU: CÔTE-RÔTIE

Among the wines of Roman Viennois cited by Pliny and other Roman authors was certainly that of Ampuis. Côte-Rôtie may be even more ancient if the theories of the origin of Syrah that say it was planted here about 600 B.C. by Phocaean Greeks, coming upriver from their colony at what is now Marseille, are correct.

It is the quintessential terraced vineyard, whose slope sometimes exceeds 60°. Traditionally two principal sectors are distinguished, Côte Brune to the north, Côte Blonde to the south. Legend has it that the Blonde was the dowry of the blonde daughter of the Seigneur de Maugiron of Ampuis, the Brune of his dark-haired daughter. The names refer to several real differences. The schistous soil of the Brune is darker from an admixture of clay and iron oxide, while the Blonde is lighter from "granulite" and some *calcaire.* It is also in the Blonde that the white *cépage* Viognier tends to be planted: up to 20% of it is allowed with Syrah in Côte-Rôtie, which is exclusively a red wine. The combination of soil and *encépagement* means, in general, that the Brune is a source of bigger-bodied, longer-lasting wines, while from the Blonde come somewhat softer, rounder ones.

Like Condrieu, Côte-Rôtie is one of those areas of the north that has come back from being a diminishing vineyard area and now attracts its young people to remain and become *vignerons.* From 59 ha in production in 1965, the figure had risen to approximately 130 by 1983. Some of this increase results from an added delimitation of parcels on flatter ground at the top of the slopes, to give the *vignerons* some ground that is easier to work. The young vines there have been coming into production. Now, I have been told, new plantation is aimed at recovering some of the best hillside sites.

The AOC requires a normal maximum productivity of 40 hectoliters per hectare and minimum natural alcohol of 10%. Chaptalization may be authorized. The communes, south to north, of Côte-Rôtie are *Tupin-et-Semons, Ampuis,* and St.-Cyr-sur-Rhône, of which those italicized are the original 1940 recipients of the AOC.

Addresses of producers are 69420 Ampuis, unless otherwise indicated.

Pierre Barge

The Pierre Barge wines of my previous experience tended to delicacy in body and sometimes color, with spice and resin more often dominant than fruit. Therefore, 1984 and 1983 were both surprises: the former, though lean, for its almost startling blend of cassis, raspberry and wild strawberry, the latter for its dark color and tannins that masked (in 1985) considerable deep fruit and suppleness. A slightly baked 1982, less structured, had a truffle nose.

The pitch of the Côte-Rôtie above Ampuis (Rhône).
Author's photo.

3 ha, most in qrt Pommière (Brune), some in Combard (Blonde). About 5% VN. ⤷ OT1 almost all in wood vats, submerged cap, 15 to 21 days; Vaslin and hand-operated vertical presses. (Son **Gilles Barge** makes Côte-Rôtie from his 1 ha in the same facility.) ⤷ Wine is lodged in oak casks for its malolactic, ages up to 3 years in casks, to which M. Barge has just added some new-oak *pièces*. Fined but not filtered.

H Emile Champet

A whiff of something stony and cinnamon are themes here, with barnyard, flowers, and an almost piquant finish in the 1983. The fruit was almost plummy in the concentrated, velvety, supple, vanilla-finished 1982. 1981 was lighter, but firm; 1980 was harder and possibly longer.

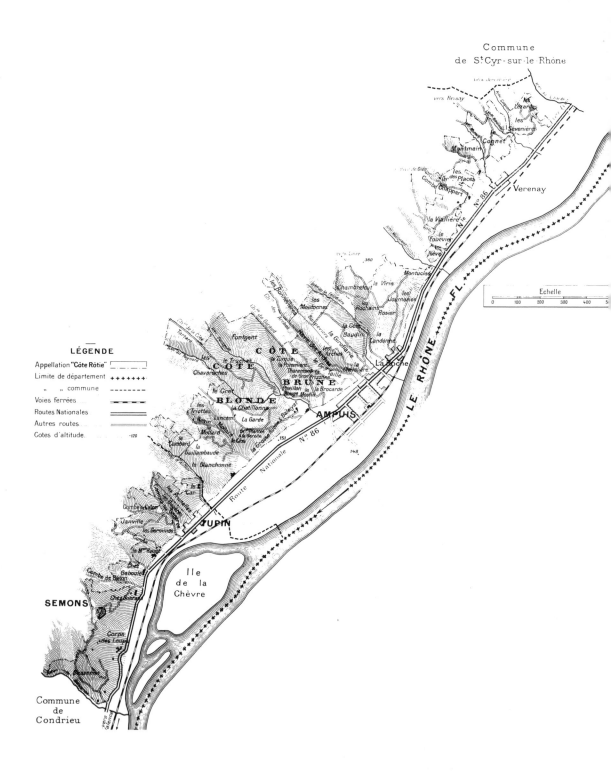

Côte-Rôtie. Reprinted with permission of *Revue du vin de France* from *Atlas de la France Vinicole L. Larmat*. Copyright 1943, Louis Larmat, Paris.

M. Champet and his son own 1.5 ha, only on slopes, in qrts Viaillère (vines 15 to 18 years old) and Mollard (vines more than 60 years old). 4–5% VN. 🌿 A little crushing occurs in the comports. OT1 in open wooden and cement vats, submerged cap, 12 to 15 days; Vaslin press. 🌿 Finished and aged in casks, hand-bottled by gravity after the fining agent (egg whites) settles.

M Chapoutier SA, Tain-l'Hermitage (Drôme)

See Hermitage.

Delas Frères, St.-Jean-de-Muzols (Ardèche)

See Hermitage.

H A. **Dervieux-Thaize,** Verenay-Ampuis

M. Albert Dervieux, president of the Côte-Rôtie growers, produces a Côte Blonde "La Garde," Côte Brune, "Fontgent," and "La Viaillère." The latter, for me his biggest and greatest wine, is epitomized in the 1983: nearly black, with even more than its usual concentration from old vines, pitchy, spicy, and long.

3 ha include 30 ares of CDR. Vines at Fontgent are 15 years old, at La Garde 25, at Viaillère 50 to 60. 🌿 OT1 in open cement vats, submerged cap, 15 to 21 days. Has changed from hand-operated vertical to Vaslin press. 🌿 2 to 2½ years in wood—first casks, then *pièces*. Fined but not filtered.

GAEC de Syrah (André et Louis Drevon)

Flowers seem to recur in these wines, sometimes with butter (1984), sometimes with meat fat, smoke, and pepper (1981), over blackberry fruit. A somewhat separate wood flavor takes time in bottle to become integrated.

4 ha in Côtes Brune and Blonde. Have both slope and "summit." 4% VN. 🌿 ST (crushed directly above vats) in open cement vats, submerged cap, 3 weeks *cuvaison;* Vaslin press (was hand-turned vertical). 🌿 18 months in oak—first casks, then *pièces*.

Edmond Duclaux, Tupin

Wines with a lively acidity and long finish have an almost always peppery nose, a hint of mineral, sometimes undergrowth and flowers, sometimes smoke and meat fat, cassis fruit, even plums (in 1982).

3 ha in qrts Maison Rouge and Coteau Tupin in Tupin (some calcareous soil). Some 50-year-old vines. 🌿 Harvest in wooden comports. OT1 in open cement vats, *pigeage* to start, submerged cap thereafter, 3 weeks *cuvaison;* "squirrel" press. 🌿 Aged 2 years in oak caks and *pièces*.

H **Marius Gentaz-Dervieux**

The recurring features of these wines, even in floral, light-bodied 1981, are a balance of chewiness with acidity, length, and rising intensity as they linger. 1982 was darker, richer, tending to spice, while 1980 added truffles to its complex bouquet. Truffles verged on barnyard and the spice was over chocolate in dense-textured 1983.

1.2 ha, all on slopes, in the Côte Brune (vines 50 to 60 years old), qrt Baudin (11 to 18 years), and qrt La Landonne (40 to 50 years). His 2–3% VN is, unusually, in the

Vin Blanc de Viognier

COTEAU DE VERNON

CONDRIEU

APPELLATION CONTROLÉE

1975

Mis en bouteille à la Propriété
VERNAY Georges, Viticulteur à CONDRIEU (Rhône)

73 cl.

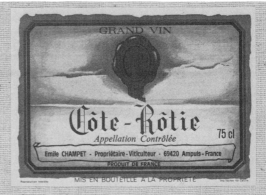

GRAND VIN

Côte-Rôtie
Appellation Contrôlée

75 cl

Emile CHAMPET - Propriétaire - Viticulteur - 69420 Ampuis - France
PRODUIT DE FRANCE

MIS EN BOUTEILLE À LA PROPRIÉTÉ

PRODUIT DE FRANCE

CHATEAU DU ROZAY
CONDRIEU
APPELLATION CONDRIEU CONTROLÉE

Mise en bouteille au Domaine

75 cl

P. MULTIER — Viticulteur — 69420 CONDRIEU (Rhône)

GRAND VIN FIN

Côte Rôtie

Appellation Côte Rôtie Contrôlée

JASMIN, Propriétaire-Viticulteur - Ampuis (Rhône)

Mis en bouteille à la propriété   75 cl   PRODUCE OF FRANCE

LA LANDONNE

CÔTE-RÔTIE

APPELLATION CÔTE-RÔTIE CONTROLÉE

RÉCOLTÉ, VINIFIÉ, ÉLEVÉ ET MIS EN BOUTEILLE PAR
E. GUIGAL à AMPUIS - Rhône - France
PRODUIT DE FRANCE

75cl

PRODUCT OF FRANCE

Côte-Rôtie

APPELLATION CÔTE-ROTIE CONTROLÉE

« La Viaillère »

MISE EN BOUTEILLES À LA PROPRIÉTÉ   750 ml

A. DERVIEUX-THAIZE, Propriétaire-Viticulteur, VERENAY-AMPUIS (Rhône) FRANCE

PRODUIT DE FRANCE

Grands Vins   d'Origine

Côte-Rôtie

APPELLATION COTE-ROTIE CONTROLÉE

"Côte Brune"

GENTAZ - DERVIEUX Propriétaire Viticulteur
Ampuis (Rhône) France   750 ml
MIS EN BOUTEILLE À LA PROPRIÉTÉ

"Ce vin du Viennois   à odeur de violette"
(Pline le Jeune)

CÔTE-RÔTIE

COTE BLONDE

APPELLATION CÔTE-RÔTIE CONTROLÉE

R. ROSTAING, Propriétaire à AMPUIS (Rhône)

Mis en bouteille à la propriété

Brune. 🙌 Harvested in plastic cases, crushed a little there and in the vat. OT1 in open cement vats, submerged cap, 18 to 21 days. Wine finishes in *pièces*. 🙌 Receives 15 to 18 months in *pièces*, is bottled by hand after the fining agent (egg white) settles.

Domaine Gerin

Earlier, the Gerin wines seemed to lack concentration and had a stone-dusty mineral smell and feel untypical of Côte-Rôtie. Was the explanation overproduction, youth of the vines, or the proportion of land above the classic slopes? In any case, there are signs of improvement in the somewhat Bordeaux-like 1983 and 1982 tasted in 1986. While both were more substantial than formerly, the 1983 was perhaps duller and still a little dusty, and so yielded place for me to the longer, more pungent, and fungal-to-barnyard 1982.

The former sole proprietor, M. Alfred Gerin, mayor of Ampuis, has been joined in the present society by a group of investors that includes Americans. From one of them I learn that the domaine now has 10 ha of Côte-Rôtie in cultivation, of which 2 are Blonde, 4 Brune, and 4 at the top of the hill. Average age of the vines is 17–18 years. 🙌 ST now includes some destemming, 7 days in cement and stainless-steel vats, Vaslin press. 🙌 Wine is aged about 3 years in cask.

E. Guigal, Propriétaire-Négociant-Eleveur

Excellent winemakers, Guigals are perhaps even more the great masters in the Rhône Valley of *élevage*, and particularly of all that maturing a wine under suitable conditions in oak can do. This makes their Côte-Rôties less rustic than some, and places them recognizably in the company of great wines as measured by what are today called "international" standards. From a regional standpoint they may not be the only great Côte-Rôties, but great they are, especially La Mouline. This is consistently distinguished by concentrated fruit, probably black raspberry; fine tannic structure that remains liquid, elegant, and round; and intense aroma, usually deeply floral, resinous, verging on cinnamon and salt with a flattering hint of volatility. La Landonne makes these characteristics darker, more compact and forceful, even aggressive at the start. 1985 suggests that La Turque may go even further in that direction.

As proprietors Guigals owned 3 ha of vine in Côte-Rôtie, all slopes, before their purchase of Vidal-Fleury. The Guigal-labeled wines that come exclusively from their properties are:

H Côte-Rôtie **La Landonne**
    First wine 1978.
H Côte-Rôtie **La Mouline**
    From the Côte Blonde. First wine 1966. Has Viognier.
Côte-Rôtie **La Turque**
    From the Côte Brune, a property recently acquired in the purchase of J. Vidal-Fleury. 1985 was first wine after replantation.

In addition to their proprietary wines, two Guigal wines are entirely of their own making, although they include purchased grapes:

Côte-Rôtie Brune et Blonde
Condrieu

❧ For reds, OT2 in closed vats, 2 to 3 weeks cuvaison; Vaslin press. Condrieu is fermented 1/3 in vat, 1/3 in used barrels, 1/3 in new. ❧ Guigals bring up and bottle both their own and purchased wines, the latter including red and white Hermitage, Châteauneuf-du-Pape, Gigondas, and CDR. More and more the Côte-Rôties are aged in new oak *pièces,* in which, for example, 1981 La Mouline spent 42 months.

H Jasmin (Georges et Robert)

Deep black raspberry fruit in these wines almost fumes with complexity, and almost always includes violets, barnyard and tobacco. It can also have smoke, vanilla, licorice, tar, and cinnamon, especially in barrels with the most Viognier. Better years like 1982 and especially 1983 have more fat, scarcely less aroma than 1984 or 1981. 1980 is a study in perfection of balance on a smaller scale.

3 ha in qrts La Garde (Blonde), Chevalière (Brune) and a new parcel of 4–5-year-old vines in Coteau Tupin. 8% VN. ❧ Began to ferment in cement in 1973. OT1 in open vats, submerged cap, 15 to 20 days; Vaslin press. ❧ 15 to 24 months in oak *pièces.* Wines are unsulfured, apart from that used for sanitizing the barrels, bottled unfined (since 1979), and unfiltered.

H René Rostaing

Côte-Rôtie; St.-Joseph. **M. Rostaing makes a La Landonne, a Côte Brune, and a Côte Blonde. He had to blend the first two because of a short crop in 1984. I prefer the Blonde, which has the fullest fruit and a roundness that seems only to heighten the somewhat austere refinement and concentration that runs through all of these. A resinous reduction also recurs, which M. Rostaing attributes to the "old" Syrah.**

1.8 ha of Côte-Rôtie planted with 50–60-year-old vines of "La Sérine pointue" (the "old" Syrah), plus 10% VN in his Côte Blonde. 55 ares of St.-Joseph at Chavanay. ❧ OT1 in open cement vats, *pigeage* to start, submerged cap after. 3 weeks *cuvaison,* Vaslin press. ❧ 2 to 3 years in wood, beginning in oak casks, then in *pièces,* only 1/5 new "because Syrah does not marry well with new wood." A "maximum" of 3 rackings during this time. Bottled unfined and unfiltered.

Louis Francis De Vallouit, St.-Vallier (Drôme)

Côte-Rôtie; Hermitage red and white; Crozes-Hermitage red and white. **A Côte-Rôtie that can possess an elegant and concentrated fruit had a tar and barnyard nose in 1983—tannic, almost salty, and lively—but some berries showed, and it was nevertheless more supple than De Vallouit's red 1983 Hermitage. The latter was hard and enclosed in its tannins in 1985. Best De Vallouit wine I have ever tasted is red 1983 Crozes-Hermitage: enormously fragrant with the concentration of a "coteaux" wine, full of black raspberry, blackberry, cassis fruit and spice, smooth, vanillaed and long.**

Conducts 10 ha of Côte-Rôtie of which 8 are his property. Qrts Grosse Roche (Blonde), Viaillère, Rosier, and Le Plomb. 2 ha of Hermitage in Greffieux and l'Hermits. 4½ ha of Crozes-Hermitage in Crozes and Larnage. ❧ ST in open wooden vats, of which the youngest are 150 years old, with *pigeage,* 12 to 15 days; Vaslin press. ❧ 2 years in oak casks.

Georges Vernay, Condrieu

    See Condrieu.

J. Vidal-Fleury

    This famous old wine house (founded in 1781) with its 10 ha of Côte-Rôtie vines has been sold to **E. Guigal,** whose founder Etienne Guigal was once cellar-master here. For the last 5 years, according to Marcel Guigal, Vidal-Fleury had restricted their activity as *vinificateurs* only to the Côte-Rôties from their own properties (Domaine Vidal-Fleury), labeled **Côtes Brune et Blonde,** and **Côte Blonde "La Chatillonne."** These wines will be made by Guigal's method in a common facility reserved by Guigal for production of domaine wines, but will continue to appear under the Vidal-Fleury label. Vidal-Fleury had some unplanted property in qrt La Landonne, whose eventual production will be added to Guigals' La Landonne; and Vidal-Fleury's La Turque holdings have become Guigal's La Turque.

Selected Bibliography

Alary, F. 1966. *Quelques notes d'histoire sur Cairanne*. Edition des Amis du Vieux Cairanne.

Amerine, M.A. and Joslyn, M.A. 1970. *Table Wines: The Technology of Their Production*. Berkeley, Los Angeles, London: The University of California Press.

André, Pierre. 1976. *La vinification des vins rosés*. Les Arcs-sur-Argens (Var): Syndicat des Côtes-de-Provence.

Bailly, Robert. 1961. *Vaucluse: Dictionnaire des communes*. Avignon: Jean-Yves Baud.

———. 1972. *Histoire du vin en Vaucluse*. Avignon: Orta.

———. 1978. *Histoire de la vigne et des grands vins des Côtes du Rhône*. Avignon: Orta.

Benoit, Fernand. 1975. *La Provence et Le Comtat Venaissin: Arts et traditions populaires*. Avignon: Aubanel.

Boisse, Cl. 1976. *Guide du Tricastin: Le pays Tricastin*. Les Granges-Gontardes (Drôme): Société des Amis de l'Abbé Boisse.

Bordas, Jean. 1946. *Essai d'agronomie Méditerranéene*. Avignon: Rullière Frères.

———. 1950. *Contribution à l'étude des facteurs de la production agricole du bas-Rhône*. Avignon: Rullière Frères.

Bréjoux, Pierre. 1974. "Les Côtes du Rhône." *Cuisine et vins de France* (March through September).

Brunel, Gaston. 1980. *Guide des vignobles et caves des Côtes du Rhône*. N.p.: J.C. Lattès.

Chabanon, Puisais, Loustaunau de Guilhem, et al. 1978. *Initiation à la dégustation des vins*. Paris: ITV.

Chabaud, Alfred. l966. *L'Uzège: Le bassin et la garrigue d'Uzès, les basses vallées de la Cèze et du Gardon*. Vol. 1. Uzès: Ateliers Peladan.

———. 1967. *Les documents et la méthode pour l'étude de la structure et de l'économie agraires dans la France du sud: L'exemple de l'Uzège et du pays de Bagnols-sur-Cèze*. Vol. 2. Uzès: Ateliers Peladan.

Chapoutier, Max 1963. "Hermitage, fils sacré du soleil." Conférence statutaire, Rotary de Valence.

Charnay, Pierre. 1968–69. "The Wines and Vineyards of the Southern Côtes du Rhône." *La Revue du vin de France* (nos. 219, 224, 225, English edition).

———. 1985. *Vignobles et vins des Côtes du Rhône*. Avignon: Aubanel.

Clavel, Jean and Baillaud, Robert. 1985. *Histoire et avenir des vins en Languedoc*. Toulouse: Privat.

Cochard, M. 1865. *Ampuis: Vignoble de la Côte-Rôtie*. Notice extrait de M. Cochard, etc., etc. Paris: Typographie de Henri Plon.

"Coteaux du Tricastin: Situation géographique de l'aire Tricastine" (mimeo). N.d. [Syndicat des Coteaux du Tricastin.]

David, T., and Foillard, L. 1962. *Les cépages des Côtes du Rhône et du Beaujolais*. Lyon: Ets. David & Foillard.

De Blij, Harm Jan. 1983. *Wine: A Geographic Appreciation*. Totowa, N.J.: Rowman & Allanheld.

Dufays, Philippe. N.d. *Histoire juridique de l'A.O.C Châteauneuf du Pape*. Edited by Pierre Charnay. N.p.: les Assurances Mutuelles Agricoles de Vaucluse.

Dunn-Meynell, Nadine. 1984. "The Wines of Spain." Society of Wine Educators *Chronicle* (Autumn).

Fédération des Syndicats de Producteurs de Châteauneuf-du-Pape. 1980. "Commentaire des premiers résultats de l'enquête effectuée au cours des mois de juillet et août 1980" (xerox), together with "Etude Statistique" prepared by Benton and Bowles Publicité, Paris.

Féret, Edouard. 1982. *Bordeaux et ses vins*. Bordeaux: Editions Féret et Fils.

Flanzy, Michel et André, Pierre. 1973. *La Vinification par macération carbonique*. CNRA Versailles: Editions SEI.

Fribourg, Gilbert. N.d. "AOC Crozes-Hermitage." [Valence: INAO (typescript)].

Galet, Pierre. 1962. *Cépages et vignobles de France*. Montpellier: Dehan.

———. 1979. *A Practical Ampelography: Grapevine Identification*. Ithaca and London: Comstock Publishing Associates, a division of Cornell University Press.

Galtier, G. 1958. *Le vignoble du Languedoc méditerranéen et du Roussillon*. Vol. 2. Graille et Castelnau: Edition Causse.

"Gigondas: son vignoble ses vins." N.d. Dossier relatif à la demande d'Appellation Contrôlée Gigondas (mimeo provided by M. François Ay).

Gouron, Marcel. N.d. "Les origines des vins des Côtes-du-Rhône." Archiviste Département du Gard (mimeo).

Hallgarten, Peter A. 1965. *Côtes-du-Rhône*. London: Wineographs.

Hermitte, Jean-Paul. 1975. "La structure du vignoble à Gigondas." *Etudes Vauclusiennes*.

Huguier, Philippe. 1973. *Vins des Côtes-du-Rhône*. Marseille: A. Robert.

———. 1977. *Vins de Provence*. Marseille: A. Robert.

INAO. Various dates. AOC Fiches XI (looseleaf, regularly updated).

Jauré, Annick. N.d. "Le Viognier: Cépage unique du vignoble de Condrieu. Est-il condamné?" (typescript in the possession of M. Georges Vernay, Condrieu).

Jean, Paul. 1973. "Etudes des structures à Châteauneuf-du-Pape." Châteauneuf-du-Pape: La Fédération des Syndicats de Producteurs de Châteauneuf-du-Pape.

Johnson, Hugh. 1978. *The World Atlas of Wine*. New York: Simon & Schuster.

———. 1983. *Modern Encyclopedia of Wine*. New York: Simon & Schuster.

"L'appellation 'Brézème' vous connaissez?" 1986. *Le vigneron des Côtes-du-Rhône et du sud-est* (no. 192).

Larmat, Louis. 1944. *L'Atlas de la France vinicole: Les vins des Côtes du Rhône*. Paris: Louis Larmat.

Lavigne, S., et al. 1977. *Le vignoble des Côtes-du-Rhône*. Paris: INRA (mimeo).

Le Plâtre, Mlle, and Sarfati, Mr. 1983. *Les Côtes du Rhône méridionales: Etude du vignoble: Situation actuelle et évolution 1971–1979–1982*. Avignon: INAO (mimeo).

Léglise, Max. 1976. *Une initiation à la dégustation des grands vins*. Lausanne: DIVO.

Le Roy, Henri. [1970]. "Vinification d'hier et d'aujourd'hui à Châteauneuf-du-Pape." *Reflets Mediterranéens* (n.d.).

Le Roy de Boiseaumarié, Baron Pierre. 1932. "Documents pour servir à l'histoire de Châteauneuf-du-Pape." Extrait de la *Revue de Viticulture*. Paris.

————. 1961."Histoire Condensée de Châteauneuf-du-Pape." In *Châteauneuf-du-Pape et ses Grands Vins* (June-July). Lyon: Publicité Raphael.

Le Roy de Boiseaumarié, Baron Pierre; Kunholtz-Lordat, Georges; and Mathieu, Gaston. 1939. "Châteauneuf-du-Pape." Extrait des *Annales Agronomiques* jan.-fév. 1939. Paris: Dunod.

Lichine, Alexis. 1974. *New Encyclopedia of Wines and Spirits*. New York: Alfred A. Knopf.

Livingstone-Learmonth, John, and Master, Melvin C.H. 1983. *The Wines of the Rhône*. London: Faber & Faber.

Moison, Auguste. 1974. *Tavel: la renaissance d'un cru*. Uzès: Editions Henri Peladan.

Pagnol, Jean. l973. *La Truffe*. Avignon: Aubanel.

————. 1975. *L'Olivier*. Avignon: Aubanel.

Pitiot, Sylvain and Poupon, Pierre. 1985. *Atlas des grands vignobles de Bourgogne*. Series: "Le grand Bernard des vignobles de France." Paris: Jacques Legrand.

Pomerol, Charles, et al. 1984. *Terroirs et vins de France*. Paris: Total-Edition-Presse; Orleans: Editions du BRGM.

Quittanson, Charles. 1984. *Connaissance des vins et eaux de vie,* International edition. Paris: Les Publications Borelli.

Régis, Le Comte de. 1946. Two versions of a report accompanying the request for Lirac to be accorded its own local AOC, one dated 20 septembre 1946. (Typescripts in the archives of Château de Clary.)

"Renaissance du vignoble en terrasses du Pilat." 1985. *Le vigneron des côtes-du-rhône et du sud-est* (no. 166).

Root, Waverly. 1966. *The Food of France*. New York: Vintage Books.

Roquette, Jean-Maurice. 1974. *Provence Romane I*. Series: "La nuit des temps." La Pierre-Qui-Vire (Yonne): Zodiaque.

Roux, Claudius. 1907. *Monographie du vignoble de Côte-Rôtie à Ampuis*. Lyon: A. Rey.

Sarfati, Claude. 1981. *La Dégustation des vins: Méthodes pédagogique et exercices pratiques*. Suze-la-Rousse (Drôme): l'Université du Vin.

Sipoly, Henri. 1962. "Tavel: Ses carrières, sa pierre, son vignoble et son vin à travers les ages." Typescript seen chez Mme Sipoly of manuscript n. 62.576, Archives départementales du Gard.

Syndicat de Défense de l'Appellation St-Joseph. 1955. "Demande d'autorisation de l'appellation 'St-Joseph' aux vins des Côtes-du-Rhône produits dans les communes de Mauves-Tournon-St-Jean-de-Muzols-Lemps-Vion-Glun" (typescript).

Syndicat Régional des Vignerons des *Côtes du Ventoux*. 1972. Côtes du Ventoux. Rapport sur la demande d'appellation d' origine contrôlée des vins délimités de qualité supérieure Côtes du Ventoux. Carpentras.

Valat, Claude. N.d. "La Roussanne." Extrait du *Progrès agricole et viticole*. Montpellier: Dehan.

Vedel, André; Charle, Gaston; Charnay, Pierre. 1972. *Essai sur la dégustation des vins*. Macon: SEIV.

Viala, P. and Vermorel, V. 1901–1910. *Ampélographie*. 7 vols. Paris: Masson.

Wagner, Philip M. 1979. *Grapes Into Wine*. New York: Alfred A. Knopf.

Wasserman, Sheldon. 1977. *The Wines of the Côtes du Rhône*. New York: Stein & Day.

Yapp, Robin, and Yapp, Judith. 1979. *Vineyards and Vignerons*. Shaftesbury (Dorset): Blackmore Press.

Index of Properties, Property Wines, and Producers

Index of Communes

Only those communes are listed here that are given as addresses of producers in this book and that do not appear in the Table of Contents.